DATE DUE

2-14-80			
MAR 28 '88			
GAYLORD			PRINTED IN U.S.A.

MANAGING
to
SUCCEED

Managing to Succeed

Profiles from
The Wall Street Journal

Edited by
LAWRENCE A. ARMOUR

Published by Dow Jones Books
P.O. Box 300, Princeton, NJ 08540

Printed and bound in the United States of America
10 9 8 7 6 5 4 3 2 1

Library of Congress Cataloging in Publication Data

Armour, Lawrence A.
   Managing to succeed.

     Bibliography: p.
     1. Management.   2. Business.   I. Title
HD31.A68   658.4   78-14419
ISBN 0-87128-568-1

49,906

CONTENTS

v

Contents

INTRODUCTION

The title of this book, *Managing To Succeed,* is provocative. Intentionally so.

Success, as we all know, can be one thing to one person, something quite different to another. But in its own way, *managing* is just as illusive. What *is* management? How does one manage? And, most importantly, how does one manage to succeed?

Several years ago, I got an insight into these and a few related questions during an interview with a mutual fund manager. The assets he managed had grown in a four-year span from $40 million to $1.7 billion. How, I asked, do you account for your enormous success? And what do you look for when you make an investment?

"Several things," he replied, "but the key is management."

Fine, but how do you guage management?

"By a man's record. I don't give a hoot about the mechanics of what he does or why he does it. Just his record. If a man can run an orange juice stand successfully, he can run a steel company. The skills are not only the same. They're also totally transferrable."

Roy Ash, the man who turned Litton Industries into a large and successful conglomerate, then went to Washington to run the government's Office of Management and Budget, has similar thoughts. "At a sufficiently high level of abstraction," he said recently, discussing his plans for Addressograph-Multigraph, the company he now heads, "all businesses are the same."

All of which is good to know. And valuable. But while it sheds light on a murky area, it doesn't really tell us what we want to know. So we asked an acquaintance, an MBA who now heads a large retailing operation in the Mid-West.

"Management," he replied, "is nothing more than the ability to get people to do the things you know they should be doing. A good manager is one who gets them to do it on their own and doesn't have to guide them every step along the road."

That, in a way, seems to be how the University of Pennsylvania's Wharton Graduate School sees it. In any case, the description of a Wharton course called *Organizational Behavior and Development* reads as follows: "One of the characteristics differentiating management from other activities is that it requires an ability to organize and deal effectively with the efforts of other people. As a manager you cannot 'do it yourself.' Your success depends on the behavior of others, such as subordinates, peers, superiors, customers, creditors and the like."

Okay. We seem to be getting somewhere. But there's another problem: the study guide from which this description comes is more than 100 pages long, and it contains reviews of dozens of other courses on management, management sciences and the like. In other words, the simple answer for which we have been searching has taken on a host of complexities.

A review of the literature in the field only makes things worse. For instance, the Fall 1977 edition of the *Columbia University Journal of World Business* starts off simply enough by stating that "a common denominator among all the activities of business managers is the need to make decisions." Then, however, it goes on to talk about formalized decision making methods, noting: "These methods include a variety of approaches (such as regression and variance analysis, simulation, linear programming or multiple criteria decision making support systems) to aid in managerial problem solving. Since the inception of operations research and management science, formal decision studies have become increasingly valued. In today's rapidly changing and competitive business environment, decision analysis has become essential."

Introduction

Columbia, of course, has lots of good company. The *Harvard Business Review* regularly slides the various aspects of management under the eyepiece of a high-powered microscope. So do publications of other equally prominent colleges and universities, management associations and similar institutions. Moreover, a day rarely goes by that doesn't see the publication, with suitable fanfare, of yet another book that delves into one or another aspect of what suddenly has become the incredibly complex world of business management.

How did it all happen? And why? Here's one view, offered by a Ph.D. who runs in-house seminars for top executives of large corporations:

"From Day One, when people first developed an interest in assembling a body of knowledge about management, different schools have evolved. Each attempted, in as scientific a way as possible, to study what it felt was the heart of business management. In the beginning, that usually meant time-and-motion studies of production line operations. After a while, someone discovered that motivational factors played a role. So Freudianists contributed their theories as to what makes business tick, and behavioral scientists came up with others. Along the way, computers gave us the tools to make quantitative studies of every aspect of business. These gave birth to still more schools of thought.

"While all this was going on, the needs of the country's businesses were undergoing major changes. In the mid-1800s, the traditional American firm was a one-unit establishment run by a man who was both owner and manager. By the early 1900s, the dominant force in the economy was the multi-unit company run by salaried managers who more than likely had no ownership in the companies they were managing. This is the form that's prevalent today, but now things like stock options have shifted the focus again.

"Other changes also took place. When the country was exploring the frontiers of science and concentrating on ways to produce automobiles, synthetic fibers, electric typewriters and all sorts of better mouse traps, the men who managed the companies tended to have engineering and scientific backgrounds. At some point, marketing and merchandising became vital skills. Today, with the emphasis on consumeristic and environmental considerations on the one hand, taxes and accounting matters on the other, the business manager more often than not is now being drafted out of the ranks of the legal and accounting professions.

"That, in short, is what happened. What started out as a simple business that dealt with relatively uncomplicated matters has turned into a science with dozens of interrelated disciplines."

The Model-T has given way to sleek new chariots, but time-and-motion studies are still important. So is the technology that goes into their manufacture. And so, of course, is the ability to produce the product in a pollution free way . . . to raise the capital needed to build the plant and equipment to do the job . . . to advertise, market and merchandise the product . . . to minimize the taxes that are paid to various governmental bodies . . . and to handle the hundreds of unexpected personal and business problems that crop up each and every day.

Which means that the manager who is successful today is apt to be the one who is able to extrapolate the important elements from all the various schools and disciplines. The one who is responsive to the needs of the times, both within and outside the walls of the corporation. The one who has the flexibility to respond to change. The one who, in the final analysis, can motivate the people he supervises to do what he feels they should be doing.

That seems to be the key. "When I travel around the country," said J. C. Penney Chairman Donald V. Seibert in a recent speech at New York's Pace University, "I spend as much time as possible with our trainees and first level managers. They're bright, articulate and candid, and we can learn a great deal from them. My most personally rewarding conversations are with the young people who have their teeth into their jobs and are turned on like a light bulb by their work. I find, without exception, that these are the ones who have been given the most meaningful work with real responsibility to go along with it. We are tapping the potential of these people, and we are all the better for it."

Later, Mr. Seibert added this: "No one can tell us exactly how to create the environment we want. But every member of management knows when he or she has succeeded at it. It's an unforgettable, exhilarating experience."

That, in a nutshell, is what this book is about. It's about managers who are successful in what they are doing. It's about people who have tasted of that exhilarating experience.

It's not a how-to-do-it book. In today's complex business environment, a how-to-do-it book, by necessity, would be an encyclopedia. It's a book, however, that contains lots of common threads which, woven together, blend into a fabric with meaningful ideas that can be used by other managers, regardless of age, sex or type of business.

It's a serious book that deals with serious matters. It also has its light moments. For example, the chapter that focuses on Fusion Systems, a young company that went into business in 1971 to produce a new type of ultraviolet light, reminds us of the roots from which much of U.S. business sprung. "A number of today's most successful companies in such fast growing fields as computers, technical instruments and electronics were started in garage shops by scientists, inventors or engineers who were gambling their futures on unproven technology."

The same chapter offers practical advice. Such as how Marshall Greenblatt, one of Fusion Systems' founders, tacked an extra day onto each end of business trips he took for his former employer and used the time to do missionary work for his new company. "If the guys at work had suspected what I was really up to," he says, "I might have been fired. But they were all convinced I was merely visiting a mistress so they never said a word."

The book contains a wide variety of material that's of concern to all businessmen, big and small alike—from things like the four-day work week and executive life abroad to what it's like to work for a company that has been swallowed up by a large conglomerate and what it's like to drop out of the business world altogether. One chapter looks at the divorced executive, another at women in business, others at other minorities. Along the way we meet an executive, a bank manager from Chicago, who felt resentment at work but couldn't tell if it was because she was a woman, a black or under 30.

The heart of the book consists of profiles of successful executives. There's a section on entrepreneurial types who are planting the seeds out of which tomorrow's giant enterprises will spring; another on the middle managers who make the day-to-day decisions that keep the wheels of corporate America turning; yet another on the men at the top, the men who are actually running today's billion dollar corporations.

They have lots in common. They tend to be work addicts who get to the office early, leave late and often devote Saturdays and Sundays to company affairs. They are self-confident, well-organized and energetic. They drive their associates hard and are not always loved: "aggressive" and "gutsy" are two of the milder adjectives that run through their stories, while "ruthless" is one that appears frequently. And while they have their differences, too, they share one characteristic—an overwhelming concern with the bottom line and an almost fanatical insistance on results.

Take Don Rumsfeld, who was brought in to rescue G. D. Searle from what was diagnosed by many to be a series of fatal ills. A brash, hard-driving executive whose background includes stints in Washington as head of the Pentagon, the Cost of Living Council and the White House staff, Rumsfeld roared into Searle's Skokie headquarters with six guns blazing. Heads

Introduction

rolled, knees trembled and dozens of marginal operations were lopped off. At the same time, Rumsfeld obtained marketing rights to several new drugs and beefed up Searle's research effort. The company is not out of the woods yet, but Rumsfeld, who puts in 14-hour days and drives his people hard, seems to be what the doctor ordered. In any case, security analysts, who once were distressed with the outlook for Searle, have been writing bullish reports on the company, and its stock has bounced back sharply from its lows.

Robert C. Wilson, who was named chief executive officer of Memorex in 1974—a time at which the company was $300 million in debt, in trouble with the SEC and in deeper trouble in the market-place—calls meetings for 7 a.m. and is seen as "a ruthless S.O.B." Colgate's David Foster is described as "tough, temperamental, impatient, ruthless and restless," United Technologies' Harry Gray as "pushy," International Paper's J. Stanford Smith as "a real P. T. Barnum kind of guy."

There's more. Much more. And the fascinating thing is learning what makes these men and women tick . . . how they tick . . . and how they manage, time and again, to succeed.

Part I:

At the Top

Strong Medicine for Searle

Robert A. Moe, director of research and development for G. D. Searle & Co., was paged as he stepped off an evening flight from London to Chicago.

The phone call summoned Mr. Moe from the airport to corporate headquarters in Skokie, Ill., where he was fired on the spot by Donald H. Rumsfeld, who was in his eighth day as president of Searle.

The abrupt dismissal typifies the aggressive and sometimes insensitive manner of Don Rumsfeld in whipping Searle into shape. He is using the same six-gun management style that made heads roll and knees tremble when Mr. Rumsfeld ran the Pentagon, the White House staff and the Cost of Living Council.

The 45-year-old Mr. Rumsfeld is the first outsider ever to head the family-controlled company. He is being paid $200,000 a year to grapple with an accumulation of problems: sagging earnings, increasing product competition, mistakes of past management and a pending grand-jury investigation into allegedly sloppy drug testing. The company's stock has plunged from a peak of $41 in 1973.

Mr. Rumsfeld's take-charge performance is stirring a modest renewal of interest in the diversified pharmaceutical company in the investment community. Searle's stock has become an active trader on the New York Stock Exchange again, and it has rebounded from the low of $11 set in 1977.

Some analysts are touting Searle as "a likely turnaround candidate" because of the new chief executive's actions so far. "Mr. Rumsfeld has really taken the bull by the horns and made some tough decisions," says D. Larry Smith, an analyst at Smith Barney Harris Upham & Co.

Mr. Smith particularly admires the way Mr. Rumsfeld dis charged 150 employes to cut out $5 million of overhead and the way he acted to get rid of 20 marginal or unprofitable operations. The planned divestiture, announced Jan. 11, 1978, involves unspecified hospital-supply and diagnostic-product businesses that accounted for about $100 million of Searle's $800 million of sales in 1977. As a result of this and other charges, total 1977 write-offs will approach $95 million, plunging Searle deeply into the red. In 1976, Searle's net income fell 24% to $61.5 million, or $1.18 a share.

Despite Mr. Smith's optimism, other analysts say it's too early to get excited about Searle's prospects. "The company's overall momentum is still quite questionable," contends Wertheim & Co.'s David F. Saks.

Such critics say, for instance, that Mr. Rumsfeld really stuck his neck out by immediately firing Mr. Moe as chief of drug research, without first lining up a successor. Since the firing, executive recruiters have been beating the bushes for a new research chief, but so far there are no takers, partly because of Searle's lingering problems with regulators over drug testing.

It's a critical vacancy because Wall Street viewed Searle's research efforts as lackluster and unproductive even before the Food and Drug Administration in 1975 attacked the company's testing, which led to the pending grand-jury matter. "The pharmaceutical division has just got to do something about new products if Searle is really going to turn around," one Chicago drug-industry analyst says.

Mr. Rumsfeld, for his part, says the firing of Mr. Moe was the "easiest thing to do," considering such things as the FDA problems. The immediate dismissal was fairer than looking for a replacement and letting rumors filter back to Mr. Moe, he suggests.

The new president hopes that licensing agreements and joint ventures will provide a stopgap solution for Searle until its research can be beefed up. Searle recently announced a U.S.

licensing accord to sell a Pennwalt Corp. drug to test high blood pressure. The move also will help soften the blow of the 1979 patent expiration for the major ingredient of Aldactone and Aldactazide, antihypertensive drugs that are Searle's two biggest moneymakers, accounting for 18% of corporate sales in 1976.

How an outsider fares in taking over the reins of a troubled family-controlled company is always fascinating. In the Searle case, it is even more so because the new top man is a brash and prominent politician testing his wings in the business world for the first time. If Don Rumsfeld succeeds in restoring Searle's fortunes, friends are betting the four-term Republican Congressman will leave the company eventually to run for the U.S. Senate or perhaps the presidency.

Founded in 1888, G. D. Searle & Co. remained a small, little-known outfit for its first 70 years. It became a leading drug house in the early 1960s by pioneering the first birth-control pill and developing innovative drugs for motion sickness, diarrhea and peptic ulcer.

In 1966, 40-year-old Daniel C. Searle, armed with a Harvard MBA degree and a lifetime of exposure to the company's inner workings, took over the presidency from his domineering father, John G. Searle, who recently died at age seventy-six. At the time, the elder Mr. Searle stayed on as chairman and continued to second-guess and overrule his son just as he had ever since Dan's first job at Searle, as a 12-year-old bottle-washer in the labs. The father withheld Dan's $12 weekly wages from that summer job, doling back $5 as an allowance. He said his son wasn't worth more because he broke too many bottles. Years later, as a wedding present, the father gave the money back, with interest.

When John G. Searle finally bowed out in late 1971, most of his longtime advisers retired with him, leaving a noticeable void in the top management ranks. The Searles tried to fill the void by creating a management troika. Dan was chief executive; Dan's brother, William, became chairman, and their brother-in-law, Wesley M. Dixon, was president. The three are referred to within the company as the "Searle boys."

Finally in a position to assert full independence from his strong-willed father, Dan embarked on an ambitious diversification campaign to reduce Searle's exclusive reliance on pharmaceuticals. "There was a father-son competition going on," a longtime family friend recalls, and it was a prime reason for Dan's "strong push to grow, to acquire, to merge."

By early 1975, Searle had acquired nearly 20 companies making hospital-supply products, medical-diagnostic instruments, eyeglasses and computerized hospital data systems. But the diversification never really paid off. By the end of 1975, pharmaceuticals still provided 84% of Searle's operating profit (against 90% in 1965) despite all the new operations. The problem? Searle "bought a lot of crap," says a New York drug analyst. "And the guys running the ship weren't capable of pulling it all together." (Mr. Dixon concedes that some of the acquisitions didn't work out so well.)

Things went from bad to worse in 1975. The FDA accused Searle of misrepresenting research data on three drugs after animal tests showed they might cause cancer. The agency also discovered testing discrepancies for Aspartame, an artificial sweetener, and Norpace, a drug designed to correct irregular heartbeats.

Searle denied all but minor clerical errors. Nevertheless, the FDA asked the Justice Department to seek an indictment for possible criminal fraud. Searle was forced by the FDA to put fuller warning labels about test results on Flagyl, a drug for vaginal infections, and on Aldactone and Aldactazide. Sales of these key drugs fell off. The FDA revoked Searle's permission to sell Aspartame, and approval of Norpace was delayed by further testing until September 1977. Searle meanwhile became a pariah on Wall Street.

Dan and William Searle then turned to Don Rumsfeld, the former Secretary of Defense and President Ford's chief of staff who enjoyed a "Mr. Clean" reputation in Washington. Dan Searle had known Mr. Rumsfeld since 1962, when Mr. Searle was finance manager of Mr. Rumsfeld's first congressional campaign from Chicago's suburban North Shore.

In the spring of 1977, Mr. Rumsfeld came in as Searle's first outside president and chief executive, partly because the "Searle boys" promised him independence. Outsiders doubted he would have free rein, since the family owns one-third of the common stock. But, to prove their sincerity, the three "Searle boys" moved out of Searle's 12-story headquarters into an unmarked suite in an adjacent office tower.

The three remain directors. Dan Searle is chairman and Bill Searle and Wes Dixon hold new posts as vice chairmen. But the three have all taken significant pay cuts from their $134,000-plus annual salaries, and they apparently now take their marching orders from Don Rumsfeld. Employes recently were ordered to refer any requests from Dan Searle right up the chain of command, without taking any action on them. One middle-level executive who followed the new order after Mr. Searle sought information from him, says Mr. Searle returned a few days later to apologize for "overstepping his bounds."

Mr. Rumsfeld runs the show in board meetings as well. "Dan is in the room and acts very much like any other board member," says Reuben F. Richards, executive vice president of Citibank and a Searle director, who doubts that there will be a clash between the "Searle boys" and the new chief executive. "Don makes the decisions," he says.

The fast-talking, calculating and hard-driving demeanor of Don Rumsfeld leaves little doubt that he commands any situation. Lacking knowhow about Searle or the drug industry, he educated himself by systematically grilling scores of present and retired executives. He asked curt, probing questions with little patience for foot-dragging or ignorance.

"It was like an inquisition. You were on trial. Absolutely unnerving," a department head says. The nearby Hilton Hotel bar became the first stop for many after such intimidating encounters, he adds. One senior man's hair has turned noticeably grayer and deeper creases have appeared on his forehead, something his colleagues attribute to weeks of high-pressure meetings with Mr. Rumsfeld.

"I'm used to operating in a situation where you have a

small margin for error," Mr. Rumsfeld explains. "My task is to see that this company is a first-rate company, functioning internally in a manner we're proud of and developing products that people need and want."

One of his first actions as president was to convene a committee of top corporate officers that used to brainstorm regularly with Dan Searle. He chewed out several members who arrived 30 minutes late, then promptly disbanded the group, explaining that it was a waste of time.

Within his first month, Mr. Rumsfeld had finished his "inquisition," fired Mr. Moe and forced the resignation of Jack L. Manes, the top personnel officer. He had also begun to recruit fresh management blood.

The way Mr. Rumsfeld laid off or transferred 300 Chicago-area administrative employes also tells a lot about his management style. He told departments how many to sack and then gave managers 24 hours to tell him who should be cut and who should stay. He set up severance-pay packages, ranging from several weeks to months, depending on the position and seniority. "Don wanted to make sure the firings were as painless as possible," says Mr. Dixon.

But former employes say the purge was crudely handled. Searle is a nonunion shop with no other recent history of layoffs. Supervisors fired subordinates without warning and ordered them off the premises within a few hours.

One $54,000-a-year woman executive got a lunchtime phone call at home from her boss's boss, who simply read the following memo to her: "Because of the corporate reorganization, your position has been determined to be redundant. Effective immediately, you are terminated." She wasn't allowed back in the building.

(A company spokesman says that most of those fired were given two days to get out, and all were offered job counseling afterwards).

A letter to Searle's 21,000 employes from Mr. Rumsfeld appeared the day after the purge, which some still at Searle say further weakened morale. "These actions will strengthen the company," the note said, without a word of sympathy or thanks for those fired. The memo's cold, impersonal tone prompted at least a few other employes to quit or start looking for jobs elsewhere. "Who wants to work for a company that treats people like that?" asks one who left voluntarily.

Mr. Rumsfeld made equally hardboiled and speedy decisions to dismantle a big chunk of Dan Searle's diversification dream. In August 1977, he formed a "transitional business" task force of several dozen executives and directors and consultants from Duff & Phelps Inc., a Chicago investment-research and consulting firm. For five months, they debated the fit, profitability and cash and management needs of every Searle business, and concluded that 20 had no future. The exhausting task was "enough to run you up the wall," Mr. Rumsfeld remembers. "I would come home at night with a big briefing book, and my wife would say, 'Put your book down and say hello!' "

The president of another Chicago-based company that took two years to plan similarly big divestitures, thinks Mr. Rumsfeld acted too hastily. "I would have some reservations about being able to analyze 20 businesses so fast," he comments. "Is he really sure he has got 'dogs'?"

Asked that question, the Searle chief executive puts down his pipe and peers over his half rimmed glasses. "This is something that had to be done rapidly because of the damage to business if it dragged out indeterminately."

He won't disclose which 20 businesses are being shed. However, Searle intends to get rid of an operation that makes computerized X-ray machines, called CAT scanners, a business under tremendous competitive pressure. Smith Barney's Mr. Smith believes others tagged for disposal include: Two British hospital-supply companies, Searle's laboratory-product and scientific-instrument business and certain industrial products of Will Ross Inc., a Milwaukee-based hospital-supply subsidiary.

Like any good politician, Don Rumsfeld keenly understands the importance of a public image. So, he has been mending fences with the FDA by personally asking top agency officials what Searle should do to straighten out its reputation.

"Our whole relationship with the FDA has improved" as a result, Mr. Dixon asserts. Without Mr. Rumsfeld, he continues, "we wouldn't have gotten approval of Norpace," whose marketing go-ahead had been delayed for months.

Mr. Rumsfeld also decided to launch Searle's first corporate-identity program—after discovering that the sign at the Will Ross headquarters made no mention of its being a Searle unit. He hired RVI Corp., a Chicago design firm, to come up with a new logo, and a Searle spokesman says it will cost "a couple of million dollars" to put the new insignia quickly on everything from product labels to stationery. And the new chief is stepping up advertising, a radical switch from the low profile of the previous management. "The difference between Dan Searle and Don Rumsfeld," a veteran insider says, "is the difference between night and day."

Mr. Searle reports that he's "under less stress" now that he has left the presssure-cooker of corporate management. On the other hand, Don Rumsfeld is happier running a large conglomerate than he expected. "He was looking forward to the challenge, but he wasn't sure he would enjoy it," a close friend observes. Mr. Rumsfeld particularly relishes having more free time to read history books and play with his 10-year-old son, Nicholas, even though the executive works 14-hour days. "Compared to the Pentagon, this job is a peach," he says.

Mr. Rumsfeld hasn't adapted his life style to his $200,000 annual salary, the most he has ever earned. He bought a rambling old house with a leaky roof for $174,500 in Winnetka, his hometown and one of Chicago's most-affluent suburbs. He still drives a used Volvo. At the office, he fixes his own coffee, eats lunch at his desk and strolls about with his tie askew and his shirt rumpled. In the sole of his right shoe, there is a big hole.

Turnaround Artist At Memorex

What does the world's largest bank do when it faces one of the biggest write-offs in banking history on a corporate debt?

It can swallow its pride by accepting the loan loss. Or it can hire a high-priced trouble-shooter, throw good money after bad and hope that the corporate phoenix will rise from the ashes.

The latter route was the risky choice of Bank of America when it backed the hiring of Robert C. Wilson in 1974 as chief executive at Memorex Corp. The company was tottering near collapse under the weight of a $300 million debt—half of it owed to Bank of America, which had nursed the small computer company from infancy to stardom on the New York Stock Exchange before its swift decline.

In the view of most analysts and insiders at Memorex, the Bank of America's gamble is paying off. Indeed, Memorex may well enter business-school textbooks as an example of how prodigious efforts by bankers and hard-nosed managers can rescue a major company from the jaws of disaster.

Memorex was in deep trouble in 1971, when the Securities and Exchange Commission charged it with issuing misleading earnings reports; Memorex later consented to an injunction. But the company's nadir was reached in 1973, when it tried to enter the main-frame computer business, challenging International Business Machines Corp. At about the same time, IBM lowered prices on peripheral equipment, which had been the main source of Memorex earnings. (Such IBM actions ultimately led to a series of antitrust suits against the industry giant, and suits by the Justice Department and Memorex itself are still pending.)

The entry by Memorex into the main-frame computer field flopped, in any case, and the company's 1973 loss totaled $119.1 million. Cash on hand barely kept day-to-day operations going. Employes fled to more secure jobs. Suppliers refused to make deliveries without prior payment, and customers stretched out their payments as insurance against losses they might suffer if the company went bankrupt.

Under Mr. Wilson's highly disciplined leadership, Memorex reported 1977 first half earnings of $26.6 million, or $4.51 a share, up 40% from a year ago. Memorex has moved onto the Fortune list of the 500 largest industrial companies and received improved ratings from both Standard & Poor's and Moody's investment services. Memorex has also recently acquired two small computer-related companies for a total of about $15 million in cash and stock.

Memorex, delisted from the New York Stock Exchange in 1973 when its fortunes were ebbing, was recently approved for relisting. This was the first such relisting in the exchange since United Industrial Corp. stock was readmitted to trading in 1964.

Whether Mr. Wilson or the bank had the lead role in Memorex's recovery is a moot point. "Some might credit Wilson more, some might credit the bank more, but it was hand-in-hand," says one analyst. "Bank of America provided the financial framework to turn the company around, and Bob Wilson did it."

To woo Mr. Wilson, the bank and the Memorex board drew up a package that Mr. Wilson couldn't refuse. Mr. Wilson had just completed a rescue effort as chief executive at Collins Radio Co., Dallas, turning a $64 million loss into a $13.3 million profit in one year's time. The bank guaranteed Mr. Wilson a base salary of $200,000 a year plus bonuses and cost-of-living adjustments. (In 1976, Mr. Wilson earned a total of $708,251.)

The lucrative five-year package also included options on 250,000 shares of stock. Mr. Wilson has already exercised the option on 187,000 shares at about $3.62 a share, giving him almost $4 million in paper profits.

The bank was equally generous in its refinancing. It agreed

to convert $30 million of its debt into preferred stock and convinced other lenders to exchange an additional $10 million debt for preferred stock. The agreement also allowed the company to credit bank purchases of Memorex equipment against its debt and to request the bank to buy even more preferred when Memorex redeemed its 5¼% convertible subordinated debentures. Finally, Bank of America provided Memorex with a new $35 million line of credit.

"Wilson was given a silver platter by the Bank of America," says one informed observer. "They gave him almost a blank check to go in and fix that company. Maybe if they'd given it to Larry Spitters (the founder and former president of the company) or any other guy, the same thing would have happened."

Bank of America officials are reluctant to discuss the dark days at Memorex, although they admit that the $150 million in loans was "large enough so that we cared—and cared a great deal."

One analyst is more blunt about the reasons behind the bank's generosity. "They were hung. They were hung out to dry," he says. "If they didn't keep Memorex running, they would have written off $150 million, bang." What's more, he says, the bank was heavily invested in the computer-leasing industry at the time and feared that a Memorex failure might have a snowballing effect on the industry, causing the bank to suffer even heavier losses. Also, he says, "They were the lead bank (at Memorex); they hooked other people into it. I have a feeling there'd have been a lot of lawsuits (against the bank)."

Once the refinancing was settled, Mr. Wilson moved quickly to reorganize the company. He converted Memorex's loosely structured product groups into five autonomous units with direct lines to the president's office. He created a central nine-man management team and recruited fresh talent for the company, including three executives who came with him from Collins. He switched the company's leasing emphasis to an aggressive sales program that includes the marketing of some equipment built by other companies. And he boosted prices on all sales, leasing and maintenance operations 6% to 8%. Finally, Mr. Wilson instituted a variety of cost-cutting measures that included the renting of economy cars instead of luxury models for company use, dropping of unprofitable product lines and eliminating of 125 middle-level jobs.

The quick action resulted in an immediate saving of almost $4 million and helped the company produce a modest profit of $1.6 million, or 36 cents a share, in the 1975 first quarter. But an executive doesn't make that kind of turnaround without ruffling some feathers.

"He's a ruthless S.O.B.," says a former high-ranking Memorex employe. "He has no respect for the individual. Everybody's just a cog in his machinery. He's the kind of guy that if I were the Bank of America and I wanted to get my money out, I'd choose somebody like Wilson, but he isn't the kind of person to build esprit de corps like at an IBM."

A major concern among Memorex employes when Mr. Wilson took over was the extent of his interest in the company's future. "Was Bob's mission to pay money back or to build the company?—That was the question among thinking people," says Robert Jaunich, one of the two executives remaining who worked under Mr. Spitters. Mr. Wilson tried to alleviate fears. He sent out newsletters, held formal meetings with employes and talked to individual workers over impromptu lunches in the company cafeteria. Mr. Wilson's actions apparently have won him the faith and respect, if not the affection, of his employes.

According to one company insider, Mr. Wilson spends "an incredible amount of time" on the job, working six or seven days a week, from early in the morning until late at night. He expects similar dedication from his employes, and one former associate complains bitterly about the 7 a.m. meeting he says Mr. Wilson called on Sunday mornings. "He has no respect for your family because he has no family life for himself," the former Memorex employe says.

But in fact, Mr. Wilson's wife, Frances, often travels with him on business trips. One of their daughters is married and the other two are in school. In the past, he often lived away from the family except on weekends, and Mr. Wilson explains somewhat awkwardly, "I think being a good entrepreneur, a good businessman, a good free enterpriser does something for the society of which you are part—and in the broader sense your family."

Few quarrel at least about what Mr. Wilson has accomplished at Memorex. In addition to cutting the company's debt almost in half, to $148.9 million at the end of the 1977 second quarter, and restoring a positive net worth, Mr. Wilson moved the company into advanced product lines, increased the size of its engineering staff by 40%, beefed up its sales force and expanded facilities. This was, he says, all geared to provide tangible evidence of his concern for the company's future.

"If you Monday-morning quarterbacked him, you wouldn't find many things that you'd have done differently. Maybe a few details with hindsight, but basically he did everything perfectly," says William H. Welling, an analyst with Shuman, Agnew & Co., claims.

Some analysts disagree, and they question many of Mr. Wilson's decisions. The executive's cutback on research and development spending means that Memorex "can't build up the new technology with the kind of budget they have, so they're buying it," says one analyst. The additional technology is particularly necessary because "the survival of Memorex is based on having enough products to put through the sales system they've built up," this analyst says.

Results have been mixed in the company's marketing of products made by others. The System 1380, a telecommunications processor built by Computer Communications Inc., hasn't been as successful as its predecessor, Memorex's own Model 1270. Also, the analyst says, marketing agreements aren't very profitable, "because you only get a distributor's fee." Accordingly, the company's $75 million merger bid for Storage Technology Corp., a Colorado-based maker of computer data-storage equipment, was considered an important move for Memorex, but merger talks fell through.

Far more disturbing to another analyst is the "quality" of the company's earnings. He says that Mr. Wilson opted to write down as much as $86 million on the company's equipment inventory in 1974. The decision depressed the company's earnings at the time, but it also made it easy to rack up impressive profits in later years as the company sold the depreciated equipment. Memorex is "taking balance-sheet write-downs and passing them through the income statement. From a financial point of view, it's lousy accounting," he says. (The company denies this, claiming "everything we wrote off, we lost.")

Critics also point to Mr. Wilson's decision to pursue what he terms the company's largest future investment, a $3 billion antitrust suit charging IBM with trying to destroy competition. "The same things (IBM) did to Memorex, they did to Calcomp," one critic says. California Computer Products Inc., Anaheim, Calif., filed a $300 million antitrust suit against IBM in 1973. A U.S. federal court judge dismissed the case in April 1977, but Calcomp is appealing the decision. "If Calcomp didn't win, I don't see where the Memorex case is a hell of a lot stronger," the critic says.

Memorex claims its case is indeed stronger, and in any event such criticism doesn't ruffle Mr. Wilson, a man who learned early to make his own decisions and to pursue them hard. The son of a Long Beach, Calif., high-school principal, Mr. Wilson majored in naval architecture at the University of California at Berkeley. He abandoned that field on graduation when he discovered naval architects earned only 45 cents an hour, while General Electric Co. offered him 75 cents.

GE offered training programs in chemical engineering, advanced engineering and sales. The ambitious Mr. Wilson took all three. During a 28-year career with GE, he moved through a series of management spots in marketing, engineering and manufacturing. He worked in Europe and Asia, and he successfully tackled problem assignments such as trying to regain GE's share of the transitor-radio market when cheap Japanese imports threatened its dominance in that field during the 1950s. Eventually, the aggressive executive felt ready for the challenges that face only a chief executive, and he was eager for the position.

Aware that there were too many others ahead of him at GE to reach that goal, Mr. Wilson moved to Rockwell International, where he thought his chances at the top slot were better. An assignment there sent him to Collins to help protect Rockwell's interest in the troubled company. The silver-haired Mr. Wilson now says his only professional regret is that he didn't leave GE sooner. "I could have become a chief executive earlier," he says.

It pleases Mr. Wilson that he has removed the "bad adjectives" such as "debt-ridden" and "financially troubled" from Memorex's name. But he insists that, despite his two turnaround triumphs, "I don't like to be considered a turnaround artist. That's the drudgery. I like building for the future."

He prides himself on being a good teacher, and he says there are about a dozen chief executives of major companies who have worked under him. He also says he has never left a company or a division that hasn't continued to do well after he's gone.

Mr. Wilson will be only 59 when his contract ends in 1979, and whether he continues at Memorex or not, it is certain he won't retire. He firmly believes that "if there weren't work, somebody would invent it just for the satisfaction it gives." He has few hobbies. He jogs two or three miles each morning to keep in shape, enjoys football games, and sometimes goes fishing when Mrs. Wilson can persuade him to spend some time at their summer home in Cape Cod, Mass.

"The only retiring I'll ever do is to change my way of working," he says. Teaching a management course at a business school, writing a book about how business works (he now writes all of his speeches and letters to shareholders) and politics all intrigue him as possible options.

But he adds, "I've got a feeling I'd never be elected (to office) and if I got elected, I'd never get reelected because I have a tendency to tell it like it is. Santa Claus gets elected, but the taskmaster doesn't."

Brushing Up The Colgate Image

David R. Foster carries a stopwatch to the track meets that his company sponsors for promotional purposes. That enables him to check up on the official timers. "He does that kind of thing everywhere," a subordinate says. "We all know he notices everything."

His subordinates also know of the quickness and depth of Mr. Foster's fury when he disapproves of something. "I wrote a report once that he didn't like," an aide recalls. "So he just walked into my office and tossed it into the wastebasket. He told me the next day what was wrong with it."

But this tough and temperamental boss is respected by his aides at Colgate-Palmolive Co., the household-products giant where Mr. Foster has been chief executive officer since 1971 and chairman since 1975. For Mr. Foster has taken the formerly stodgy company—facing stagnation in its traditional toothpaste and soap markets—and launched it on a bold program of diversification into hospital supplies, cosmetics, sports equipment and foods.

Under David Foster's zealous and eventful rule, Colgate is changing itself apace. During the last five years, it has laid out $935 million in stock and cash to acquire 17 companies, including Kendall Co., Helena Rubinstein Inc. and Riviana Foods. On sales of $3.51 billion, Colgate's net income in 1976 exceeded $149 million, more than three times the 1971 level. The acquired businesses accounted for $1.22 billion of the sales and $46.7 million of the profits. And Mr. Foster says, "I'd like another $1 billion in sales from our nontraditional businesses."

And when Mr. Foster wants something, Colgate goes after

it. Says a securities analyst who knows the company well: "Colgate has been a company of dictators. More so than in almost any other company, there are very few checks and balances in Colgate. The chief really controls the company, he calls all the shots."

Around Colgate's offices everybody seems to agree with that view. Before Mr. Foster took over, the company had been dominated for a decade by George H. Lesch and for the two decades before that by Edward H. Little, who hung on until age 79. Says Mr. Foster: "I don't know if my successor will be able to carry on the kind of rule that Little, Lesch and Foster have carried on, which is a one-man kind of management."

David Foster—short, stocky and 57 years old—is a restless, impatient and resolute man who sets difficult goals for himself and his staff. "David looks for perfection in everybody and everything, and he can get very upset when he doesn't see it," says Philip E. Beekman, who resigned as a key Foster aide early in 1977 to become president of Joseph E. Seagram & Sons. Mr. Foster's strong point, Mr. Beekman says, "is the ability to rise above the daily crises and daily routine to think ahead and see where the corporation is going."

Says Mr. Foster himself, reflecting on the kind of reputation he wants: "If I felt a chief executive was looked upon as a nice guy, I would question whether he was setting the right objectives." He adds: "I don't think that you can be popular and still be a forward-looking manager. I want to be remembered for having changed the direction of the company for its future well-being."

On Wall Street, Mr. Foster is beginning to get the kind of recognition he wants. "I feel the guy has been very good for Colgate," says Hercules A. Segalas, an analyst at Drexel Burnham Lambert Inc. in New York. "He has verve and imagination and guts. He has very quickly moved the company into fast-growing areas."

Even so, Colgate's stock is down from its 1973 record of over $35. Analysts note that Mr. Foster hasn't regained much, if any, of the ground Colgate lost earlier to its archrival, Procter &

Gamble Co. Moreover, Mr. Foster doesn't intend to alter the company's heavy reliance on foreign operations, which accounted for 63% of Colgate's earnings in 1976.

"That's a real hang-up for investors who don't want foreign-currency risks," says L. Richard Wenzel, an analyst with David L. Babson & Co. in Boston.

While Colgate today has almost 50,000 shareholders, it traces its roots to a family business started in 1802 by William Colgate, an immigrant from England who began by selling soap and candles. He and his heirs struck it rich, especially after bringing out Colgate Tooth Paste—at first sold in jars rather than tubes—in 1877. The company in 1928 was merged into Palmolive-Peet Co., whose Palmolive soap, named for the oils it contained, was the biggest-selling soap in the world.

During Edward Little's rule from 1938 to 1960, the combined enterprise gained a commanding position in many foreign markets, but was clobbered by competitors in the U.S. One by one, the company's dominant products came crashing down in the market-share charts. Its leading toothpaste—by then labeled Colgate Dental Cream, but known as "Big Red" to insiders because of its red packaging—was surpassed by Procter & Gamble's Crest after Colgate initially ignored fluoride additives.

George Lesch, Colgate's next boss, is widely credited with revitalizing the company. He expanded its detergent business and imposed strong financial controls that saved the funds necessary for new-product programs. But Colgate had to settle for modest growth—net income rose 31% from 1966 to 1970— achieved largely by expanding its foreign markets.

Along came David Foster. After a fast-track Colgate career mainly in Europe, Mr. Foster had been transferred to the U.S. and became Mr. Lesch's own choice for a successor. But from the day he took over in 1971, Mr. Foster took a vastly different approach to the business.

At first, his subordinates noticed the small ways in which Mr. Foster was different from the exclusively budget-minded Mr. Lesch. Under Mr. Foster, for example, officers on company business were permitted to fly first class (more recently, Mr.

Foster went even further and ordered Colgate's first corporate airplane, a $6 million Gulfstream II jet). Colgate's Park Avenue offices also have been spruced up. ("Give George Lesch a good balance sheet and he wouldn't have cared if he were sitting in an outhouse running the business," a vice president says.)

But the biggest and most important difference was Mr. Foster's willingness—indeed, eagerness—to risk Colgate capital on major acquisitions, even if a transaction didn't immediately enhance the corporate earnings or the parent company's cash position. Mr. Foster recalls that under his predecessors Colgate rarely made an acquisition, except for an occasional small company "that came limping to us on the way to the grave."

Yet, as Mr. Foster saw it, Colgate's businesses faced stagnation; the soap and toothpaste markets were saturated in many countries, and there were just so many new places Colgate could go. Procter & Gamble, as the bigger and wealthier company, was almost certain to win any serious contest over U.S. market shares. And Colgate's repeated efforts to develop new lines of business on its own, without acquisitions, had failed.

On the basis of what he saw as their growth potential, Mr. Foster picked several new businesses for Colgate to enter— health care, cosmetics and a few others were on the initial list— and the company started seeking acquisitions. In 1972 it outbid Textron Inc. to acquire Boston-based Kendall Co., maker of Curad plastic bandages and other hospital supplies. The price: $514.6 million in stock. Six more companies were acquired by the end of 1974.

It was a rapid pace, and Mr. Foster—apparently because of his tendency to dominate all aspects of the growing company— soon ran into trouble with some directors who were souring on one-man rule. At a stormy session in 1975, directors forced him to give up one of his titles (he had been president as well as chairman and chief executive). Some of the 16 operating units that had been reporting to Mr. Foster then started reporting to Keith Crane, the new president. Even so, "David didn't lose an iota of his power," one insider says, explaining that Mr. Foster still makes all the important decisions.

On other fronts, things were going more smoothly. At first, Colgate's plans to improve Kendall, its new subsidiary, had been delayed by disagreements between Mr. Foster and Willard Bright, the Kendall president, but Mr. Bright resigned ("Colgate wasn't big enough for two chief executive officers," he says) and Colgate made big changes in Kendall's operations. More efficient management allowed—at a time when the business was growing—a $42 million reduction in the funds tied up in raw materials, packing materials and accounts receivable. This money was then used to reduce debt.

As Kendall profits zoomed, Colgate was also injecting new life into the U.S. operations of Helena Rubinstein, which was in the red when the cosmetics producer was acquired for $142.3 million in stock in 1973. These operations returned to the black after Colgate lopped off hundreds of products, introduced some promising new ones (including a skin cream priced at $50 for a two-ounce jar) and took numerous financial and marketing measures. "We can say quite categorically that a turnaround has happened," says Peter H. Engel, the Colgate vice president now in charge of Rubinstein.

Encouraged by its progress with the companies acquired early, Colgate is plunging ahead to buy more. Foods had been one business that Mr. Foster thought Colgate could enter without acquisitions, and it tried to do so by marketing in the U.S. a cereal (Alpen) produced in England. But this pet Foster project collapsed because of inadequate supplies and fierce competition. ("It was supreme egotism," a Colgate vice president says, "to think we could cart a product from England to here and run up against the big food companies.") So Mr. Foster in 1976 paid $179.3 million in stock for Riviana Foods, the Houston-based producer of Carolina Rice and other products—thus using acquisition after all to enter the food business.

Colgate has also been buying some small producers of sports equipment and athletic clothing, building up a new "leisure and entertainment" division whose products include Bancroft tennis rackets. Now, Colgate says its U.S. acquisition program is substantially complete. "We aren't finished, but the frame is pretty well made," says Mr. Crane, the Colgate president.

Mr. Foster says Colgate now will concentrate on acquisitions overseas. Of his 16 acquisitions to date, seven have been overseas, but they account for less than $40 million of the company's $935 million in outlays for acquisitions. (In addition, Helena Rubinstein's business is largely overseas.)

Making acquistions is by no means Mr. Foster's only goal. He is attempting to increase the company's profitability by continuing and expanding on Mr. Lesch's practice of appointing special "task forces" of managers to ferret out waste. As the result of one such task force, the company now expects to save $750,000 yearly by making its own plastic bottles in Portugal, Spain and Brazil. An additional $1 million a year in savings is expected in Belgium because Colgate now is making polyfilm there for use in disposable diapers.

Colgate's return of profit on sales has improved under Mr. Foster to 4.3% in 1976 from 3.4% in 1971, and Mr. Foster says his goal from the start has been a 5% return on sales by 1980. He adds, however, that soaring energy costs probably will prevent him from achieving that, making 4.7% a more realistic expectation.

With all the acquisitions, Colgate Dental Cream remains the company's No. 1 product. Other products include Ajax, Fab and Cold Power detergents; Irish Spring, Palmolive and Cashmere Bouquet toilet soaps; Palmolive dishwashing liquid; and Ultra Brite toothpaste.

The company's promotional and advertising efforts have been changed considerably under the Foster regime. "Colgate had an image of an old, rather stuffy company," Mr. Foster says. "It wasn't seen as a swinging company, a young people's company." He tackled that problem mainly by sponsoring women's sports events and using sports figures rather than professional actresses for TV commercials (many of which are seen on "The Doctors," the soap opera that Colgate produces and sponsors). Mr. Foster insists that the strategy is working, although at least one securities analyst has questioned whether

Colgate is making "optimum use" of its promotional dollars.

Perhaps Mr. Foster's most criticized move was the payment of $5.5 million late in 1974 for the Mission Hills, Calif., golf course (and surrounding subdivision), for use by the company for promotional purposes. Mr. Foster, a crack golfer himself, has often been accused of having bought the course for his own pleasure, But the company insists that the transaction was justified and that Colgate will even make some money selling condominiums in the subdivision.

David Foster was born in England in 1920 to American parents, and thus was recognized as a citizen by both countries. (He renounced his British citizenship in 1953.) His father, Robert Foster, was with Palmolive-Peet, but the son had no particular career in mind when he attended Cambridge University and studied economics and history. Then he spent six years during World War II as a Royal Navy pilot; he received the highest decorations after combat missions mainly in the Middle East and the Pacific.

At his father's invitation, David Foster joined Colgate's British unit in 1946 as a management trainee ("It was a bit embarrassing—there were ugly words about nepotism," he recalls) and soon proved an able salesman. After Robert Foster's retirement in the early 1950s, as managing director of Colgate's British operations, David Foster kept rising in the company. By 1965 he headed the parent company's key household-products division in the U.S., where he impressed associates with his decisiveness. "He was a natural leader," one subordinate recalls.

While it was obvious that Mr. Foster would get Colgate's top job, at present it is far from obvious who will succeed him, in part because the president, Mr. Crane, is only a year younger. But Mr. Foster insists the succession question isn't urgent yet because he plans to stay about five more years, probably retiring at age 62, or three years short of the mandatory retirement age.

Some associates doubt that Mr. Foster will retire early—"his total life is tied up in the business," one acquaintance says—but Mr. Foster says he has enough other interests, such as art, architecture and his family, to make retirement attractive. He is married to Patricia Anne Firth (an earlier marriage, to the actress Glynis Johns, ended in divorce) and has two children. The couple has a New York City apartment and a house at Nantucket, Mass.

Mr. Foster's subordinates don't seem eager for him to go. Despite his toughness and aloofness, they say, he is loyal to industrious employes and has done a lot to improve salaries. (Mr. Foster's own salary and bonus last year totaled $320,667.) They also say he is building a company with more opportunities for advancement and for "psychic income"—the feeling that you're working for a company that's going somewhere. Richard J. Vail, a vice president, adds:

"He wants it to be said that he's moving the company forward faster than anybody else who ever ran Colgate—and I think it's true."

Quiet Growth at Teledyne

In 1966, Henry Singleton, chairman of Teledyne Inc., told the owners of Aqua Tec Corp. that his company wanted to buy theirs. They had a question. "Tele-who? That's what we said," recalls Eugene Rouse, head of the company then and now.

Aqua Tec did enter the Teledyne fold and was renamed Teledyne Water Pik, after its well-known dental-hygiene product. But its owners could be excused for not recognizing Teledyne then; only six years old, it was something of a corporate pup, with only $86.5 million in 1965 sales.

No more. Under the reins of its founder, the ambitious Mr. Singleton, Teledyne has exploded into a $2 billion giant with more than 130 subsidiaries and divisions. They churn out microcomputers and insurance, drone aircraft and shower massagers, specialty metals and stereo equipment. But the company is still "Tele-who?" to much of the investing community.

Teledyne officials don't address analyst groups or grant many interviews. Press releases and stockholder reports are models of brevity. Even some securities analysts who follow conglomerates have all but given up on Teledyne, complaining that they can't get enough information. "When it comes to being quiet, they're way off by themselves," says one. "Their view is, if you don't like it, sell the stock."

If you do sell the stock, Teledyne itself may wind up with it. The company in recent years has gobbled up big blocks of its own stock. It has also bought major interests in other big concerns; this reflects the strategic thinking of its scientist-chief, who sees corporations as "just so many chips tossed on the ocean wave" of an ever-changing business environment they cannot influence. Instead of breasting the wave, they have to take whatever bargains float by at the moment and, to Mr. Singleton, that means undervalued stocks.

His success in swimming with the wave has given Teledyne an enviable record in sales and earnings growth, though its changes in course have sometimes bewildered Wall Street. In the soaring sixties, for example, when merger mania sent conglomerate stocks skyward (Teledyne stock at one point was selling at 60 times its annual per-share earnings), the company was a voracious acquirer, issuing rafts of new shares in an acquisition binge that pushed it into the billion-dollar class by 1969.

Sensing the impending recession and the end of the go-go years, Mr. Singleton abruptly ceased acquiring companies, paid off $180 million in debt, and turned to cash management and internal growth. This turnabout helped the company weather the 1970-71 recession and add almost a billion dollars more to sales since. A few years ago, Teledyne began a new investment strategy, buying back its own stock. From a peak of about 40 million shares in 1971, the number outstanding has been pruned to less than 12 million today.

The company's continued strong earnings gains, coupled with the big buybacks, have sent per-share net for existing stockholders through the ceiling. Teledyne ranks as No. 115 in sales in Fortune magazine's list of industrial concerns; in per-share earnings growth over the past 10 years, it is No. 5, with an average annual rise of more than 30%. Per-share net, only 66 cents in 1966, was $10.21 in 1976 and exceeded $15 in 1977.

Why, then, isn't Teledyne out trumpeting its virtues on Wall Street? Mr. Singleton shrugs; with the entire market depressed and the conglomerate group long out of vogue, he considers it a waste of breath. "To say we lost our popularity," he comments in a rare interview, "would be an understatement."

He is trying, however, to position the company for an eventual market rise, not only by buying back its own stock but with quiet, open-market purchases of other shares through Teledyne's insurance subsidiaries. Now the company is an invisible but formidable presence in many a boardroom: Through the insurance units, it controls more than 20% of Litton Industries

Inc., Curtiss-Wright Corp. and Walter Kidde & Co., and has lesser interests in a dozen other firms. All are just investments, Mr. Singleton insists, not spearheads for later takeover attempts.

Teledyne's big stock purchases have nevertheless aroused criticism from people who complain that the quiet giant has been far too tight-lipped. Former Teledyne stockholders, for example, are suing the company, charging that in tender offers to repurchase its stock, it failed to adequately disclose all its favorable prospects for the future—information that might have induced them to hang on to their shares instead of selling out. Teledyne denies it.

The Securities and Exchange Commission, meanwhile, has put Teledyne on the carpet, charging that the insurance subsidiaries that made the stock purchases didn't adequately inform the SEC about the influence of the parent company and Mr. Singleton on those investment decisions. The agency accused the company of "concealing" the chief executive's key role in buying the stock, thus hiding Teledyne's control over the securities.

As a boy growing up on his father's Texas ranch, Mr. Singleton enjoyed reading about captains of industry, but he originally wanted a Navy career and got an appointment to Annapolis. A stomach ulcer interrupted his studies there and he later attended Massachusetts Institute of Technology, where he got three degrees, including a doctorate in electronics, and a teaching appointment in the department of electrical engineering.

In 1951 he started working at Hughes Aircraft Co., then moved to North American Aviation the next year. In 1954, he was hired by Charles (Tex) Thornton, chairman of Litton Industries then and now. Mr. Thornton calls his former associate "a very able scientist, realist, and a straightforward guy." After building Litton's important guidance systems division from scratch in four years, Mr. Singleton became Litton's vice president and general manager.

Former associates say that a personality clash with Roy Ash, then Litton's president, was one factor in Mr. Singleton's decision in 1960 to leave and start his own company, Teledyne.

He and Litton colleague George Kozmetsky each invested $225,000 in the new venture, which they hoped would attract some of the many government electronics contracts being let then. There was no grand design for growth; Mr. Singleton says he even flirted with the idea of developing a business-machine company competing with IBM.

By the mid-1960s, however, Teledyne was swimming along with the conglomerate merger wave—but with a difference. While many budding conglomerates bought companies for the cash in their treasuries or their sexiness on Wall Street, Mr. Singleton focused on mostly privately owned companies, usually small- to medium-sized, with executive teams that had been able to give their concerns strong positions in their fields but who needed more financing to expand. Teledyne provided it and let the managers go on managing.

This hands-off approach helped win over many concerns fearful of losing their identity or being dismembered in a merger. "We were thought of as a technological company, not just a stock-market company," says Teledyne President George Roberts, who works in tandem with Mr. Singleton and who himself came to Teledyne through a merger.

Observers believe that the quality of Teledyne's acquisitions and its freehandedness in financing its units are responsible for a good part of its success. The rest, according to Robert Hanisee, a securities analyst who follows Teledyne for the Los Angeles brokerage house of Crowell, Weedon & Co., results from the parent company's careful cash-management program, installed by Mr. Singleton in 1969.

Mr. Singleton named his company from Greek roots meaning "force applied at a distance," and that neatly summarizes the supervision he and Mr. Roberts apply to the subsidiaries. How they manage their units is up to them—"Henry and I try very hard not to create ideas for our companies," Mr. Roberts says—so long as they meet present goals.

Company presidents must submit to headquarters, every fall, exhaustive budget plans that generally run from 50 to 100 pages. An equally voluminous profit plan has to be submitted in the first quarter, with an update in May. These standardized reports "put every bit of our thinking about our company into numbers and ratios," says one subsidiary executive. This executive quickly learned of Mr. Singleton's emphasis on the reports when Mr. Singleton rejected his first one.

Mr. Singleton spends much of his time personally reviewing these reports and quizzing the subsidiary chiefs. His voracious appetite for detail and numbers is coupled with powers of recall that sometimes astound subordinates. (A chess fiend, he often plays a variation of the game in which neither player can look at the board but must commit the changing position of the pieces to memory.)

During profit-plan reviews he will sometimes pounce on obscure statistics—sales per employe, for example—and compare them accurately with year-ago figures committed to memory. "Then he'll say something like, 'It looks as if you have too many people lying around.' He's a human computer," says Mr. Rouse of Water Pik.

A cool man, Mr. Singleton is not given to back-patting. At one recent meeting, Mr. Rouse was praised by President Roberts for a sharp increase in Water Pik's cash flow. Mr. Roberts then asked Mr. Singleton if the performance didn't merit his congratulations, too. The chairman replied crisply: "The fact that I didn't comment otherwise should be congratulations enough."

Cash takes the place of compliments. Under the company's incentive plan, the heads of subsidiaries who keep inventories in hand, make the best use of their capital spending and show healthy cash flow can earn performance bonuses that may equal their annual salaries.

The hundreds of subsidiary reports and plans submitted yearly also help the parent company spot trouble early, say Teledyne's top executives. When trouble does arise, Mr. Singleton is likely to deal with it abruptly and radically. In 1972, for example, Teledyne's Packard-Bell unit was suffering losses on its home TV and stereo operations; Mr. Singleton shut them down permanently. The Packard-Bell acquisition, he says, was the only one he is sorry he made.

But Teledyne's most severe problem cropped up in 1974 when its Argonaut Insurance Co. unit, a major medical-malpractice insurer, was inundated with hefty judgments against many of its physician-clients. Mr. Singleton descended on the company, sacked its managers, slashed costs to the bone and drastically cut back the writing of new malpractice insurance.

Teledyne's chief is still bitter about the Argonaut debacle, which resulted in a $105 million pretax writeoff that slashed net 50% below the previous year—only the second year in the company's history that it failed to show earnings gains. Other malpractice insurers had had losses too, "but our people compounded it by trying to be the low bidder on every contract that arose," Mr. Singleton says. "We were at fault in our personnel decisions there."

But Argonaut is back in the black again. Teledyne's profits are rising, and Mr. Singleton can say that his company has met the goals he set for it a decade ago. Still fit and trim at 61—he is an avid jogger—he has no thought of retirement.

Some in the investment community can't believe that the intense, competitive Mr. Singleton will be content just to go on managing what he already has. Rumors that Teledyne will be bidding for this company or that frequently run up and down Wall Street, and "deal men"—finders who earn a fee bringing prospective merger partners together—still call him and offer their blushing brides.

All are rejected. "They're professionals and they should know better," Mr. Singleton says. "We aren't an acquiring company." The climate, he says, is bad; attempts to buy companies outright now often result in competitive bidding wars between rival suitors that drive the target's price far above market value.

Mr. Singleton prefers to buy low-priced minority interests on the open market—and wait. "I won't predict the future," he says, "but it's unlikely that we'll be active in acquisitions in the next few years."

He didn't say never.

Sleeping Giant Named International Paper

J. Stanford Smith loves the showy gesture. During a speech not long ago to a paper-industry conference, he wheeled a nine-foot-wide bookcase onto the platform, then, midway through his talk, whipped off the cloth to reveal a stack of books—the amount of paper work required to get an environmental permit for a mill.

"Smith's a real P. T. Barnum kind of guy," says another executive in the industry.

Mr. Smith's appointment as chairman of International Paper Co. at the beginning of 1974—he had been a top executive at General Electric Co.—followed an exhaustive executive search for a man who could demonstrate some fairly fancy footwork. The world's biggest paper company was in the doldrums.

Major capital projects were far behind schedule and had huge cost overruns. Budgeting procedures were lax. Management development was weak. Perhaps worst of all, corporate morale was suffering from severe losses in some of the company's businesses and executive shakeups that followed them.

Now, three years into the job, Mr. Smith and his team have chalked up some substantial achievements. They have undertaken one of the more ambitious reorganizations in corporate history. They have set up a management-information system that centralizes computer operations, introduced more stringent criteria for capital appropriations, substantially tightened budget controls—and improved the corporation's financial position.

But the industry agrees that IP still isn't where it should be. "The company simply doesn't have as much clout as some other companies in the industry," says a competitor. "They could be the IBM of the paper industry and bury every one of us, but they're still a sleeping giant."

That IP is a giant is undeniable. It is North America's largest private owner of forest lands and the world's largest producer of paperboard, paper and pulp. It owns outright 8.5 million acres of forest land and has harvest rights on another 12.4 million acres, primarily in Canada. With more than 50,000 employes, it manufactures newsprint, paper towels, pulp, white papers, linerboard, boxes, lumber, plywood and a variety of other products—leading, in 1977, to profits of $233.7 million on sales of $3.7 billion.

But its relative lack of clout has been demonstrated by various IP price increases that other, smaller, companies declined to emulate, often costing IP critical shares of market. The company's industrial packaging group, for instance, tried and failed to get through box price increases in 1975 and late 1976.

"We were amazed that nobody else in the industry went along with these increases," says James Malloy, IP's head of those divisions. "We just didn't know what to make of it."

Others think they know. They point to Mr. Smith and his vaunted reorganization program. The thrust of it has been to shift emphasis away from paper (which still constitutes 87% of IP's business) into the broader area of land-resource management, including real estate and oil.

The underlying motive is to cushion the company from the cyclical nature of the paper business. Indeed, chairman Smith says, "I won't even refer to papermaking as an industry because it's merely one part of the larger forest-products industry."

But the result, say industry analysts, has been to give short shrift to pulp and paper—to the point that untimely pricing decisions are routine, market shares have been lost, and management expertise in paper is sorely lacking at the highest levels. "IP hasn't had a chief executive in years who knew one end of a paper machine from the other," says a former company executive.

International Paper Co. was created in 1898 by the merger

of 20 paper mills in New England and New York. For the period 1943 to 1961 it was run as a feudal empire by the Hinman family, the sole purpose being to cut trees to keep the mills running. In 1963 John Hinman, the family sovereign, retired from the chairmanship, leaving a company that was rich in assets and debt-free. His son Edward eventually took over as chairman.

By the late 1960s the younger Mr. Hinman began to worry that the company was vulnerable to a takeover, and he started acquiring debt, at exorbitant interest rates, to finance what turned out to be a disastrous acquisition program. Between 1968 and 1970 he and his colleagues engineered three major acquisitions: Davol Inc., a manufacturer of surgical items, for $98.5 million; American Central, a Michigan-based developer of second homes, for $17.8 million in stock; and Donald L. Bren Co., a California developer of second homes in planned communities, for $34 million in stock. In addition, IP built a $50 million tissue plant in Oxnard, Calif.

Davol turned out to be a solid though unspectacular acquisition. However, between 1970 and 1971 the bottom dropped out of the residential housing market, and IP proved to be a late entry in the consumer-tissue business, which had been largely preempted by Kimberly-Clark Corp. and Procter & Gamble Co. Then the paper market dropped because of oversupply and a depressed economy.

Earnings plunged in 1970. In February 1971 IP's board of directors met at the Yale Club in New York City and voted to fire Edward Hinman. At the same meeting Paul Gorman, who had been president of Western Electric Co. and then chief executive officer of Penn Central Co., was introduced to the board and immediately made chairman, chief executive officer and president.

Mr. Gorman began a cleanup operation, establishing an $81 million reserve fund to facilitate writeoffs of unprofitable operations. It is agreed that Mr. Gorman brought the company a long way towards recovery. But he had stipulated at the time of his appointment that he be allowed to retire at the end of 1973.

Enter Mr. Smith, to take on the massive task of ensuring IP's growth and profitability in the future. He is an energetic and extroverted man, now 62 years old, with gray hair and a generous girth, described by friend and foe alike as a person with a large talent and a large ego.

"Smith demands unmitigated loyalty," says an executive who used to work with him at IP. "He's one of the most brilliant executives I ever met, but his demands aren't always reasonable." The IP chairman denies that he is difficult to work with. With each new assignment, he says, he gets "scores of letters and phone calls from employes asking to work with me again." He adds, "People with ability welcome responsibility."

Mr. Smith brought with him from GE the reputation of a man who could fix ailing businesses. Most notably, he was credited with saving GE millions of dollars by reorganizing its money-losing computer business so that it later could be sold at a profit.

He also brought the reputation of a man who devises catchy schemes to motivate the staff. At GE, he was remembered for giving out "tiger tail" awards to the most productive departments and "turtle" awards to the laggards. "Stan used to invite the employes out to his home in Greenwich, Conn., and stand on the balcony and throw down the tiger tail awards to the winners," says a former colleague.

At IP it has been "Operation Breakthru . . . an extra effort to serve customers. . . ." This is a program to improve company morale, with buttons, charts and a device called a "cost monster." It attempts to give employes more insight into quality and cost control problems at the mill and corporate level.

Mr. Smith saw his chief task at IP as bringing the company "into the mainstream of modern management." That meant reorganization. He says he quickly decided on a marketing orientation that would extract maximum value from the company's vast resources. If more could be realized by using timber for lumber or plywood than for papermaking, then IP would go after the higher value.

IP therefore has been expanding its lumber and plywood

operations. It acquired General Crude Oil Co. of Houston for $489 million. And it developed its real-estate operations. To implement the new approach, Mr. Smith restructured the company into three basic businesses: forest products, international and diversified. He also decentralized profit and loss responsibilities to rest with the executives in charge of each product group within the various businesses.

Most of those responsibilities previously had been in the office of Judson Hannigan, IP's president. Not surprisingly, Mr. Hannigan quit in January 1976. He was known as a man who "could tell you who made a piece of paper just by putting it between his fingers."

That kind of feel for papermaking, the biggest portion of IP's business, is just what is lacking in many members of the new top management team, say critics. "IP is well staffed with paper experts," counters Mr. Smith. But only two of the company's four executive vice presidents are considered to have a real working knowledge of the industry, and the fifth executive vice president's position, for forest products, remains glaringly empty.

Mr. Smith's philosophy is that a good man can perform well in any business, and he brought in a number of men from other industries, a process that Mr. Gorman had started. This created some confusion. A former employe recalls, "Some guys were running around, saying, 'This is the way we did it at General Electric.' Others were saying, 'This is the way we did it at Western Electric.' And one guy from an oil company kept referring to the paper mills as refineries."

That lack of depth, say industry observers, is what led IP to make some bad pricing decisions. Mr. Smith replies that "somebody has to be bold enough to go out there and get the prices." And he defends his approach to the business in general by saying it "is the only way to achieve a decent return for investors."

As the chairman points out, earnings have more than doubled in the 1972 to 1976 period compared with the previous five years. However, in the 1977 first quarter, IP's earnings dropped by 23.6% from the year-earlier results to \$48.6 million, and in the second quarter they fell by 29.6% from the year-earlier figure to \$59.1 million.

This certainly resulted in part from factors that were affecting other big papermakers too—bad weather, customer resistance to price increases and a generally sluggish market. But competitors didn't experience the same kind of drops as IP. Union Camp Corp., for instance, recorded earnings drops of only 2.5% in each of the first two 1977 quarters.

The IP downturn revived a running battle between the company and the securities analysts who follow its fortunes. The analysts have been complaining that IP didn't alert them late last year to an impending downturn, but, says Mr. Smith, "We don't make projections on the up side, so we're not going to make them on the down side."

A year ago, however, IP was sufficiently perturbed by its relations with the analysts to commission Opinion Research Inc. to study the situation. The report concluded that in analysts' perceptions IP isn't "considered a real leader or ahead of its other major competitors" in a variety of performance factors. The company gets average ratings from analysts on such items as competitive position, financial performance including diversification, and earnings growth potential for the next five years.

If the analysts are critical of IP, so is Mr. Smith critical of the report. He says, "The sample of only 15 respondents as well as the methodology and write-up were grossly inadequate."

The situation may be, as analyst Lawrence Ross of Mitchell Hutchins Inc. puts it, that because of IP's enormous assets, "the company doesn't have to have above-average management to achieve above-average results."

But, adds Mr. Ross: "Some of IP's top managers don't have the business in their blood, and that's never a good thing."

Master Marketer Who Tries Harder

A few years ago, a magazine cover featured a picture of a smiling, well-tanned David J. Mahoney superimposed on the labels of such Norton Simon Inc. products as Hunt's tomato sauce, Canada Dry ginger ale and Johnny Walker scotch.

The montage was appropriate. For few men have put more of a personal stamp on their companies than David Mahoney, chief executive of Norton Simon. Since 1969, he has taken a grab bag of marginal businesses collected by the company's founder and namesake, disposed of 21 of them, redeployed some $450 million in assets and spent $660 million in advertising to make NSI a leading purveyor of consumer products.

Now, the flamboyant 54-year-old Mr. Mahoney is poised to put his personal stamp on his latest acquisition—Avis Inc. The company previously acquired 47% of Avis from International Telephone & Telegraph Co. (which was ordered by the Justice Department to dispose of its holding). Mr. Mahoney's $22 per shareoffer for that block abruptly ended a bidding war by two other companies, who were offering around $21. The balance of the stock was acquired through an offer, also at $22 a share, to other stockholders.

"Like Avis, we just tried harder," Mr. Mahoney says about the transaction, which cost about $174 million all told.

Avis, of course, says it tries harder because it is a clear No. 2 to RCA's Hertz Corp. in the car-rental business. "I don't think Dave will be satisfied that Avis is only No. 2," says an NSI executive who has seen Mr. Mahoney's handling of earlier acquisitions.

Any serious challenge to Hertz's supremacy would take a lot of doing, but if Mr. Mahoney's past performance is any indication, Avis will be making a run for it. In Europe, Avis is already No. 1 among car-rental companies.

With his Madison Avenue roots, Mr. Mahoney's corporate strategy to date has been to concentrate on big brand-name, high-profit consumer products and to battle intensely through advertising, promotion and new-product development to gain bigger chunks of the particular markets.

Increasing a product's market share involves "cool nerves, cold cash, hot products and creative marketing," he says, clearly reflecting his Madison Avenue background.

Whether the techniques he has used successfully in the cosmetics, fashion and wine industries will succeed similarly in the car-rental business is arguable, and some have their doubts. Richard Sondheim, an analyst for Dean Witter Reynolds, notes that Avis is far afield from NSI's consumer packaged goods, with bigger capital investments and bigger risks involved. Avis's fortunes depend greatly on fluctuations in interest rates and used-car prices, for example.

But Mr. Mahoney doesn't see a lot of differences, and his present and former colleagues at NSI predict he will soon be deeply involved in Avis affairs and applying to the car-rental business many of the same techniques he has applied to say, McCall patterns and Wesson vegetable oil.

"I think Avis' management is scared of Mahoney," one former NSI executive says. "I think they understand that when Mahoney buys something, he jumps in with both feet."

That doesn't necessarily mean major changes immediately. "I don't foresee Dave sending storm troopers into Avis," says E. Garrett Bewkes, vice chairman of NSI. "That's not his style."

Mr. Bewkes and others say that Mr. Mahoney typically gives the management of an acquired company considerable autonomy and time to meet his expectations. But he doesn't hesitate to ax the top brass if they can't live with his profit-or-perish style over a period of time.

Take Chester Firestein, who became president of Max Factor & Co. shortly after it was acquired by NSI in 1973. He was slow to invest in new products, NSI sources say, and Max Factor's earnings were stagnant for two years, so he left in December 1975. Mr. Mahoney calls it an "amicable divorce."

Mr. Firestein's successor was Samuel Kalish, a hard-driving taskmaster not unlike Mr. Mahoney. Mr. Kalish, who had been president of Revlon Inc.'s International unit, recalls that Mr. Mahoney said to him, "I hear that if you come to Max Factor, 50 people will leave." To which Mr. Kalish replied, "I hope it's the right 50."

After Mr. Kalish took over, indeed, more than 75 Max Factor managers either quit or were fired. "I don't know if it's ruthlessness or pragmatism with little emotion," Mr. Mahoney says about such shakeups. Decisions of this kind "really hurt," he says. "Nobody wants to be Genghis Khan."

To help build up Max Factor, NSI acquired Halston Enterprises to enter the fragrances market and Orlane of Paris, a maker of skin-care products. Prestige items of these companies helped Max Factor get its foot in the door of such stores as Saks, and Max Factor then introduced a new "Maxi" cosmetics line priced at $2 or less. Illustrating Mr. Mahoney's emphasis on new-product development, 20% to 25% of Max Factor's sales each year comes from new products.

The addition and transformation of Max Factor wasn't the only change at NSI after Mr. Mahoney assumed full command in August 1969. First, he pulled the company out of such erratic businesses as publishing, printing and packaging, shedding such properties as Redbook and McCall's magazines and David Susskind's Talent Associates Ltd.

With the funds from these divestitures, NSI bought not only Max Factor, Halston and Orlane, but also Alexis Lichine, the No. 3 importer of French table wines; San Martin Vineyards, a premium California wine company; Tanqueray gin; Old Fitzgerald bourbon; Reddi Wip; Orville Redenbacher's gourmet popcorn, and others. NSI also added such new NSI products as Barrelhead root bear and Hunt-Wesson's Prima Salsa spaghetti sauce.

The financial results have been impressive during Mr. Mahoney's tenure. For the fiscal year ended June 30, 1976, Norton Simon Inc. earned $92.4 million on sales of $1.74 billion—hefty increases from fiscal 1970's $37.7 million profit and $1.08 billion sales. Record results also were scored in fiscal 1977, with sales climbing to $1.81 billion, earnings to $101.8 million.

Impressive as they are, the results aren't quite up to the 15% annual earnings growth once projected by Mr. Mahoney. And there have been some minor setbacks along the way. Promoting of Canada Dry ginger ale as a soft drink instead of just a mixer hasn't had any significant success, for example. (Mr. Mahoney himself, because of an ulcer, shuns Johnny Walker and Tanqueray in favor of Canada Dry, which he drinks from a pewter mug at his favorite haunt, New York's "21" restaurant.)

Whatever the current growth rate of NSI, Mr. Mahoney has every intention of building it into a marketing giant on the scale of a Procter & Gamble Co., and the executives at Avis can be forgiven if they are indeed "scared" of David Mahoney.

Many NSI executives have come and gone since 1969, with as many quitting as were fired. Leaving in the past few years have been two presidents of operating companies, including Max Factor's Mr. Firestein, a senior vice president and several vice presidents. On July 1, 1978, Samuel Kalish, the man who took over the Max Factor presidency from Mr. Firestein, also stepped down.

Current and former executives describe NSI as a highly pressurized environment. "Dave operates by fear," says one ex-employe. "He likes to put two or three people in conflict and let them fight it out." One analyst who is friendly with Mr. Mahoney adds, "When there is a decision to be made, Dave will marshal his staff rather brutally to gather the information bearing on the decision." For example, he put 25 lawyers to work for four straight days to prepare the Avis tender offer.

Richard C. Beeson, Canada Dry's president, says, "I don't think Dave's ever been unfair. But he's an absolutely crazy man if someone screws up. He has the knack of making you feel he's your best friend, even though you know he's not. He motivates the hell out of people. He might get mad at me because we disagree, but the next day it's all kiss and make up."

For his part, Mr. Mahoney says, "Difficult? Yeah. But we're not going to be a P&G by sitting back in the status quo."

As NSI's chairman, president and chief executive, Mr. Mahoney doesn't like to have his one-man domination challenged. When he felt Joseph H. Gamache, his friend and senior vice president, was pushing too hard to be president, a "shootout" took place, NSI insiders say. Mr. Gamache says only that he had differences with Mr. Mahoney. Mr. Mahoney says, "Joe felt he should be president, and I just wasn't ready to put him in that position."

In any case, NSI sources say, Mr. Gamache was given the "golden handshake"—he was allowed to stay on for about a year with his salary and bonus totaling about $200,000, before departing in June 1975.

Mr. Mahoney has been shopping for a marketing man from outside the company to be chief operating officer. He confirms that when he heard rumors that Philip L. Beekman, a strong marketing executive from Colgate-Palmolive, was going to become president of Seagram Co., he called Mr. Beekman, an old friend, about the possibility of taking the NSI job instead. But Mr. Beekman had already committed himself verbally to Edgar Bronfman, chairman of Seagram. "I would've loved to have had Phil," he says.

Mr. Mahoney is paid handsomely, and he believes his key executives should be paid handsomely. Along with Mr. Kalish, he hired Earle K. Angstadt Jr., former president of Abercrombie & Fitch, to head McCall Patterns, and John E. Heilman, former president of Seagram Distillers, a unit of Seagram Co., to head Somerset Importers Inc., a leading liquor importer. Although NSI won't disclose their salaries, it's believed each makes well in excess of $100,000 a year plus bonuses and stock options.

Mr. Mahoney's salary and bonus, which totaled $844,444 in 1976, has often been criticized by shareholders as excessive, and one shareholder suit was settled recently with a small cutback in his total compensation.

The son of a New York crane operator, Mr. Mahoney has clearly come a long way. A talented athlete, Mr. Mahoney went to the University of Pennsylvania on a basketball scholarship, and after college went to work for a New York ad agency.

He eventually opened his own agency, and it was tough going at first. After work, Mr. Mahoney would hang out at the "21," often nursing one drink for the entire evening. But his easy going charm, big smile and flattery weren't lost on the influential businessmen who frequented the club. Later, some of those businessmen helped Mr. Mahoney to get a succession of top corporate jobs—president of Good Humor Corp., executive vice president of Colgate-Palmolive Co. and chief executive of Canada Dry Corp.

He was at Canada Dry in 1968, when NSI was founded through the consolidation of McCall Corp., Hunt Foods & Industries Inc. and Canada Dry.

After founder Norton Simon bowed out of the company in 1969 to pursue his art interests, the company was run by a troika of William McKenna, chairman; Harold Williams, finance committee chairman, and Mr. Mahoney, president and chief operating officer. A fierce struggle ensued that lasted a year. "McKenna and Mahoney disliked each other intensely, and Dave wanted to be No. 1," an observer says.

Mr. Mahoney became No. 1, largely by winning support of NSI's operating companies, and the other two left the company. Mr. Williams, who remained friendly with Mr. Mahoney, was retained as a director and consultant until his recent appointment as chairman of the Securities and Exchange Commission.

Despite his image as a bon vivant, Mr. Mahoney considers himself a fiscal conservative, as befits a child of the Depression. He points to NSI's buildup of working capital, including $266 million in cash, before the Avis purchase.

"He's got a fetish about keeping cash on hand," one NSI executive says. "He never wants to be subservient to the bankers." Mr. Mahoney says he has noticed "a lot of companies selling off acquisitions made during the halcyon days," and doesn't want to be in that position.

He admits he may have been too prudent at times. He rejected the chance to purchase International Playtex Co. in 1975 as potentially a slow-growth company, but the company has prospered under Esmark Inc.

Even with the big outlay for Avis, Mr. Mahoney says he is ready to buy another big company tomorrow if it fits into his marketing strategy. And chances are the takeover will be friendly. Talks with Miles Laboratories Inc. were dropped awhile back, he says, because "they made it pretty obvious they didn't want to sell."

Not surprisingly, business is most of Mr. Mahoney's life. Though he is comfortable with the so-called beautiful people who frequent places like the "21," his friends see him as essentially a "steak and potatoes man." He says his best friends are mostly business associates or other executives like Pete Rozelle, commissioner of the National Football League.

He spends two hours a night with his children, David, 17, and Barbara, 15, at his Park Avenue apartment, and he generally spends weekends with them at his home at Bridgehampton, Long Island. He had been divorced from his wife when she died several years ago. He recently married Hildegard "Hillie" Merrill, a former Miss Rheingold.

He is about as competitive in sports as he is in business. Before he gave up golf for tennis, he tried fervently to improve his golf game. A former golfing companion of his observes, "Dave couldn't understand why the golf ball wouldn't behave for him like everybody else."

Making Things Pop At Pillsbury

In late December 1972, William H. Spoor, head of Pillsbury Co.'s international operations, was driving Arthur Rosewall, president of the company's Burger King subsidiary, to the airport in Minneapolis.

The conversation inevitably turned to topic "A" at Pillsbury: selection of the next chairman and chief executive. Robert J. Keith had just resigned. He would die of cancer five months later.

"It it were up to me," Mr. Rosewall said, "I'd just put Terry Hanold (Pillsbury's president) in there and get it over with."

Mr. Spoor recalls that he peered sideways at Mr. Rosewall and squirmed. He had just learned that Pillsbury's new chairman and chief executive would be William H. Spoor.

It was a choice that would surprise not only Mr. Rosewall but almost everybody familiar with the company. Pillsbury's international operations were anything but impressive, contributing in 1973 just 8.5% of the company's earnings—less both in dollar and percentage terms than they accounted for five years earlier. Aside from a vague reputation as sort of a wheeler-dealer, Mr. Spoor was largely an unknown quantity and certainly wasn't a member of Pillsbury's inner circle. Nevertheless, he was the choice. The board of directors elected him on Jan. 3, 1973.

For better or worse, Pillsbury Co. will never be the same. The stodgy, old-line flour miller that sat on its hands while competitors raced forward in the 1960s is "at last a hopped-up company," says one longtime employe. "Spoor's got the guts to make significant moves. That's the big difference in this company. We're not just bumping along anymore."

Not everyone agrees that Mr. Spoor's moves are all to the

good. The story of Pillsbury under Bill Spoor is still unfolding, skeptics say. Whatever its outcome, it should provide a classic case study of what happens to a conservative company that is suddenly thrust into the hands of a tough, aggressive executive who effects deep and rapid change.

As measured by profits at least, what has happened so far has been very good. Pillsbury's earnings from continuing operations in its last five years have grown by an average of more than 20% a year, to a record $57.8 million on $1.46 billion in sales in the year ended May 31, 1977. That compares with an average annual gain of just 9% in the last five pre-Spoor years. It also is better, a company memo delightedly notes, than the gains posted by such top food companies as Beatrice Foods, Ralston Purina, Carnation and—sweetest of all to the folks at Pillsbury—Twin City rival General Mills.

Mr. Spoor can't be given all the credit for that; some of that growth would have taken place without him. But the 53-year-old executive seems determined to make such gains commonplace. "This is going to be a first-class company in all respects," he says. And the kind of company investors swarm to. "Yes, damn it," he says, "All my stock options were underwater when I took this job."

Through acquisitions, Mr. Spoor has accelerated Pillsbury's move into restaurants and has led it into the frozen-foods business, something the company had been contemplating for years. More acquisitions are on the way, he says; among other things, he hopes to acquire some European company "close to ourselves in size."

Mr. Spoor has pulled Pillsbury out of its erratic poultry business and some other pursuits, such as flower selling, low-cost housing, publishing and wine making. He has stepped up Pillsbury's spending on research and development, plans to build a new research center and has given a research man one of the company's top executive posts, all in an effort to improve the 107-year-old company's mediocre record in developing new products.

In personnel matters, Mr. Spoor has shown little of the sentimentality of past Pillsbury chiefs, who often placed longevity above talent and promoted from within accordingly. Mr. Spoor, himself a career Pillsbury employe, tapped another career employe, Winston Wallin, to take over the presidency and day-to-day operations in June 1977. At the same time, he has recruited vigorously from outside Pillsbury, and with notable success. He also has carried out some notable dismissals. "People aren't exactly trembling, but everybody is keeping a scorecard," says one middle-level executive. "They know who has come and who has gone, and they know there's a pressure to perform in this company like there never has been before."

Mr. Spoor also has appointed six of the company's 14 directors; only one of the six was a Pillsbury insider. Mr. Spoor hired Philip D. Aines, formerly director of food-products development at Procter & Gamble Co., to head Pillsbury's research and engineering. He named Walter D. Scott, an associate director of the federal Office of Management and Budget, to be Pillsbury's chief financial officer. He lured Raymond F. Good from H. J. Heinz Co., where he was president of Heinz's U.S.A. division, to take charge of Pillsbury's consumer division. In January 1977, Mr. Spoor scored another coup when he persuaded Donald N. Smith, senior executive vice president at McDonald's, to head up Pillsbury's Burger King subsidiary.

"We were too inbred," Mr. Spoor says in explaining his outside recruiting. "And when I stacked up the credentials of the people we were looking at, against those of people we already had, the outsiders won, hands down."

But some people who follow the company's fortunes are concerned about possible management disruption at Pillsbury. They wonder if the outside people will mesh well with key inside people. They wonder if some of the outside recruits might chafe under Mr. Spoor's strong rule.

They also remember the Jimmy Peterson affair. James Peterson, "Jimmy Pete" as Mr. Spoor sometimes called him, was once the company's rising star. In 1972, at the age of 45, he was head of the consumer division, the company's largest, and was regarded by some as a top candidate for the chairmanship. Instead, he was elected president when Mr. Spoor was elected chairman.

Mr. Spoor and Mr. Peterson simply didn't function well as a team. One former employe says the two argued openly and often bitterly at management meetings. He describes their reign as "a repeated collision of egos."

Around that time—and some attribute this to the Spoor-Peterson friction—Mr. Peterson reportedly grew overly demanding and even abusive of his subordinates. There were morale problems. They peaked in the winter of 1975, when George Masko, head of the lucrative refrigerated-foods division, resigned. Within a few days Mr. Peterson was gone—"asked" by the board to resign—and Mr. Masko was back in the fold.

To the casual acquaintance, Mr. Spoor appears as warm and affable as the Poppin' Fresh Doughboy who appears in Pillsbury advertisements. He hardly seems a ruthless terminator of men's careers. As a young man, he considered being a minister, and he has said that he still wonders occasionally if he is doing enough to help people. "You die when you have to let someone go," he says. "You're up all night."

As a corporate tactician, on the other hand, Mr. Spoor apparently rests easily. "Outsiders say, 'My, look at Pillsbury, all that turnover,' " he says. "They don't look at the people who've left as a strengthening of the company. I do."

Mr. Spoor's reorganization moves have left Pillsbury with three major divisions: consumer, which accounted for about 36% of profits in fiscal 1977; restaurants, also about 36%; and agricultural products, 28%. "We've got no dogs," Mr. Spoor says. "Every business is making money."

Burger King, the 1,700-unit hamburger chain, is Pillsbury's chief restaurant operation and the company's major growth vehicle since it was acquired in 1967. But Mr. Spoor expresses dissatisfaction with Burger King because it fares poorly in virtually all financial comparisons with McDonald's, the industry leader. Burger King is No. 2.

Among other things, "We just haven't done the job with the kids that McDonald's has," Mr. Spoor says. He and Mr. Rosewall, who moved up from Burger King president to Pillsbury executive vice president for restaurants, blame that partly on Burger King's advertising. They have dumped the subsidiary's former ad agency, Batten, Barton, Durstine & Osborn, in favor of J. Walter Thompson.

Mr. Spoor broadened Pillsbury's restaurant involvement in May 1976 with the acquisition of Steak and Ale Restaurants of America Inc., a 120-unit chain with one of the industry's highest profit margins. Pillsbury paid about $100 million in stock, making the deal its most expensive acquisition yet. Pillsbury also operates an internally developed chain of 23 Poppin' Fresh Pie Shops that has done very well. The company hopes eventually to operate 250 pie shops.

The movement of large food companies into the fast-growing restaurant field is nothing new, but none has moved as rapidly as Pillsbury. "We missed the golden age of the '60s (when competitors jumped into some areas Pillsbury ignored), but we're ahead of the pack in restaurants and we're going to stay there," Mr. Spoor says. He figures that Pillsbury several years from now will make at least half its earnings from restaurants.

Pillsbury's consumer-food operations, plagued a few years ago by flat earnings and a poor new-products record, have perked up. Starting in 1973 with Bundt, a popular cake mix developed out of the company's annual Bake-off contests, Pillsbury has posted a string of successful new products. These, along with a resurgence of demand for traditional products like flour, have contributed to a near doubling of consumer-food earnings in the last two years.

Mr. Spoor got Pillsbury into frozen foods with the November 1976 acquisition of Totino's Frozen Foods Inc. Totino's is a frozen-pizza maker that Pillsbury says is the market leader almost everywhere it competes. The frozen-pizza market is growing rapidly and is already larger than the cake-mix or refrigerated-dough markets, previously Pillsbury's major consumer-food areas. Mr. Spoor says Totino's first priority will be to broaden its product line beyond pizzas.

Pillsbury's agricultural-products operations were once even

more worrisome than consumer foods. This was largely because of Pillsbury Farms, a poultry-raising subsidiary that made handsome profits in the high-price phase of any broiler-chicken cycle but was a heavy drag on growth whenever chicken prices were down.

Pillsbury in the past posted earnings declines with maddening frequency: in fiscal 1962, 1964, 1967 and again in 1971. Inevitably the explanation was a poor year in broilers. Just as inevitably, the company would contend that it was coming up with ways to beat the broiler cycle.

Whether that was indeed possible caused great division within the company. "We were deluding ourselves," Mr. Spoor says. He sold the business in 1974 for $22 million, which he says is nearly three times as much as Pillsbury thought it could get. The sale drew wide praise from the company's followers, some of whom think it is the most significant move Mr. Spoor has yet made. "We wouldn't have had that decision without him," one executive says.

For all his apparent single-mindedness, associates describe Mr. Spoor as a complex, even paradoxical man. They say he is an almost compulsive worker—arriving shortly after 7 a.m. and often leaving after everyone else—who nonetheless rarely takes work home. Once he is back at his lakeside residence in nearby Wayzata, he prefers poring over his collection of books by and about Lincoln (he is a self-described "history nut") to reading company reports.

Mr. Spoor is an organized man who creates the impression he isn't. He jams things into the airline flight bag he uses instead of a briefcase, and he strews papers all over the floor of his office. He operates with shirt-sleeve informality, often conducting business from his office couch. Though associates say he isn't a screamer or a desk pounder, he at times severely tongue-lashes subordinates for perceived shortcomings.

Finally, says one associate, Mr. Spoor is "an outwardly confident guy who lives in constant fear of failure. Something like a bad earnings drop could shake him up badly, I think."

Even as a youngster growing in Colorado (as, ironically,

the son of a flour salesman), "Bill wouldn't stand for anything mediocre, anything that wasn't done well," says Mr. Spoor's brother Richard, who is vice chairman of U.S. Trust Co. His competitiveness and athletic skills earned him an athletic scholarship at Dartmouth, where he was an outstanding hurdler and a starting football player.

One former employe describes Mr. Spoor as "an ex-track star who is still running the big race." Winston R. Wallin, Pillsbury's vice president for agricultural products, recalls spending some time with Mr. Spoor at a management meeting in Miami: "He beat the hell out of me in tennis, and that was the highlight of his stay in Florida."

Mr. Spoor is married and has three children, one of whom is an aspiring actress. He and his wife, a former New Yorker, are said to be somewhat private people who limit their participation in Twin City social affairs. Mr. Spoor proudly describes his family as being "very close."

Mr. Spoor's competitiveness and drive bother some observers. "He's bound and determined to succeed big," a Minneapolis executive says. "You've got to wonder if that's going to lead him into some big mistake."

Some Pillsbury observers believe that Mr. Spoor almost made a costly mistake when he tried to acquire Weight Watchers International for 795,000 Pillsbury shares. They suggest that Mr. Spoor offered too much, overestimated Weight Watchers' growth prospects and overlooked the difficulties Pillsbury would have in obtaining the right to produce Weight Watchers' food line. (Weight Watchers had licensed such production indefinitely to two other companies.)

The deal fell through when Pillsbury's stock subsequently rose in a bull market, raising considerably the price it would be paying. "That gave Spoor an out and he took it," one securities analyst says, noting that Wall Street was sharply critical of the proposal. A Minneapolis executive adds: "There was lots of concern about this guy when he came out of left field to head the company. What was he going to do? Then the first really big deal he tries to pull off is Weight Watchers. A lot of red flags started waving."

Mr. Spoor says he told Weight Watchers the price had become too high largely "because they weren't meeting their own (earnings) projections." He says he didn't reevaluate the deal otherwise and he shrugs off criticism of it. "We've certainly got to know more about our business than securities analysts do," he says.

Similarly, he dismisses speculation about possible morale problems. An outside study of Pillsbury shows that company morale "is as good as IBM's and way ahead of any other food company," he says. He adds:

"My style obviously doesn't suit everyone. That's OK; most people will like the results."

Odyssey of an Inventor

Stanford R. Ovshinsky. A slim, dark-complexioned man of 54 with fuzzy hair and a predilection for dark suits. A voluble talker. In scientific circles, his name calls forth the most amazing differences of opinion.

"His critics generally picture him as a glib con man and promoter," the respected journal Science has noted. "His supporters picture him as an oppressed genius who is being persecuted by the forces of status quo in science and industry."

The uproar precipitated in the scientific world by Mr. Ovshinsky began in 1968, when he announced he had developed new materials—"glass transistors," the newspapers dubbed them—that could be used as electronic switches and memories. The glasslike devices, he said, were cheaper and in some ways better than the tiny transistor-type crystals used by the electronics industry.

This news wasn't received kindly by the giants of that industry, which had invested billions of dollars in the crystalline transistors. "Old hat," said the laboratory chieftain at one major electronics concern. Another executive said, "Unless you can crank them out like jellybeans, it's not worth much."

Many considered Mr. Ovshinsky's claims close to scientific heresy—compounded, in his case, by what seemed like a special audacity. Mr. Ovshinsky not only lacked a degree in physics but also hadn't even been to college (in fact, as he has acknowledged, he even flunked two grades in secondary school).

Moreover, his announcement made him paper-rich for the moment, by triggering speculation in the stock of Energy Conversion Devices Inc. (ECD), the small company he had set up to exploit his invention. Today, Stan Ovshinsky isn't rich, and

ECD has an accumulated deficit of more than $20 million. But it looks as though he is going to be vindicated.

In fact, he may be emerging as a kind of middle-aged Tom Swift who, despite a lack of conventional credentials, has made a basic scientific discovery missed by some of the best brains in science, one that now is leading to firm practical applications.

Within the next few months, record keepers from secretaries to archivists may get an entirely new kind of microfilm system using one of Mr. Ovshinsky's glassy materials instead of conventional photographic film. The system allows, say, a secretary to add new correspondence to a microfilm card daily or to erase previously microfilmed correspondence—all done with only a flash of light. The film develops instantly without any chemical processing.

Minnesota Mining & Manufacturing Co. is expected to be selling that system. In another application, a new kind of high-capacity computer memory based on the Ovshinsky materials is under development by Burroughs Corp.

And recently in London, Mr. Ovshinsky announced a new version of his materials that can convert heat or sunlight directly into electricity—a development that could prove a major advance toward economical solar energy.

For Mr. Ovshinsky, however, the most satisfying victory would be acceptance of himself and his theories by the scientific priesthood. "I'm tired of being looked upon as some kind of eccentric who operates outside the establishment circle," he says.

There is progress on that point. Reports in scientific journals suggest with increasing frequency that his concepts of electronic behavior in glassy materials may well be correct. "On every single point of controversy, it now is clear that Ovshinsky has been correct from the very beginning, and it is about time that the scientific community acknowledges this explicitly," says David Adler, professor of electrical engineering at Massachusetts Institute of Technology.

In a lesser triumph, Mr. Ovshinsky has won recognition from the second college edition of Webster's New World Dictionary. "Ovonic," a word taken from his name that he uses to describe the glassy materials, is included therein with a credit to "Ovshinsky . . . U.S. inventor."

Why have Mr. Ovshinsky's theories encountered such resistance among more orthodox scientists? For one thing, he has failed to follow the usual stately procedure of publishing in scientific periodicals each new step of his work. Speaking of his critics, he now says, "I didn't speak their language, and they didn't understand me."

And Mr. Ovshinsky's personal history is altogether unconventional. His father, a Lithuanian emigre, was a scrap collector in Akron, and the young Ovshinsky, though a prodigious reader and enthusiastic amateur scientist ("A friend and I blew up part of our basement," he recalled), wasn't much good at school.

"I was just not interested in school; it was never a force in my life except as a negative one," he said several years ago in a long taped interview with Joseph J. Ermenc, a professor of engineering and technology historian at Dartmouth College.

"I never thought of going to college," Mr. Ovshinsky added in that interview. "It wasn't really part of our culture in those days." This was during the Depression. "I knew I had to make a living," Mr. Ovshinsky said, so he became a machinist, graduating from a trade school in the same year that he finished high school.

In that humble trade, his knack for innovation began to emerge. He fondly recalls modifying an ordinary metal-working lathe so that it would do tricks for which it hadn't been designed. He conceived and patented an automated lathe in the mid-1940s, long before "automation" was a household word.

After some marginally successful ventures in the machine-tool business, Mr. Ovshinsky was hired in 1952 by Hupp Corp., an automobile-parts maker, as a research director to help automate machine tools. There he began the strange intellectual sojourn that led to his new electronic materials.

Prof. Ermenc suggests that Mr. Ovshinsky is one of those inventors distinguished by the ability to see immediately an analogy between two apparently unrelated phenomena. In this case, it was the automatic control of machines and the workings of the human brain.

Automated machines basically involve arrays of electronic switches, constantly turning on and off, that create patterns of electric circuits. To Mr. Ovshinsky, the brain seemed to involve a similar principle. It is a vast collection of nerve cells, or neurons, billions of them, each continually switching from a conductor of electric nerve impulses to a nonconductor.

This, in a sense, was "thought." Intrigued, he plunged into a study of the neuron and eventually decided to build an electronic switch that would mimic its action. Scientists in the field frequently have built such models, but ordinarily they have turned to the electronics laboratories for their switches; the switching capability of semiconductors such as the transistor is the keystone of modern electronics.

Semiconductor technology, however, is based on the use of crystalline solids whose atoms are linked in near-perfect symmetrical order. But, as Mr. Ovshinsky noted, the membranes and other parts of neurons are made of disordered or "amorphous" materials whose atoms are in jumbled disarray.

The former machinist, therefore, began casting about for amorphous solids. Tantalum oxide was the substance he chose for his first device.

It was quite clear in his mind, Mr. Ovshinsky maintains, just how the electrons would behave in his device. But it wasn't clear to others. The whole theory of semiconductors was based on crystals (except for the Xerox photocopier), and the idea that noncrystalline materials could be semiconductors had been ignored by the scientific community.

However, Mr. Ovshinsky gradually won the support of three prominent physicists, Hellmut Fritzche and Morrel Cohen of the University of Chicago and Sir Neville Mott, head of Britain's famed Cavendish Laboratory. Their prestige is said to have helped Mr. Ovshinsky get a paper on his project published in the Physical Review Letters, a journal devoted to theoretical physics.

That was in 1968. By then Mr. Ovshinsky and his wife, Iris,

a trained biologist, had set up Energy Conversion Devices Inc., with a small plant and laboratory in Troy. The paper in Physical Review Letters, heralded by newspaper headlines after a well-timed press conference, caused ECD's stock to triple in one day, to as high as $150 a share, in the over-the-counter market.

However, many in the world of science were furious. Ordinarily a scientist would spend months or years in meticulous experimentation before propounding such a new theory. But Mr. Ovshinsky's report, after describing his switches, merely made a flat statement on why they worked.

And the inventor was an unknown. To many scientists, saying that electrons could be juggled around in amorphous solids as easily as they could be in crystals was like saying that croquet could be played on a potato field as well as on a manicured English lawn.

Mr. Ovshinsky had developed two switches. One was a "threshold" device that would switch from nonconductor to conductor the moment an electric current reached a certain intensity. The other was a "memory" device—one version of which was an opaque film that responded to flashes of light.

The "ovonic" materials are mixtures of such elements as sulphur, selenium and tellurium, melted together and then rapidly cooled before their atoms have lined up in crystalline structures. (Chemists and geologists call such substances "glasses," hence the term "glass transistor.") Unlike crystals, which have to be meticulously "grown," and "doped" with impurities, the ovonic materials can be mixed to order and poured out by the square foot.

Amid the scientific furor, Mr. Ovshinsky was sewing up his patent positions and trying to eke out a living by offering licenses to such companies as Xerox Corp., Eastman Kodak Co. and IBM. Intrigued, they separately advanced a total of several hundred thousand dollars but then lost interest.

"I don't know how we managed," says Mr. Ovshinsky, looking back over the last few years. From the beginning, he says, "I've wanted to build a manufacturing business," rather than a "think factory" that develops new technology and sells it by licensing to others. But plans to market many potential products have had to be shelved because of lack of funds and uncertain markets.

Scraping along on loans, some secured by stock and patents, with lenders often getting warrants to buy ECD stock, ECD by the end of September 1976 had an accumulated deficit on operations of $19.7 million, with the figure increasing at the rate of $185,000 a month.

The company then raised a crucial $2 million by selling 100,000 shares of stock to warrant holders. (The Ovshinskys retain voting control with 28% of the shares.) The highly cautious prospectus on the sale warns that unless ECD is able to commercialize some of its products, a minimum of $1.9 million is required to keep its operations going through mid-1978.

So ECD's immediate fate may rest heavily on the new microfilm system and the plans of Minnesota Mining & Manufacturing Co. to market it. The system uses a silverless film that develops instantly, based on one of Mr. Ovshinsky's "memory" materials that changes from opaque to transparent when struck with a predetermined level of energy, either heat or light—and changes back with another flash of energy.

The "MicrOvonic File" is a desk-top device that permits an "active" record, with as many as 98 pieces of correspondence to be filed on a single microfiche—and changes made as desired. With the conventional microfiche, users must wait until enough correspondence is available to fill the microfiche, and then send it to a darkroom for development. Once exposed, the conventional microfiche can't be changed.

Minnesota Mining has promised an initial order worth more than $4 million if the system meets certain specifications. ECD meanwhile has worked out licensing agreements on its imaging films with Asahi Chemical Industry and Fuji Photo Film Co. of Japan and with Agfa-Gevaert NV in West Germany.

Another critical decision rests with Burroughs Corp. The ability of ovonic materials to switch from nonconductor to conductor makes them potentially ideal for storing the "on-off" language of computers. Burroughs has been working on tiny ovonic "chips" for high-capacity computer memories that would retain information even in power failures and could be reprogrammed by the user.

Although by necessity Mr. Ovshinsky has to struggle with financial concerns to keep ECD alive, his heart is still in the laboratory. "If I couldn't work in science, I couldn't work in the company," he says. "Science is my relaxation."

Where he now is headed isn't certain. But in the May 1977 issue of Scientific American, MIT's Mr. Adler published a lengthy article on the promise of amorphous semiconductors. In it he notes that Mr. Ovshinsky recently made an additional advance that "promises to open up a new area of commercial applications, from low-cost solar cells to all-amorphous solid-state devices." At about the time the article appeared, the inventor gave a talk at Wayne State University on the potential use of modified ovonic materials to convert heat or light directly into electricity, suggesting the possibility of a new, cheap type of solar cell.

Anyone watching a black-and-white image appear almost instantly on one of the ovonic memory films, such as that used in the microfilm system, is tempted to ask whether it could be done in color and, if so, whether Mr. Ovshinsky could make a new type of "instant-picture" camera to compete with Polaroid and Kodak. "I think it could be done; maybe when I've got time, I'll do it," the inventor replies.

Empire Builder of United Technologies

At first glance Harry Gray, a lanky, grinning 57-year-old, seems like an easy-going salesman, retaining a touch of the "aw shucks" manner from his home town of Milledgeville Crossroads, Ga. But he is the financial world's latest empire builder. As chairman and president of United Technologies Corp., the shrewd, hard-driving businessman is turning the once-sleepy company into one of the biggest and fastest growing corporations in the country.

In the process, Mr. Gray has been pushing more than a few noses out of joint. He has upset General Electric Co. with some competitive maneuvers GE felt weren't quite cricket. He has infuriated executives at Babcock & Wilcox Co., the power-plant builder that United Technologies is trying to acquire. And he has drawn the attention of antitrust officials at the Justice Department, who are studying the bid for Babcock.

Whatever hackles may have been raised along the way, they haven't seemed to slow Mr. Gray. When he took over United Aircraft Corp. in 1971, the company consisted of divisions such as Sikorsky helicopters, Hamilton Standard propellers, Norden electronics and a unit making rocket fuel. The main operation, however, was Pratt & Whitney Aircraft, a competent but stodgy maker of airplane engines.

Mr. Gray reorganized key parts of United Aircraft and installed tight financial controls. At the same time, he put the corporation on the acquisition trail, in 1974 buying Essex International, a maker of electrical products with $845 million in sales, and in 1975 acquiring Otis Elevator with $1.2 billion in sales.

By such moves Mr. Gray has pushed the company, rechristened United Technologies, from $2 billion to $5.2 billion in sales in the last five years. Profits have more than tripled, from $50 million to $157 million. United has jumped from the 59th biggest industrial company in the U.S. in 1973 to 35th today.

"Mr. Gray's performance," says Wolfgang Demisch, a securities analyst at Smith, Barney, Harris, Upham & Co., "is very, very impressive."

If Mr. Gray snares Babcock & Wilcox, a producer of nuclear and coal-fired power equipment with $1.7 billion in 1976 sales, United Technologies will rank as the 19th biggest corporation in the country, ahead of companies like Boeing, Kodak and RCA.

But whether or not he succeeds in acquiring Babcock, Mr. Gray's style in building a new industrial empire is worth watching. After leaving Georgia to study marketing at the University of Illinois, he sold trucks for a Dodge dealership, then moved to Greyhound Corp. in Chicago, where he became general manager of the moving division. In 1954 he joined Litton Industries in Los Angeles. There, he established and built up the components group, which, among other things, sold microwave tubes to the Air Force for electronic-warfare devices. By 1969 Mr. Gray was senior executive vice president in charge of three major Litton groups—industrial, marine and machine tools. "They called me the super-group chief," he recalls.

Mr. Gray decided he wanted to be president of Litton. But Tex Thornton, chairman, and Roy Ash, president, weren't interested in retiring. In the meantime, United Aircraft's management was reaching retirement age, and the company hired Booz, Allen & Hamilton Inc., the consulting firm, to find a new chief executive. A Booz, Allen man contacted Mr. Gray, and on Aug. 31, 1971, Mr. Gray dined with United Aircraft executives at the Mayflower Hotel in Washington.

"It was just a general discussion of business philosophies, and I told the United people that if they wanted to discuss a job possibility for me, they should first let Thornton know," Mr. Gray says.

Shortly afterwards Mr. Gray made a move that set teeth on edge at General Electric. Litton's marine division, which was building destroyers for the Navy, was purchasing $130 million of turbine engines for the ships from GE's big turbine plant at Evendale, Ohio. Litton requested a management review of GE's operation, including a tour of the Evendale plant.

On Sept. 17 Mr. Gray journeyed to Evendale, was briefed on the turbine program by GE executives and toured the GE plant. "Gray was a major customer, and we rolled out the red carpet for him and told him some of our long-range plans," says a former GE man.

The core of the turbine made at Evendale is used not only in marine engines but also in GE's jet engine that powers such airplanes as McDonnell Douglas DC10s. A main product at United's Pratt & Whitney division is a competing jet engine for airplanes.

On Sept. 23 — six days after his visit to Evendale — Mr. Gray says he agreed to become president of United Aircraft. On Sept. 27 the United board ratified the agreement and the company announced it publicly.

GE executives were livid. Jack Parker, vice chairman of GE, fired off a blistering letter to William Gwinn, then chairman of United Aircraft, protesting Mr. Gray's Evendale visit. Mr. Gwinn replied in a letter that Mr. Gray was still employed by Litton at the time of the visit and was only doing his job.

For his part, Mr. Gray says he got no inside information from the GE briefing. "From time to time I asked if I was getting any proprietary data, and if the answer was 'yes,' I requested that that part of the discussion be stopped." During the plant tour, he adds, certain items "which looked like they might be jet engines" were shrouded.

Mr. Gray also says that Litton had been concerned about GE's performance on the engine contract for a long time, and a tour of the Evendale facility had been planned for months. He also adds that in connection with the contract, "we had a Litton man practically living at the GE plant, and if I wanted to get anything sub rosa, I could have gotten it through him in spades."

(Once at United, Mr. Gray quickly took care to shroud that company's operations from the gaze of competitors. To avoid disclosing financial results of individual divisions such as Pratt & Whitney, Mr. Gray lumped them into groups; United has since been reporting financial figures only on a group basis.)

For a time after the GE incident, things went more smoothly for Mr. Gray. The acquisition of Essex was friendly from start to finish. Acquisition of Otis Elevator at first provoked vehement resistance from Otis, but after United sweetened its offer for Otis shares, directors of the elevator company voted acceptance. Along the way Mr. Gray picked up the reputation of being able to buy companies at almost bargain-basement prices.

Then came the Babcock bid. Proceedings in the bitter struggle help to shed light on Mr. Gray's methods and motivations.

Testimony at the Ohio securities division hearing on Babcock and depositions for the federal case in Akron indicate that United, ironically, wasn't even interested in Babcock at first. United coveted Combustion Engineering Inc., which like Babcock builds electric generating plants for utilities.

"We thought all along that Combustion Engineering was the better company," Mr. Gray said at one point in his testimony. Mr. Gray added he had even held some preliminary talks with Arthur Santry, president and chief executive of Combustion, but Mr. Santry wasn't inclined to go along with a merger.

Then, on Dec. 10, 1976, Paul Hallingby, chairman of White, Weld & Co., the investment company, dropped in on Edward Hennessy Jr., United's senior vice president for finance, in Hartford. According to a subsequent Hallingby memo, "Hennessy (of United) reiterated his interest in acquiring 'one more big one' . . . and gave Combustion Engineering as a random example. I responded that I saw no chance of knocking over Combustion . . . and urged him to consider Babcock & Wilcox." Mr. Hallingby left some annual reports and other materials on Babcock with Mr. Hennessy, urging that he read them.

Mr. Hennessy and Mr. Hallingby met again, this time in New York on Jan. 11, 1977, and Mr. Hallingby offered to have White Weld perform a study for $20,000 that would prove Babcock was a better acquisition target than Combustion. After the meeting, Mr. Hennessy joined Mr. Gray for a taxi ride across Manhattan, and during the ride Mr. Gray told Mr. Hennessy to proceed with the White Weld study.

Then a setback. On Feb. 8 a number of White Weld officials presented their study to Messrs. Gray and Hennessy at United's headquarters in Hartford. Among the White Weld men were Mr. Hallingby and Charles Tillinghast, former chairman and still a director of Trans World Airlines and now also a vice chairman of White Weld. Mr. Hallingby made a lengthy presentation.

Mr. Gray testified that Mr. Hallingby then suggested a price of $45 for Babcock, at a time when Babcock's stock was trading on the New York Stock Exchange at around $35. Mr. Gray added, "I am normally a kind of quiet guy and don't get excited, but I got excited at this point. I said, 'Where in God's name did you get that?' . . . . I said, 'I don't think we want to discuss that anymore, and if that's what you are going to talk about, I think maybe the meeting ought to be adjourned, because I have some other things to do.' To me it was an outlandish number and nothing that he said would, in my opinion, support it.

"I kind of then went back to talking to Mr. Tillinghast about (TWA's requirements for) jet engines. I think that upset the White Weld people because they came in with these very careful presentations, and I was not paying much attention to them."

All the same, a Babcock acquisition was beginning to intrigue the United executives, and they discussed the possibility in a series of subsequent meetings. By Feb. 15 it was decided that Mr. Gray would make a friendly overture to George Zipf, the bluff engineer who is chairman and chief executive of Babcock. (And just in case the friendly approach didn't work, an outside law firm was instructed to begin drawing up papers for a tender offer for Babcock stock.)

Mr. Gray's opening gambit with Mr. Zipf involved a research effort on a more efficient way to burn coal. Mr. Gray telephoned the Babcock executive, explaining United researchers wanted to spend $30 million to $50 million on the project.

According to Mr. Gray's testimony, he told Mr. Zipf, "When somebody makes that kind of recommendation to me, that is pretty serious, and I think I would like to know more about it. Would you be willing to talk to me about it? And he (Zipf) said, 'yes.'"

On Friday afternoon, Feb. 25, Mr. Gray met with Mr. Zipf in Babcock's midtown Manhattan headquarters. For nearly two hours the two talked about research on coal and other fuels, how United spent more than Babcock on research, and then how United might somehow assist Babcock on research. At that point Mr. Gray suggested the two companies might do "something together."

Mr. Zipf's testimony indicates he was startled:

"I said, 'What?'"

"He (Gray) said, 'Well, us doing something together.'"

"You will have to define. I am not sure I understand what you are talking about, doing together."

"He said, 'Putting our two companies together.'"

"I told him very emphatically that . . . if he was talking about a contemplated merger of our two companies, he can forget it. . . ."

The meeting broke up, but United continued moving forward anyway. On March 21 United's management and White Weld's Mr. Hallingby presented a Babcock merger proposal to United's directors, and the United board approved any offer up to $42 a share.

Two days later, Mr. Gray met with Mr. Zipf again. According to Mr. Zipf's testimony, Mr. Gray said if a merger took place, United would add $10 million to Babcock's research budget. Mr. Gray also suggested the presidency of the combined companies might go to Mr. Zipf. The Babcock executive still resisted. "I suggested maybe he (Gray) ought to buy Combustion Engineering." Mr. Gray replied he didn't think that would work out.

Again the meeting broke up. Subsequently, Mr. Gray tried to reach Mr. Zipf by telephone, but for days Mr. Zipf dodged Mr. Gray's repeated calls. On Monday, March 28, Mr. Zipf finally returned a Gray call. Mr. Zipf testified, "I told him if he really was looking for trouble and wanted a fight, that we were ready to deal with him; we had the guns ready and the guns pointed; if he wanted to pull the trigger, go ahead; he was asking for it. . . . And I hung up."

Later that day, Babcock shares suddenly began moving up in price. Fearing a leak of United's takeover plans, Mr. Gray called Mr. Zipf again and said he was sending him a copy of a letter and a press release on a proposed offer for Babcock.

"You really are pushy," Mr. Zipf snapped back.

The next day, United publicized its offer of $42 a share, or a total of $512 million, for Babcock.

Editor's note. Babcock & Wilcox was not to be. Although United Technologies overcame a series of legal hurdles thrown in its path during the summer, a new element entered the picture—namely, J. Ray McDermott & Co., which decided it too wanted Babcock & Wilcox. After a spirited battle in which the bidding for Babcock soared to $65 a share, United withdrew from the race.

The following month, however, United announced the acquisition, for roughly $20 million, of Dynell Electronics, a producer of shipboard radar equipment. It then made a $210 million acquisition of Ambac Industries, a producer of diesel fuel injection systems. At its 1978 annual meeting, the company displayed its faith in the future by boosting the dividend. Mr. Gray also told stockholders that while United's sales were then running in excess of $5.5 billion a year, "our goal is to expand this figure by 50% by the mid 1980s."

Top Bananas at United Brands: The Street Fighter

Some of his fellow executives were surprised when, in January 1977, Wallace W. Booth resigned as president and chief executive officer of United Brands Co. after a falling out with the chairman. But even more were surprised when the vice chairman, Seymour Milstein, stepped out of the shadows and into the top slot.

Mr. Milstein's abrupt ascendancy in the $2.3 billion food concern, one of the world's largest banana producers, took even Mr. Booth by surprise. "There wasn't any indication he wanted the top job," he says.

But now that Mr. Milstein is in control, shareholders and even employes are asking, exactly who is Seymour Milstein? Amazingly for the chief officer of a major, publicly traded corporation, he courts anonymity, won't allow himself to be interviewed, won't talk about his background and prefers to be known as a businessman and investor rather than as a professional manager. But what really concerns some observers is that he has no previous experience in running a large company, much of his operational experience having been gained in running a small family business.

Thus the question is being asked in the investment community, can the 56-year-old Mr. Milstein do the job, particularly since United Brands is a troubled company that has been suffering both marketing and management problems. Some company officials say he has made a respectable beginning. But others say that his background hasn't provided him with the skill to manage such a large concern. "He's trying to run it like a corner grocery store, and you can't run a $2 billion company that way," says one disenchanted former United Brands official.

"It's a potentially explosive situation," says Prof. Eugene E. Jennings, a management expert at Michigan State University, who knows the company well. Mr. Booth, he believes, was a professional manager who failed to understand the banana business. But Mr. Milstein, he says, "not only doesn't understand the banana business, but he also doesn't have a track record as a professional manager."

Mr. Milstein, a slight, bespectacled man with an almost scholarly appearance, hasn't revealed his attitude to such criticism. Declining a request for an interview for this story he said, "You've described me as a private person and I'd like to keep it that way."

But in a company as big and as troubled as United Brands, Mr. Milstein probably won't be able to keep his customary low profile for long. The problems go back to February 1975 when Eli M. Black, then chairman and president, leaped to his death from his 44th-floor New York office. Shortly after came the disclosure of a United Brands payment of a $1,250,000 bribe to a Honduran official in return for tax concessions.

Since then, life hasn't been easy at United Brands. In particular, there are both morale and marketing problems at the company's United Fruit subsidiary, the banana concern that contributes 75% of corporate profits and 30% of sales. In 1973, United Fruit's Chiquita brand bananas slipped in the marketplace to number two in competition with Castle & Cooke Inc.'s Dole brand. Chiquita still hasn't rebounded. The reason, say both insiders and outsiders, is that United Fruit simply doesn't have the management talent at the top and middle levels.

Shortly after Eli Black's suicide Mr. Milstein began amassing United Brands stock. In April 1975, he and wealthy Detroit investor Max Fisher, another large holder, were named directors.

At the time, no one was clearly in charge of running United Brands, and the board was split over who should be named chief executive. As a compromise candidate the board hired Mr.

Booth, who shortly before had held the post of senior vice president of Rockwell International Corp. and was known as a tough financial man. Three months later, in August 1975, Mr. Fisher was named chairman, and Seymour Milstein became vice chairman.

But in January, only halfway through his three-year contract, Mr. Booth stepped down in a major disagreement with Mr. Fisher over how to run United Fruit. Only the previous month, Charles M. Waite, senior vice president of United Brands and president of United Fruit, had taken an indefinite leave of absence after disagreements with some subordinates. Mr. Milstein has since taken over the United Fruit presidency, and Mr. Waite's departure has been made permanent.

The situation on the board has been equally unstable. In the past year, seven directors have left the board and five new members have joined, including Mr. Milstein's brother, Paul, 54. It is thought that the company is being run largely by the Milstein brothers, who own nearly 10% of the stock, Mr. Fisher, who owns over 4%, and another director, Carl Lindner, chairman and president of American Financial Corp. whose Great American Insurance subsidiary owns 25% of United Brands stock.

Such is the influence of this group of men that, a former director says, Mr. Booth would eventually have been "tossed out . . . whether or not he did a good job." Prof. Jennings, for one, questions Seymour Milstein's motives. "Is he working for the long term or the short term?" he asks. "He could be acting on behalf of a powerful block of investors." However, one source recalls hearing Mr. Milstein say he has committed the next 10 years of his life to running United Brands.

Whether he will be able to bring stability to United Brands is now of vital importance to the company's future. Prof. Jennings believes there is a clue in his personality. On the one hand he is a soft-spoken introvert (who is said to be considerably influenced by the more aggressive personalities of his brother, Paul, and of Mr. Fisher, the chairman). On the other hand he is "a street fighter who won't be reined in," says Prof. Jennings.

But some United Brands executives, both past and present, clearly have serious doubts about his management ability. While they give him top marks as a quick study and as an energetic, bright and well-organized person, they feel that he exhibits the traits of the manager of a small firm. One former executive complains that both Mr. Milstein and Mr. Fisher nagged him with frequent telephone calls from the day he was hired.

Even worse, says this former executive, Mr. Milstein would telephone subordinates to verify one employe's information with another. This, he says, "introduced tension" and created a situation where "politically savvy" subordinates began "planting ideas" that would enhance their standing in the company.

Seymour Milstein was born in New York City and earned a bachelor of science degree at New York University in 1941. His father, Morris Milstein, had helped found two building materials companies, Circle Floor Co., a floor and ceiling contractor, and Mastic Tile Corp. of America, a maker of floor tiles. Both companies flourished in the postwar housing boom.

The Milstein brothers took over the companies from their father, and Seymour managed Mastic while Paul ran Circle Floor. The Milsteins apparently were paternalistic managers. "Sometimes we were on the road for long periods, and the company would rent temporary quarters for us and pay the costs of bringing our wives along," a former Mastic employe recalls.

In 1959, Mastic was acquired by Ruberoid Co., a building products concern, in an exchange of 290,000 shares of Ruberoid stock valued at $12 million. Seymour was named a Ruberoid director and vice president, and later became senior vice president. Ruberoid prospered, and in 1967 it was acquired by GAF Corp., the maker of chemicals and photographic supplies. The Milsteins became major GAF holders.

But Seymour Milstein didn't step into a top slot at GAF as easily as he had at Ruberoid. He was offered the post of vice president of personnel, a post he apparently felt was beneath him.

GAF says it had consulted Ruberoid executives as to what

Seymour was best suited for. "It was hard to find out just what he did there," says Juliette Moran, GAF's executive vice president. It apparently didn't involve major executive responsibility. "I couldn't tell you what Seymour's managerial talents are, he only had a few people under him," says a former Ruberoid official.

Apparently, it was this slight that was a major cause of a costly and bitter proxy battle. It was spearheaded by the Milsteins in 1971, who aimed to unseat the GAF board and put in their own slate. The Milsteins cited their unhappiness with a decline in GAF's earnings and stock price, after it had acquired Ruberoid. GAF countered with a lawsuit, alleging that the Milsteins were trying to seize GAF "for their own personal and private purposes." Ultimately, the Milsteins' slate was defeated by a two-to-one margin.

The Milsteins had sold Circle Floor for $15 million in debentures to Kinney National Service Inc. in 1968. Paul stayed on as Circle's manager until 1971. When Kinney spun off a building maintenance unit called National Kinney Corp., Paul became president. In 1973, National Kinney acquired, for $63 million, a 54% interest in Uris Buildings Corp., owner of several prime New York office buildings. Paul promptly named his brother president of Uris.

Uris, too, presented problems for the Milsteins. Shortly after the acquisition, National Kinney announced that Uris would adversely affect its 1973 results and got Uris to agree to a $12.5 million cut in the purchase price. Problems with Uris were further aggravated because National Kinney had financed the acquisition with bank borrowings at interest rates pegged to the prime rate. When the prime rate climbed to nearly 10% from 6%, borrowing costs soared. In November 1973, both Milsteins quit their posts.

At the time, Seymour also had other interests. He was a member of the advisory board of the Chase Manhattan Bank and chairman of Bronx-Lebanon Hospital Center (he has since left both posts, although he remains a director of the hospital). But he and Paul Milstein are still partners in One Lincoln Associates, owners of Manhattan's One Lincoln Plaza apartment building.

Exactly why the Milsteins chose United Brands for their next investment isn't known, but Milstein Ventures, jointly owned by the two men, amassed 1,020,700 shares of the company's common stock and smaller amounts of the three series of preferred. Some United Brands executives say that Seymour was positioning himself for the top job from the day he came in. At a May 1975 meeting of executives (and before Mr. Booth had been named), a former executive recalls, Seymour announced that he would be the next chief executive.

"He would have been willing to take over then. He had run companies. He was financially successful, he had time on his hands," another former executive says. Or, as a Milstein family friend puts it: "He really didn't have anything to do. It must be terrible to be rich and bored."

He apparently was surprised by the choice of Mr. Booth, some sources say. But he kept his composure. "Seymour was very careful not to rock the boat. He was a gentleman all the way," says a former director.

Throughout the nearly two years of Mr. Booth's tenure, Mr. Milstein, as vice chairman, apparently kept his hands off the day-to-day company affairs. But some United Brands officials say he gradually assumed more control. As chairman of the board's executive committee he was, of course, deeply involved in company policy, such as dividends and legal affairs.

For a while it seemed as if the two brothers, Seymour and Paul, had gone their own ways in business for the first time. After Seymour joined United Brands, Paul became chairman and co-chief executive of Starrett Housing Corp., a New York building concern.

But in May 1976 Paul was named to the United Brands board, and last December he was named to the executive committee. Paul Milstein declines to be interviewed, but it is assumed by observers that he wants to take a greater interest in United Brands. A family friend notes that "Seymour and Paul stick together like glue, but not as equals. Paul always seemed to be the power in the family."

Seymour also has a close relationship with United Brands' chairman, Mr. Fisher, a 68-year-old multimillionaire whose interests include helping rebuild downtown Detroit and raising money for Republican candidates. Mr. Fisher "is aggressive, bold and authoritative. He doesn't give a damn if he's liked, he speaks his piece," says a former executive. Seymour, says another ex-company officer, "is tolerantly respectful to Max as a son to his father. They are an odd couple."

Top Bananas at United Brands: The Quiet Operator

In August 1975, Max M. Fisher accepted the chairmanship of Boston's scandal-tarnished United Brands Co., the big banana and meat-packing concern. At the time, the $2.3-billion multinational firm was still reeling from the suicide of its previous chairman and the subsequent disclosure of a $1.25-million company bribe to a Honduran official.

To many in Mr. Fisher's home town of Detroit, his decision to take the job came as a surprise. The burly Mr. Fisher, then 67 years old, had always preferred to operate quietly, staying primarily in the background. This time, he was moving into a highly visible, potentially explosive situation where he would be scrutinized by shareholders and the press.

Max Fisher did not need the job. For long ago, Mr. Fisher became one of the wealthiest and most influential men in America. In the best Horatio Alger tradition, he built a fortune from an independent oil business and successful investments in real estate and stocks. Then, without benefit of any high political or corporate position to use as a springboard to power, he became an adviser to two Republican Presidents and a leader of the U.S. Jewish community.

"Max Fisher is one of those rare men who become respected and influential at the national level despite the lack of any official office," says Paul W. McCracken, University of Michigan economist and former head of the President's Council of Economic Advisers. "During both the Nixon and Ford administrations, he was a welcome visitor at the White House."

Not only was he welcome; his counsel was sought. "Because

of his role in the American Jewish community and his broad friendships in Israel," says former President Gerald R. Ford, "Max was invaluable in offering very factual input on Middle Eastern affairs." A Nixon White House staffer adds: "Mr. Fisher was our dominant nongovernmental adviser on American-Israeli affairs."

Mr. Fisher doesn't have easy access to the White House these days, but he still moves in powerful circles and at a pace equaled by few men half his age. A director of half a dozen major corporations, active in Republican and Jewish affairs, an unabashed cheerleader for Detroit, he rarely relaxes.

When he does, he is likely to look for new real-estate ventures, a pursuit he calls his hobby. In the summer of 1977, this "hobby" led him to join a group of private investors who bought the land-rich Irvine Co. in Southern California for $337.4 million, outbidding Mobil Oil Corp., the fifth largest corporation in America.

"When he took over United Brands, I thought he would give up some activity," says Maurice Schiller, a longtime friend and former business associate. "So far, I can't see that he's dumped anything."

Some think Mr. Fisher may be overextending himself. His keen sense of timing—the key to much of his success—may be waning, critics argue. "Was his timing on United Brands a stroke of genius or a disaster?" asks one former company official. Similarly, Mr. Fisher's detractors say failure to break ground on a $100 million riverfront apartment project he is backing in Detroit, which has been in the works for more than two years, is another sign the multimillionaire's touch may be slipping.

"My mind is a little ahead of my body right now," Mr. Fisher concedes. (A recent cataract operation on his right eye, however, kept him out of his office here for only three days.) "I need to slow down, but I won't give up any activities I feel are important."

Mr. Fisher's friends say he is particularly suited to situations where factions exist. He serves as a patient conciliator and orchestrator, seeing opportunities where others see only problems. "Max functions best in a crisis," says Leonard Garment, former counsel to President Nixon. "He has the capacity to dissect very large, difficult questions, and he enjoys that."

He is firm and decisive once a course is set. Some people who have worked with him call him strong-willed, opinionated and impatient with those who don't agree with him. These characteristics, they say, have occasionally pitted him against colleagues.

"My long suit is bringing people together," offers Mr. Fisher. "If you have that ability and can help a bad situation, you can't turn your back." He adds: "Once I take on that responsibility, I stick it out. I'm not a quitter."

That became evident early in Mr. Fisher's life. He was born in Pittsburgh of Russian immigrant parents but grew up in the small, eastern Ohio town of Salem, where his father owned a retail clothing store. In the fall of 1926, young Fisher went off to Ohio State University to get an education, aided by a football scholarship.

"I broke my shoulder the first year, had a bad knee my last year and lost four front teeth blocking a punt one day," he says, "but football enabled me to get through school." He washed dishes in a fraternity house during the school year and carried ice in Cleveland during the summers. In 1930, he graduated with a business degree in accounting and economics, but no varsity letter.

The day he graduated, Mr. Fisher's parents moved to Detroit, where his father had purchased an oil-reclaiming plant for the depression price of $500. Fascinated by the business and needing money (he had to give up his Ford Roadster because he couldn't afford the $15-a-month payments), Max Fisher immediately went to work for his father, processing used auto crankcase oil collected from gas stations.

In the late 1920s, crude oil had been discovered in Michigan, and Max Fisher sensed an opportunity for a local independent refinery. He learned refining from experts at the University of Michigan and then persuaded Henry Wenger, a Detroit gasoline broker, to back him in building a small, 100-barrel-a-day refinery on the site of his father's plant. The two men bought out the elder Mr. Fisher and in 1932 formed the Aurora Gas Co., which grew into the largest independent producer and distributor of petroleum products in the Midwest.

For 25 years, Mr. Fisher ran Aurora. "He handled every phase of the operation," says Mr. Schiller, one of the company's first employes. "Max was demanding. He ran so fast you had to work like crazy just to keep up." He adds: "He has always been a stickler for details: he can tear apart a budget or a balance sheet as fast as anyone."

Not only did Mr. Fisher prove to be a tough executive; he soon demonstrated the foresight that characterizes him still. In 1938, crude oil was plentiful in the country and refiners could buy all they needed at a discount. That year, Mr. Fisher called on the Ohio Oil Co., now known as Marathon Oil Co., and offered to buy crude oil at the listed price. "In return I wanted to be taken care of when supplies became scarce," Mr. Fisher recalls. "As a result of our deal, I never had any trouble getting oil during the war years."

That transaction also started a relationship that culminated in mid-1959: Marathon bought Aurora, which by then had about a 65,000-barrel-a-day refining capacity and nearly 700 service stations, in an exchange of stock valued at more than $39 million.

The sale did two things. First, it provided a handsome independent financial base that Mr. Fisher, a shrewd investor and entrepreneur, has today parlayed into a fortune many times its original size. At the same time, it freed Mr. Fisher of daily business responsibilities, permitting him to immerse himself in civic, philanthrophic and political affairs and gain a national reputation as a fund-raiser. In the last 15 years or so, he has helped raise millions of dollars for everything from local United Funds to the national United Jewish Appeal.

Mr. Fisher formed what he calls his "first big political partnership" with George Romney, the former chairman of American Motors Corp. "We just hit it off," Mr. Fisher says. From

1962, when Mr. Romney was first elected Michigan governor, to 1968, when he dropped out of the Republican presidential race, Mr. Fisher served as the governor's campaign finance chairman. "Romney and Fisher rebuilt the party in this state," says Michigan Republican Chairman William McLaughlin.

After Mr. Romney faded, Mr. Fisher became an avid supporter of Richard Nixon. In pre-Watergate days, he gave $150,000 to Mr. Nixon's 1968 campaign and then $250,000 to his 1972-73 war chest. "I was willing to do whatever I could, because I believed in the cause," says Mr. Fisher. "I was offered ambassadorships and Cabinet positions, but I turned them down because I felt I could be more effective outside of government."

The downfall of President Nixon was a severe blow to Mr. Fisher. "Watergate and the ensuing mess was a great disappointment," he says, "but if things go wrong, you either run or stay and try to do something about it." Mr. Fisher decided to stay and work for the party. "In the spring of 1976, when we were trying to reorganize my finance committee for reelection," President Ford recalls, "Max worked almost full time on it for three or four months."

Similarly, Mr. Fisher wouldn't give up on Detroit despite its reputation as a dying city. In 1969, he served as the second chairman of New Detroit Inc., an urban coalition formed after the city's devastating 1967 riots. During his chairmanship, Mr. Fisher solidified the coalition's goals, raised $10 million for it and got long-term pledges of financial support from local businesses. Since 1971, he has served as chairman of Detroit Renaissance Inc., a group of business leaders who are trying to find ways to pump economic vitality into the city's downtown.

Some critics wonder whether Mr. Fisher's commitment to the city isn't sometimes undermined by his instincts as a profit-minded businessman. When he was chairman of New Detroit, he was also developing a major suburban apartment and shopping-center complex. When S. S. Kresge Co. (now K Mart Corp.) decided in 1969 to move out of its downtown Detroit headquarters, Mr. Fisher sold Kresge the land across from his suburban complex.

"Max always has some kind of deal or angle going that will ensure his return," says one disillusioned Detroit businessman. "That's all right, but you shouldn't let yourself be painted at the same time as a savior of the city."

That isn't to say that every investment Max Fisher proposes pays off. In late 1974, he and Adolph Komer, a local developer, announced plans to build a $100 million riverfront apartment project near downtown. Blocked by the recession, charges of scrimping on planned amenities and unable to persuade federal officials to insure it, the project probably won't get off the ground, skeptics say. "It's been frustrating, but I'll break my neck trying to get the financing," Mr. Fisher says. "I don't need the project for my economic survival. I just want it because it's important to the city."

Similarly, some real-estate men wonder about Mr. Fisher's latest venture, the Irvine Co. land in California. One real-estate expert who was close to the Irvine talks says, "I can't see a quick return on any one's money there: just servicing the debt will be a monumental task." Mr. Fisher says he isn't worried. "The Irvine deal is strictly an investment, principally for my children," he says. "It may take a few years for a return, but it's the best piece of property in America. Besides, it won't take any of my time."

That is in sharp contrast to Mr. Fisher's involvement at United Brands, which takes a lot of time. When Mr. Fisher joined the company's board in April 1975, United Brands was leaderless and its board was split into two warring camps. "I opened my mouth," he recalls, "and both sides asked me to be acting chairman."

Mr. Fisher couldn't resist the lure of trying to straighten out the company. Besides, he had some personal reasons for taking the job: He had known Eli Black, the United Brands chairman and president who jumped from an office window to his death in February 1975; he also had a financial stake in the company, owning about 73,000 shares at that time. (He has since increased his holding to nearly 700,000 shares or more than 5% of the company.)

So far, the jury is still out on Mr. Fisher's performance at United Brands. Certainly he has calmed the storms and brought order to its board. Most of the 10 current directors are friends of his, having replaced others who had been there for years. "He's an effective chairman," says E. Robert Ross, vice president for material management. "He has created a working environment. The feeling of 'We want to get the job done.' "

Mr. Fisher himself sees progress. He points to the company's profit of $7.6 million in 1977, compared with a loss of $13.2 million in 1974. "We've made money every year since we took over," he says. "It'll take another two or three years before we're a top-notch company, but we're making progress."

Some sources don't think so. They point to the company's lackluster stock price, the fact that the company hasn't resumed dividend payments on its preferred shares, losses at its meatpacking subsidiary, inability of the United Fruit Co. unit to regain first place in the banana market, and what some critics see as a general lack of management direction.

Critics object to the management style of Mr. Fisher and Seymour Milstein, the 57-year-old president and chief executive officer. Some executives say the two men pay attention to detail at the expense of the big picture.

Mr. Fisher, for example, is said to telephone executives at all levels any time of day, confronting them with minute details of reports. "It's easy to tell the coach how to manage the team from the sidelines and save $100,000 on a minor issue," one executive says. "but he doesn't comprehend how a professional manager manages a multinational" with companywide systematic controls.

Mr. Fisher sees the situation he inherited at United Brands a little differently. "The company wasn't mismanaged: it was never managed at all," he says. "We've tried to get the right officers, develop a sense of urgency and bring in young, bright people."

As far as his and Mr. Milstein's style is concerned, he

counters: "You have to pay attention to details in a business like this, where profit hinges on the weather and rapid changes in commodity prices." He adds: "Sure I call my executives, and I don't talk to them about their golf games."

Mr. Fisher, who says he doesn't get involved in day-to-day operations, nonetheless is said to have clashed openly with some subordinates, resulting in resignations of even a few of the top people he himself recruited. One executive privately concedes that his departure was "rooted in a single problem—the enormous participation of the chairman in day-to-day affairs."

Another bone of contention has been the company's recent move to New York from Boston. Critics say the move could cost as much as $5 million and drain additional management talent when the company can least afford it. One executive charges: "In truth, we're going because senior management wants to live there."

"I don't want to live there," replies Mr. Fisher, who argues that the move will improve access to Latin America and financial institutions, facilitate recruiting and help create a new atmosphere.

"People were discouraged in Boston," Mr. Fisher says. "They would come in late and clear the office by 4:30. This will inject new life into the corporate bureaucracy."

Mr. Fisher lives with his second wife, the former Marjorie Switow, in a large white-brick Georgian home in Franklin, Mich., a northern suburb of Detroit. A shy man socially, he enjoys entertaining their five children and their families when they are in town. Two of the children are from the present marriage, one is from Mr. Fisher's previous marriage, and two are from a previous marriage of Mrs. Fisher's. Mr. Fisher's first wife died in 1952.

The Fishers also own a contemporary home in Palm Beach, Fla., which the family uses primarily as its winter residence. "Max is happiest when his children and grandchildren are around him," says one friend of the family.

Private Affairs of Curt Carlson

Curt Carlson seems obsessed with setting higher goals for himself.

When he started working, more than 40 years ago, he would write his next goal on a piece of paper and put it in his wallet. Once he reached the goal, he would replace the slip of paper with another one.

Well, Mr. Carlson is so rich now that he isn't bothering anymore with the paper-in-the-wallet routine. But he is still lifting the sights up and up for the Carlson Cos., his solely owned enterprise that operates a wide range of businesses. Among them: trading stamps, catalog showrooms, restaurants, hotels, candy and tobacco wholesaling and the importing of optical and tennis equipment.

He created a stir in Minneapolis in 1975 by announcing that the company was aiming for $1 billion in annual sales by 1981, more than double the sales figure at the time. As things are turning out, Carlson Cos., skeptics notwithstanding, is well ahead of schedule; it will hit the $1 billion mark in 1978. Not one to allow his executives to relax, 63-year-old Curtis LeRoy Carlson is dangling a new target to shoot at—$2 billion by 1982.

That may seem heady for a company that had sales of $120 million in 1968 and for a one-time soap salesman whose first goal was to earn $100 a week, yet Mr. Carlson fully expects to attain the objective. And by then, he will have his eye on a new sales peak.

"I believe that you should never be content with reaching a goal," he says. And to sustain a company's success, he feels, the chief executive has to set higher goals for his subordinates than they set for themselves.

To illustrate the point, he recounts a recent management meeting at which the head of one of the company's two restaurant chains was outlining plans for opening 50 new units this year. Mr. Carlson says, "I kept asking, if the chain could open 50 new units, why not 100? And he finally agreed. Now he's more enthusiastic than ever."

Such prodding has had a lot to do with making Carlson Cos. one of the nation's largest privately owned businesses. Observers figure that it will be in the top 20 or so in 1978, with at least $1 billion in sales. In 1977, Mr. Carlson says, sales totaled $755 million and profits were "the best ever." Today the company has more than 70 subsidiaries and divisions and it employs more than 10,000 people.

Mr. Carlson, who is chairman and president, concedes that much of the company's growth in recent years has come through acquisitions, and he expects acquisitions to be a big part of the drive to $2 billion of sales. But he believes that sustained growth requires keen management, and one of his criteria for acquisitions is that the companies should have capable executives willing to stay at their jobs. "I could never run any of these businesses we acquire," he says.

He prefers to keep his company privately owned for the usual reasons. There are no stockholders to criticize management or clamor for dividends; privileges such as use of the company's plush lodge in northern Wisconsin aren't subject to the scrutiny they might receive if the company were publicly owned; and Mr. Carlson can wheel and deal without worrying about reactions of directors or stockholders.

"Several years ago I reached an agreement to acquire a company in a few hours of phone-calling after I learned it was for sale," he recalls. "Usually I can convene a meeting of a few executives here on a moment's notice if I need advice. If we were a public company, it might take weeks to make a deal, or we might lose one by not moving fast enough."

The rapid buildup of his company has enabled Curt Carlson to achieve a net worth that outside sources estimate at well over $100 million. This has brought him a commensurate style of living. He has a family compound of three large homes near Minneapolis, two of which are occupied by the families of his two children, married daughters Marilyn and Barbara. Mr. Carlson and his wife, Arleen, play tennis on their private court and take daily dips in a heated indoor pool at their home. Another luxury is a television set that is recessed in the ceiling above his bed and descends to viewing height with the touch of a button.

Mr. Carlson travels a lot, much of the time in the company's jet plane, and he takes cruises on an 85-foot yacht that he keeps based in Florida. For socializing, his preference seems to be get-togethers with his family, particularly his eight grandchildren. One ritual of recent years has been a Christmas-week gathering of about 50 Carlson clan members at the company lodge, which is called Minnesuing Acres. Minnesuing is an old Indian word that means land surrounded by water.

Getting where he is today didn't come easy for Curt Carlson. After working part of his way through the University of Minnesota, he got a job with Procter & Gamble Co. in 1937 selling soap to stores for $85 a month. While working for P&G, he soon noticed that a Minneapolis department store had considerably increased its sales by offering trading stamps. He also observed that few grocery stores in the area offered such stamps, and he decided there might be room for another trading-stamp company, one that concentrated on lining up grocers.

A trading-stamp company makes its money by selling stamps to merchants, who give them away to customers—so many stamps per so many dollars in purchases. When they have collected a bunch of them, customers turn them in for merchandise at a redemption center run by the stamp company.

With $50 in borrowed capital, Mr. Carlson set up such a company, which he occasionally had to subsidize by persuading his landlord to wait for his rent. On evenings and weekends, he made the rounds, persuading one and then another small grocery store to try trading stamps. It was strictly a small-scale operation.

By 1939, the outlook was promising enough that Mr. Carlson quit P&G and went into business for himself full time. He formed the Gold Bond Stamp Co., which had tough going for more than a decade, including the World War II years when most stores, because of shortages, had little reason to stimulate sales. Gradually the business expanded out of Minneapolis to become a regional operation and then, in the early 1950s, a national company.

A breakthrough came in 1952 when Mr. Carlson signed up his first large grocery chain, Super Valu. Many others followed suit, and Mr. Carlson soon had made his first million.

In the mid-1960s, trading stamps began losing favor among supermarkets, something that generally happens when consumers worry about inflation and think that stores might be able to hold their prices down if they dropped stamps. With the stamp business declining, Mr. Carlson saw need to diversify. He entered the hotel business in 1962 by acquiring the Radisson Hotel in Minneapolis and building it into a 20-unit chain. Then followed other acquisitions.

Among his other large units today are Ardan Wholesale Inc., which specializes in jewelry; Premium Corp. (sales incentive programs); Indian Wells Co. (tobacco and candy wholesaling); Jason/Empire Inc. (importer); the two restaurant chains, Country Kitchen International Inc. and TGI Friday's Inc.; and Naum Bros. Inc., a catalog-showroom retailer.

Like most salesmen, Mr. Carlson seems like an affable optimist, a practitioner of positive thinking. But to hear some present and former underlings tell it, he isn't easy to work for.

"I'm not used to being screamed at," says the president of one subsidiary whose company was acquired by Carlson Cos. Mr. Carlson's methods of motivating executives are more than he had bargained for. But this officer figures he can put up with a short-tempered chief executive because selling out to Carlson Cos. has proved profitable for himself.

A former Carlson Cos. executive says, "Curt has a computer mind and is probably the smartest businessman I've known, but I couldn't handle the way he treated some of his people." He recalls how he and other executives were grilled for hours by

Mr. Carlson as they made presentations at company conferences. He says that it didn't bother him too much but that some of his colleagues wilted under the constant needling.

Having heard about Mr. Carlson's volatility, an executive recruiter says he offers a piece of advice to Carlson Cos. job candidates: "I tell them to pay attention to what Curt has to say, not the way he says it."

Mr. Carlson brushes aside talk about his outbursts in meetings with executives. Even if he does find it necessary to push his executives, he says, it is obviously worth it to them. He says that their pay and benefits are competitive with those of most major companies in this area.

Also, he widely dispenses one lavish perquisite: He gives each of his top 20 executives the use of a new luxury car. The cars are all the same model and color, and you can see them lined up in a row outside the company's headquarters. This year Mr. Carlson selected cinnamon-gold Lincoln Continentals for his executives; last year he chose maroon Cadillacs. "If they like those cars as well as they say they do," he says, "you can see I'm not so hard to get along with."

Mr. Carlson invites a reporter to sit in on a company conference to observe his style. He obviously holds back on fireworks, but exhibits a flair for showmanship. Donning a yellow hard hat along with the other executives (at another recent conference, they all wore railway engineers' caps), he mixes in some ribbing of subordinates with announcements of new goals for them. He soaks up applause as he reveals a plan to take his executives on a round-the-world trip to reward them for reaching $1 billion in sales. Then he brings out the stick to go with the carrot:

"Of course, some of you may get left at home if you don't meet your targets."

He saves the big moment for near the end. He points to a giant wall chart that lays out company goals by years, then walks over to the chart and begins chalking up a new set of higher figures. As he comes to 1982, a well-rehearsed aide rushes to the front with a big new sign: "Billions—TWO in '82."

More applause and a big smile from Mr. Carlson. Finally, a group picture is taken. Mr. Carlson is still very much in charge, directing this person to move here and that person to squeeze in there.

While the company seems like a one-man show, Mr. Carlson says he has turned to professional managers for such specialties as financial planning, acquisitions and legal affairs. He also says he has learned to delegate more authority as the company has grown. "But I'll never delegate goal-setting," he says.

Mr. Carlson has a reputation for being a work addict, and can frequently be found at his office on evenings and Saturdays. He doesn't seem to ease up much when he is on vacations, which tend to be brief anyway. "I call in every day when I'm away," he says, "and usually do it early in the morning so I'll feel better about taking the rest of the day off."

Success enables Curt Carlson to cut a wide swath in Minneapolis, but some people say he is looked down upon as nouveau riche by older wealthy families. "Until recently at least, Curt may have been a little too brash and brassy for some rich types," one executive says. This executive tells a story, which may be apocryphal, that a leading businessman said there were at least 50 people in town who would like to see Curt Carlson fall on his face in business.

Raymond O. Mithun, an advertising executive who has known Mr. Carlson for years, tends to dismiss that. "There are always some people jealous of a fast-rising businessman," he says. Mr. Mithun believes that Mr. Carlson has gained wide acceptance in Minneapolis for his work in civic affairs and generous donations to the arts and to charity. He is now heading, along with Irving S. Shapiro, chairman of Du Pont Co., a $20 million drive to finance the Hubert H. Humphrey Institute of Public Affairs at the University of Minnesota. Mr. Carlson has helped the cause with a $1 million donation.

As in any private company, succession weighs heavily in the future of Carlson Cos. Lack of an heir, or lack of interest among heirs, often leads to the sale of family-owned companies. Mr. Carlson says Arleen and his daughters would inherit the business, and if that should happen soon, he has a plan, contained in a sealed envelope, for continuity of management. His wife and daughters would go on the board of directors, and one of his present officers would become chief executive.

In time, he expects 37-year-old Edwin C. Gage, who is married to his daughter, Barbara, to head the company. He thinks his older daughter, Marilyn, who is married to Dr. Glen D. Nelson of Minneapolis, may eventually assume a key role in management. Then, some day, he would like to see one of his four young grandsons take charge, "so he can feel the thrill I've felt as an entrepreneur." Mr. Carlson concedes that that is one goal that can't be reached well ahead of schedule.

Maverick Banker From Chicago

It was August 1977, and A. Robert Abboud, chairman of First Chicago Corp., the holding company for First National Bank of Chicago, was in high dudgeon.

For days Mr. Abboud and the bank had been the target of insinuating news stories as a result of a $3.4 million personal loan the bank had made to President Carter's then budget director, Bert Lance, whose tangled financial affairs ultimately led to his resignation.

Shortly after a report from the U.S. Comptroller of the Currency absolved the bank from impropriety in connection with the loan, Mr. Abboud struck back. In a series of interviews he attacked the news media for being "irresponsible," claiming that the possibility of adverse publicity would deter banks from making future loans to public figures. For good measure he took a swipe at the Comptroller, the primary regulator of national banks, bitterly complaining about that official's public release of what Mr. Abboud considered confidential bank memoranda.

The performance was classic Abboud; it typified the aggressive, truculent style that the bantam 48-year-old former Marine has displayed during the nearly four years that he has served as deputy chairman and later chairman of the U.S.'s ninth largest bank holding company, with assets at the end of 1977 of $22.6 billion.

That style and the controversies it has generated have made Mr. Abboud the talk of U.S. banking, an industry in which tact and decorum are hallowed traits. "Bob is certainly a colorful, distinctive personality—a man of 90-degree angles rather than gentle curves," observes Gabriel Hauge, chairman of Manufacturers Hanover Trust Co., a major New York bank holding company, who is an Abboud admirer.

Mr. Abboud has indeed proved at times to be a fractious member of the tight-knit banking fraternity. Some examples:

In late 1975, enraged over Lockheed Aircraft Corp.'s foreign payoffs, Mr. Abboud demanded ouster of Lockheed's top management, threatening otherwise to pull First Chicago out of the 24-bank consortium that was keeping the company afloat. After much grumbling, the other banks grudgingly acceded to the demand and joined in forcing the ouster.

Then there was the time, also in late 1975, when Mr. Abboud testified before Congress against the federal loan program to save New York City from default. The move incensed a number of New York banks, whose investment portfolios were loaded with the city's debt securities.

Early in 1978, First Chicago stole the march on such big rivals as Bank of America and Chase Manhattan Bank by winning favored status with the People's Republic of China. Mr. Abboud did it partly by ordering a curtailment last fall in the bank's Taiwan operations. Several other banks grouse that the curtailment was largely a public-relations ploy, given the fact that First Chicago, unlike most of its major bank rivals, has only minor loan exposure in Taiwan and no offices there.

Mr. Abboud's celebrity rests on more than his maverick reputation, though. He has succeeded, in just two years as chairman, in stabilizing the operations of First Chicago, which had emerged from the 1974-75 recession with a shaky loan portfolio and badly overextended.

First Chicago's recovery hasn't been painless. Over the three years from 1975 to 1977, the company's earnings growth rate, which has been sharply reduced by big loan-loss provisions, has been one of the lowest of the nation's top 10 banks. This is a disappointing performance indeed for a company that boasted one of the highest profit growth records in the industry during the 1968-74 go-go banking era.

Even more embarrassing, First Chicago's 1977 operating earnings of $111.1 million, though a record, fall far short of the

$144.2 million in operating earnings posted by Continental Illinois Corp., a rival Chicago bank holding company of almost comparable size and serving the same markets.

In spite of this, many observers give Mr. Abboud high marks. "He has had the guts to face up forthrightly to the terrible problems in the bank's loan portfolio, ruthlessly cut costs and tighten what had grown to be very lax lending procedures," says Harvey Bundy, a bank-security analyst with the Chicago investment house of William Blair & Co. "While he hasn't made many friends doing it, he has done a first-class job."

Many present and former First Chicago officers complain that unlike his genteel predecessor, the now-retired Gaylord Freeman, Mr. Abboud is autocratic, given to intimidating subordinates and involving himself in the pettiest of details. Critics also claim that he has hurt the bank's business by his notoriety and arbitrary stands on the granting and pricing of loans. One veteran First Chicago lending officer says:

"On a personal level Bob is charming, but he has emasculated the organization by his abrasiveness and meddling. The bottom line under Bob will be acceptable. What it won't show is the talent, corporate loan business and potential we're losing on account of him. I see nothing but drift in the organization."

In fact, more than 200 officers have left First Chicago since 1975, including two of Mr. Abboud's former rivals for the chairmanship, Chauncey E. Schmidt, who now heads Bancal Tri-State, a San Francisco-based bank holding company, and Robert Wilmouth, president of the Chicago Board of Trade, the giant futures exchange.

Also, First Chicago's commercial- and industrial-loan volume, the best measure of business-loan strength, has remained sluggish while rival Continental's has grown.

Mr. Abboud dismisses such criticism as that voiced by the lending officer. "Sure we've lost people and some corporate loan business, but this was largely by design. We haven't felt that overstaffing or reaching for new business was appropriate in today's banking environment," he says. "I'm not abrasive, but I do get frustrated frequently when I find my people giving me a snow job about a particular problem rather than the unvarnished facts."

However Mr. Abboud's management style is viewed, few dispute the flair and energy that he has brought to the job. But he also embodies much of the new conservatism that has swept the U.S. banking scene after the excesses of the go-go era.

Conservatism had been the hallmark of First National Bank of Chicago for most of its 105-year history. During the 1950s and early 1960s, for example, it never joined in the pell mell overseas expansion of other major U.S. banks. And it couldn't participate in the post-World War II rush to open domestic branch networks, either, because of stringent branching restrictions in Illinois. Instead, it jealously guarded its strong capital position, remaining content to concentrate its lending activities on the market it had long served—the manufacturers, retailers and finance companies of the Middle West.

All of this changed in the late 1960s and early 1970s under the dynamic leadership of Mr. Freeman. The bank was transformed into a holding company that diversified into an array of businesses, from auto leasing to servicing of student loans.

At the same time, First Chicago built a network of branches and offices in 35 countries and also opened some 10 loan-production offices around the U.S. Loan volume boomed, nearly tripling between 1969 and 1974 to eclipse the growth rate of any of the other top 10 banks.

The Freeman years were a heady period. First Chicago became a haven for ambitious business-school graduates, who were advanced on a special "fast track," shuttling from division to division and making $20 million and $30 million loans on their own authority just two to three years out of school. At his Friday morning executive meetings, Mr. Freeman invariably began by flashing First Chicago's latest stock quote on the screen. The meetings had a pep-rally aura, with booming applause often accompanying the announcement of each new corporate loan relationship.

But by the mid-1970s, the cheering stopped at First Chicago. For in the wake of the 1974-1975 recession, the bank's total of uncollectable loans soared ominously, and problems developed with a number of the bank's other borrowers.

The bank was especially hard-hit because more than 10% of its loans were to the troubled real-estate-investment-trust industry or were backed by shaky condominium and land-development projects and the like.

To make matters worse, rumors of First Chicago's difficulties spread to the money markets, and for a scary couple of weeks in 1974 it wasn't clear that First Chicago would be able to attract sufficient new money in the certificate-of-deposit (CD) market to meet its rising loan commitments. That ability was crucial because First Chicago, like many other major banks at the time, relied heavily on constant borrowings of short-term 30- to 60-day CDs, or loans from corporations and others, to finance a substantial hunk of its generally longer-term loan portfolio.

Understandably, most of Mr. Abboud's efforts since he became chairman in 1975 have been directed toward cleaning up First Chicago's loan portfolio and revamping its lending procedures. He has stiffened lending standards, required elaborate documentation on each loan ("You wouldn't believe how skimpy the files on some of our problem loans were," says one high-ranking First Chicago official) and tightly controlled the lending authorities of his underlings.

He has also brought back many of the veteran credit officers who had been shunted aside in the go-go days, and he has ended the musical-chairs shuffling of the business-school graduates.

Mr. Abboud has taken an active role in riding herd on the bank's many problem loans. For example, he played a key role in rescuing Genesco Inc., which early in 1977 was floundering following the unexpected ouster by its directors of its chairman and chief executive officer, Franklin Jarman. As the retailing conglomerate's lead banker, Mr. Abboud pushed Genesco directors to hire as chairman John L. Hanigan, who in the mid-1960s was the savior of another First Chicago customer, Brunswick Corp. Mr. Abboud then put together a new multi-bank lending consortium to back the new management, which since has been credited with turning around Genesco.

"Bob proved to be a banker in the finest sense of the word with his grasp of Genesco's problems and the courageous help he gave," says Pierre Rinfret, the economist and Genesco director.

Along with all this, Mr. Abboud has cut costs with a vengeance. First to go was Mr. Freeman's pride and joy, the bank's leased BAC-111 jet liner, which cost the corporation $1.3 million a year. Also chopped were such executive perquisites as free subscriptions to business periodicals and first-class travel on domestic flights. ("Bob's so short that he has no problem fitting in a tourist seat," one subordinate acidly notes.)

The Abboud regime is pinching pennies on pay increases, too. During 1977, most raises for officers barely kept pace with the rise in the cost of living, and some were substantially lower. Mr. Abboud's own salary went up 6.4%, to $232,280.

Finally, First Chicago's balance sheet has been materially strengthened under Mr. Abboud to avoid a repetition of its near-disastrous liquidity problems in the 1974 credit crunch.

Mr. Abboud's retrenchment program hasn't been an unalloyed success. Banking sources say that First Chicago has become overly cautious in such areas as leasing and real-estate lending because of Mr. Abboud's conservatism. And corporate treasurers still talk bitterly of Mr. Abboud's attempts a few years back to raise bank profits by jacking up the required compensating balances, or interest-free deposits, for unused corporate lines of credit. The policy backfired and was ultimately dropped after such long-time bank customers as Inland Steel Co., Deere & Co. and Cargill took some of their business elsewhere.

Overriding many of his operating accomplishments is the issue of Mr. Abboud's style and personality. Banking is a business in which image is crucial since there is no difference in the product banks offer—money—and precious little in their level of services. Mr. Abboud's image, both inside and outside First Chicago, is one of abrasiveness and pugnacity.

Stories abound of Mr. Abboud's epic blowups. Angered by an unflattering personal profile in Business Week in 1976, he yanked First Chicago's $300,000-a-year advertising program from the publication. He has yet to reinstate the program.

Lewis H. Young, editor in chief of Business Week, says First Chicago also "shut us off editorially" because of the profile, and at a time when the Chicago bank was "setting the prime rate in this country." In February 1977, Mr. Young made a fence-mending visit to Mr. Abboud. "We got into a shouting match," Mr. Young says. He maintains that only editorial matters, not advertising matters, were discussed.

In the fall of 1977, Mr. Abboud reportedly subjected his top operations officers to almost ritualistic daily tongue-lashings following the embarrassing and still-unsolved theft of $1 million in currency from First Chicago's vaults one weekend.

"Bob has a petty side to him where he always has to find a scapegoat for anything that goes wrong and then publicly chew him out," one bank source says. "He often forgets the whole thing a couple of weeks later, but the subordinate doesn't."

Another factor contributing to Mr. Abboud's controversial image, especially in the generally Republican business community, is his active involvement in Democratic Party politics. He is a friend of Chicago Mayor Michael Bilandic and appeared at a party slatemaking meeting in 1976 to second Mr. Bilandic's nomination to run in a special mayoral election.

Mr. Abboud's rise to business prominence was anything but easy. The grandson of Lebanese immigrants, he remembers vividly the time his family's car and furniture were repossessed during the Depression after his father's heating and ventilating business in Boston failed.

"My father went under because First National Bank of Boston turned him down for a $5,000 loan to carry his receivables," Mr. Abboud says. "The banker told him that they just don't make loans to people of Arab extraction."

But the son, by dint of his intellect and boundless energy, succeeded. He won a scholarship to Harvard (where he earned a letter in wrestling); he fought and was decorated in the Korean war; and he worked his way through both the Harvard law and business schools. He joined First National Bank of Chicago in 1958.

Gaylord Freeman, who personally recruited him and became almost a father figure, matter-of-factly told Mr. Abboud early on that he probably would never get the top job at the bank because of his ancestry and height. First Chicago's public-relations department always describes Mr. Abboud as 5 feet 6 inches, but he appears to be a couple of inches shorter than that. Bank photos usually show him seated with other seated people or, as in a recent picture used in Business Week, standing on a higher stair than the other subjects.

Mr. Abboud rose quickly in the organization, riding the very fast track he is now dismantling. He made his reputation in the late 1960s by building the bank's overseas network. This won him a spot in an unusual, four-man competition for the top job that Mr. Freeman openly declared in 1972. The other candidates were Richard Thomas, now First Chicago president, and Messrs. Wilmouth and Schmidt, who left the bank. Less than three years later, Mr. Abboud emerged the victor.

Mr. Freeman declines to discuss what lay behind his apparent change of heart over Mr. Abboud. The latter cites the changing social mores of the 1960s as facilitating his rise. But according to some observers, Mr. Freeman's choice arose in part from a maverick streak of his own.

These days, Mr. Abboud spends most of his free time at his sprawling converted farmhouse home in Chicago's posh northwest suburb of Barrington Hills, where he lives with his wife, Joan, a son and a daughter. Another son is away at Purdue University, where he studies engineering. Proudly surveying his 17-acre domain, Mr. Abboud tells a visitor: "I couldn't be more satisfied. I have exactly the job and the life that I've always wanted."

Part II:

The Middle Managers

Big Gun In Explosives

Atlas Powder Co. had a problem that was threatening to cost it business. Its salesmen were complaining that they needed a new, inexpensive dynamite product to sell to their strip-mine customers. The salesmen wanted to know what Atlas could do to prevent customers being lured away by competing products.

Atlas, a division of Dallas-based Tyler Corp., turned to Chester A. Hoffman, manager of its huge plant in Tamaqua, located in the Pocono Mountains of northeastern Pennsylvania. Mr. Hoffman designed a 25-pound stick of dynamite that was stout enough for stripmining, cheap enough to be competitive and waterproof for use in wet holes where other explosives would get soggy.

Then, he set his plant to work: the engineers to adapting equipment to handle the new product; the powder line to mixing the dynamite; the shell shop to turning out the casings, and the box factory to making shipping cartons. Within two weeks, the truckers of Mr. Hoffman's 18-van fleet were loading the new dynamite for delivery. Today, it is the Tamaqua plant's biggest volume item.

"That's one of the joys of the job." says Mr. Hoffman, a bespectacled 55-year-old manager whose mild manner belies the fact that he is a $50,000-a-year big gun at an explosives plant. "I have a hand in everything that goes on here," he says. Mr. Hoffman's responsibility for his plant is, in fact, a 24-hour assignment and of a complexity that top corporate executives rarely have to face.

Yet despite his wide-ranging responsibilities, his acknowledged expertise in his field and his 35-year career with the company, Mr. Hoffman, like most of the nation's plant managers, remains far down the corporate ladder. He has met Tyler's top officers only twice, has never visited the corporate office and made his first and only trip to the Atlas division's home office in Dallas just last winter.

The plant manager is a pivotal figure in American industry and ranks among the most highly paid and valued of all middle managers. What's more, his responsibilities seem to be growing. "The able manufacturing man recognizes more and more that the name of the game is profit and loss," says R. J. Wytmar, president of Wytmar & Co., a Chicago recruiting firm that regularly surveys companies on the movement and duties of their executives. "In the past, all a manufacturing man had to do was to produce a product. Now he has to explain what it cost and why."

Few details escape the plant manager's eye. As one example, Fred Scharer is manager of the Oregon, Ill., plant that makes mowers for the Woods division of Hesston Corp., a farm machinery maker. Mr. Scharer is charged not only with making the mowers but also with designing, testing, advertising, marketing and selling them. "I see a Woods mower working in a field and I know that I've supervised every aspect of getting it there," he says.

But when it comes to making major corporate decisions, the plant manager usually has little say. Some managers contend they don't want anything more than the chance to give a little advice. "It wouldn't be good business to do anything in the plant without asking the plant people," says Raymond Shelmire, manager for operations for three Johns-Manville Corp. glass-fiber plants in Defiance, Ohio. "But we already have a lot of responsibility, and I'm not sure we could do justice to the job if we took on any more."

Atlas' Mr. Hoffman says that he is content to "have enough input to affect the decisions concerning this plant." But making decisions, he says, is "the most challenging part of any job, and only the dullard doesn't want to be the top dog and make the top decisions."

Norman B. Keider, Atlas' president, rates Mr. Hoffman's chances of moving into upper management as "reasonable": one chance in three of becoming an Atlas executive, one in five of becoming a top manager at another Tyler subsidiary and one chance in 10 of moving into the corporate offices at Tyler.

As it is, it would seem that Mr. Hoffman's duties are considerable. They range from ordering the raw materials for dynamite, nitroglycerin, blasting caps and slurries (gelatinous ammonium nitrate-based explosives) to delivering the finished goods to customers in construction, mining and quarrying. He oversees the safety of 950 employes, the profitability of an operation that will report about $50 million in sales this year, the reliability of dangerous products and the general care and security of 500 buildings, a 2,700-acre wooded site and over a ton of stored explosives.

At times, his responsibilities even include the dramatic and the droll. When a forest fire threatened the plant, Mr. Hoffman manned the fire lines. When smoke began wafting from a dynamite magazine, he chopped open a rooftop vent to find the source. And when a herd of deer living on the grounds threatened the flower beds, he ordered protective fencing.

But while Atlas leaves all production policies up to Mr. Hoffman, it keeps the purse-string policies for itself. Thus Mr. Hoffman was powerless this winter to hire a badly needed draftsman until Atlas authorized creating a new salaried position, a process that took over two months.

Sometimes, though, Mr. Hoffman does find himself in a position to influence the company's course. He argued at a December 1975 meeting with Mr. Keider and fellow plant managers that a new explosive developed and patented by Atlas researchers was ready for commercial production at the Tamaqua plant. Atlas had been working on a product to combine the best characteristics of old-fashioned dynamite with the newer, safer slurries. But to put it into production would cost $550,000 for a new building and equipment.

"I asked Chet's advice and listened to what he had to say,"

recalls Mr. Keider. Before the meeting ended, Mr. Hoffman had approval for the project.

Mr. Hoffman's career with Atlas began in 1942 after he had graduated from Lehigh University with a degree in chemical engineering. He was assigned to a bomb plant in White Haven, Pa. (Atlas has only made ordnance during wartime.) After Navy duty during World War II, Mr. Hoffman rejoined the company at its Joplin plant and eventually became assistant manager.

In 1960, with the dynamite market on the decline, Atlas moved him to Senter, Mich., to close its plant there. A year later he transferred to Tamaqua as blasting supply supervisor. In 1962, he was made plant manager.

His 15-year tenure has been far from carefree. The boom went out of the dynamite industry in the late 1950s as cheaper ammonium nitrate products, which can be whipped up in automated chemical plants, gained in popularity over dynamite, which is made in small batches by crews of two or three men. In little more than a decade, two dozen dynamite plants closed nationwide.

The plant at Tamaqua survived by changing with the market demands. In the 1950s it began manufacturing ANFO, an ammonium nitrate-fuel oil compound that has captured most of the nation's explosives market. In the 1960s, it added slurries, and last year it began marketing its emulsion (an ammonium nitrate-based explosive with the consistency of soft rubber).

Additionally, while the world market for dynamite continues to dwindle, Atlas has picked up a larger share of what is left, its uses being mainly in road-building, quarrying and strip-mining. Dynamite production at the plant has averaged about 180,000 pounds a day for the past five years and probably will stay at that level for another three years, Mr. Hoffman predicts.

But more than just the explosives market has changed since Mr. Hoffman joined Atlas; so has the company's ownership. In 1971, Atlas Chemical Industries Inc., then an independent concern traded on the New York Stock Exchange, was acquired by ICI America Inc., a subsidiary of Imperial Chemical Industries Ltd., the big British concern which is a major explosives maker.

company, as individuals they often face the frustration of little or no supervisory authority and working with little visibility in a position that isn't well understood. It isn't always easy for a knowledge specialist to feel appreciated or to see a bright future ahead of him in such a position. A specialist must constantly be building his own expertise. Yet to rise very far in management, says James E. Dunlap, TRW's vice president of human relations, "the specialist has to somehow or other get broader and become more of a generalist."

Nowhere is the impact of an emergent corporate staff of specialists in widely diverse areas of expertise more evident than at TRW, an innovative multinational concern with $3 billion of annual sales, ranging from auto parts and electronics systems to aerospace and industrial products. TRW's knowledge specialists range the globe, giving money to orchestras, colleges and hospitals, arguing with tax officials in Singapore, lobbying elected officials in California and creating computer programs to do such things as automatically audit purchases and sales between divisions.

As one example, TRW's human relations staff has grown to 20 from seven in 1967. One of its newest members is Paul D. Hubert, 41, the director of productivity projects. He is one of five behavioral specialists immersed in questions of how to restructure work to make jobs more efficient, more productive and more satisfying. Shirley A. Curry, 41, corporate manager of employe benefits, spent half of 1976 supervising the preparation of new slides, booklets and memos required by the Employe Retirement Income Security Act of 1974.

TRW's finance staff is probably the most highly specialized arm of the corporate staff and numbers 92, up from 43 a decade ago. Dennis G. Tischler, 34, manager of international taxes, is one of three tax managers reporting to the director of taxes. Mr. Tischler and his seven tax specialists pay $100 million a year of TRW's taxes in 30 foreign countries and file TRW's federal tax return, a document that fills four two-inch binders and takes two man-years to prepare.

In the cramped little office where he daily pores over computer readouts, John Armbruster compares his work to the microwave oven his wife would like to buy. "I'm caught up here in providing something no one would miss if it weren't provided," he says.

Ruben F. Mettler, president and chief operating officer of TRW, calls Mr. Armbruster's contributions "very real and very large, but also diffuse and subtle." Over the past few years, he says, his work has had "a very positive effect on the bottom line," which rose 12% in 1975, 28% in 1976, and 16% in 1977, when net income was $154 million.

Mr. Armbruster is an intense, fussy man with dark, piercing eyes and nervous hands that are constantly drawing diagrams in the air. He worked summers in TRW's mail room while he was earning a degree in mechanical engineering at Case Western Reserve University. During six years in the Air Force he immersed himself in analytical research work and statistics. He earned a master's degree in industrial engineering and management at Oklahoma State University and later added an MBA degree in marketing and finance from Case Western. The advanced degrees, he believes, helped him "avoid being pigeonholed as a computer jock" early in his career at TRW.

That career began in 1965 as a reliability engineer in TRW's aircraft propulsion group. But that wasn't what he really wanted, so in 1967 he applied for a computer modeling job on the corporate staff and got it.

Computer modeling was then in its infancy as a forecasting tool for making long-range strategic decisions and for separating internal growth expectations from forecasts based on growth through acquisitions. A series of top-echelon memos and meetings had created the job. TRW's founder, Simon Ramo, in a 1966 memo first cited the need to start plotting mathematical growth curves that would project TRW's financial and operating results far into the future under different economic conditions. By the time Mr. Armbruster had been appointed a year later, the scope of the job had broadened considerably, but it was still very fuzzy.

"I've been doing about the same kind of work since 1967,

but I've been doing it in a lot of different offices, because they didn't quite know where to put me," he says. First it was the data processing department, then the controller's office, then with the vice president of finance. "That was the first real recognition of the nature of my work," says Mr. Armbruster. His next boss was the vice president, economics, another step up in status. In 1973, a new post was created, vice president, corporate planning and development, and Mr. Armbruster has been director in this office ever since.

Mr. Armbruster's salary is in the $40,000 to $50,000 range, and he participates in TRW's management incentive bonus program, which is based on annual profit gains. "I don't know where the topside is on this job," he says. "I think I could have a very fulfilling career right here."

Certainly, the moves he has made so far have been significant. "It isn't uncommon to find people like me stagnating in an accounting department somewhere," says Mr. Armbruster. "My product isn't something that can be pushed up through an organization. Top management has to understand it and want it enough to reach down and get it."

The main product Mr. Armbruster and his young MBA assistant, John Keogh, produce is TRW's "top-down forecast," a half-inch sheaf of typewritten pages, financial tables, charts and graphs that is delivered to Mr. Mettler three times a year. It forecasts key financial and operating data, including profits, working capital requirements and return on assets as far as five years ahead and separates TRW's sales into 15 different business areas.

"The object is to be able to understand how much of TRW's performance is really under the control of management and how much is subject to the vagaries of the economy," says Mr. Armbruster. "It gives top management an idea of what's possible under five or six different conditions. They can select the preferable future and see what actions to take to attempt to reach various goals, rather than just let the corporation meander off on its own."

For instance, "Rube (Mr. Mettler, the president) can look

at the forecast and tell an operating guy: 'Forget those plans, that business is strictly at the mercy of the economy. Use your creative management time to concentrate on this business, where what you do can make a difference,' " says Mr. Armbruster. "We've found that management can exercise far more control over a company's fate than was thought possible before."

Over the past three years, the short-term quarter-to-quarter portion of the top-down forecast has come closer to forecasting actual operating profits than have the traditional "bottom-up" forecasts prepared quarterly by the operating divisions.

The forecast doesn't just spring out of the computer room 250 feet down the hall where Mr. Armbruster spends a big chunk of his day. Building the various computer models that make the forecast possible has been a painstaking research and development process. The forecast still is evolving, growing more detailed and refined all the time. "The data that are generated to meet federal requirements, the SEC, IRS, EPA or whoever, usually are not the most useful data for running a company, so we have to go out and develop most of our own," he says.

That takes lots of time on the phone, "digging out stuff like how many pumps they moved out the door last quarter," he says. Sometimes it requires personal visits to operating divisions' financial staffs "to make friends and convince them to pull the stuff I need out of their archives," says Mr. Armbruster. "The people down below are very sensitive about requests from the corporate staff for data that are going to require their time and effort to put together. It's always a question of how far can I go without stepping on the toes of the operating people."

The quality of the information is a constant worry. "We're trying to look at the future with pretty flaky data sometimes," he says. "I have a high tolerance for ambiguity, but sometimes it gets very frustrating to never be sure what's out there." He has built up his credibility carefully over the years, "and I guard it very jealously," he says. Still, bad information sometimes gets into a forecast because of aberrations caused by internal reorganizations, acquisitions and accounting changes over the years, and it can make things hot for an operating man who is meeting with top management. Recently a division vice president "phoned and really chewed my ear for a long while because I had bad data," says Mr. Armbruster.

Another worry is time. Mr. Armbruster, his assistant, Mr. Keogh, and TRW's econometrician, Van Bussmann, have spent about 80% of their time working together as a team lately in an effort to meet top management's increasing requests for more and faster information. "We're in danger of being loved to death," says Mr. Armbruster. "We just can't keep up with everything we want to do." Instead of going to lunch, he often sneaks off to the computer to run his own analyses.

Mr. Armbruster concedes that some of the time pressures he feels are self-imposed. "Sometimes if I didn't generate some particular report nobody would miss it because they don't even know it's coming," he says. "But I know it ought to be done and I feel like I've got to. My wife says I get compulsive when I have a project going. I enter into a one-track mind mode until I either solve the problem or fall over in complete frustration."

"That Was No Secretary— That Was My Boss"

"Your secretary came outside to inspect the no-parking signs we put up at the drive-in teller," the police lieutenant told Martin Hartmann, an assistant branch manager for Continental Bank.

"Hey, that was no secretary," objected Mr. Hartmann. "That was my boss."

His boss is Challis M. Lowe, a 31-year-old black woman who earns more than $25,000 a year running the bank's first branch office, which opened September 1976 in a skyscraper lobby at the north end of Chicago's financial district. Well aware that Mrs. Lowe is in charge, her staff of 26 bankers, tellers and clerks have dubbed the branch "Challis' palace." But outsiders, unaccustomed to dealing with a woman executive, sometimes mistake her for a secretary.

More women than ever before are working in the executive suite. Antidiscrimination laws, pressure from women's groups and changing social values have encouraged concerns to open up management ranks in recent years. And the results are beginning to be evident.

The U.S. Bureau of Labor Statistics reports that in 1975 about 19% of the nation's 8.9 million managers and administrators were female, up from 16% in 1970. A recent study by the Council on Economic Priorities, a private research group, found that at 24 large U.S. banks the proportion of women officials and managers has grown to 26% from 16% five years ago.

However, the vast majority of women managers in both banking and other industries are concentrated in entry-level, supervisory or management training jobs. It's estimated that at present, women hold only 6% of all middle-management posts and just 1% of vice presidential and higher posts in major U.S. corporations.

So while the woman middle manager may no longer be her concern's only female executive, she remains a relative newcomer who is often viewed with a mixture of sexist attitudes and cautious acceptance. And the hurdles she must overcome may be greater than those facing women in senior management, who already have achieved a degree of success.

In middle management, "there's the greatest pressure to compete. You've got a glut of people and only a few of them will make it to the top," observes Francine Gordon, assistant professor of organizational behavior at Stanford University's school of business. "A woman in that position is more threatening to men," she says.

Some experts believe that female middle managers encounter difficulties because their upbringing and training haven't prepared them for a lifetime of work, much less a management career. Women tend to have narrow horizons that don't go beyond "limited and discrete time intervals," such as marriage and a family, whereas "a man expects to work all his life," notes Margaret Fenn, associate professor at the University of Washington's Graduate School of Business Administration.

Such are the strains of management, that some women executives suffer considerable guilt about being considered bad mothers because they work long hours. For example, Kay K. Mazuy, senior vice president of Shawmut Corp., a Boston bank-holding company, gets upset when schoolteachers or pediatricians want to discuss her two children in the middle of the afternoon. She feels they are really giving her "little jabs that say, 'if you were being a good mother you would be at home.'"

Female executives report that the predominantly male business world puts them at a disadvantage in another way. They complain that they are often isolated from informal social contacts by being excluded from lunches, drinking sessions or weekend golf with fellow executives. Such contacts form traditional "old boy networks" that provide critical advice about how to get things done and who is important to know for advancement in a company.

For the same reason, women in management say they have trouble finding a corporate sponsor, a senior executive who will encourage them and bring them along as his career advances. The protege system is one way that men have typically moved up the corporate ladder. But if a man sponsors a woman, Prof. Gordon says, "people are likely to ask, 'what's going on between them?' "

The small number of female executives also means that they are expected to perform better on the job than men. "We're still in the super Bionic Woman stage," observes Janet Jones, chairman of Management Woman Inc., a New York executive search concern for women. Fortune 500 companies constantly ask her to find someone who is guaranteed to be successful, she says. "There's no margin for error."

The special burdens of being an isolated female, plus the normal tensions of middle management, often combine to place tremendous emotional stress on women executives. Consequently, physicians report, they are starting to fall prey to such traditionally male stress-related diseases as heart attacks, ulcers and high blood pressure.

Statistical evidence of the trend doesn't exist yet. But as more women move into management-level jobs "I think we will see an increase in coronary heart disease" among younger and younger women, says Dr. Ray Rosenman, associate director of San Francisco's Brunn Institute for Cardiovascular Disease.

The pressures and frustrations of being a woman middle manager are clearly apparent in Challis Lowe's career. But there also is satisfaction, and her experience suggests that some aspects of corporate life may get easier as the ranks of female executives swell.

At first glance, Challis Lowe doesn't appear to fit the part she plays: an ambitious, hard-driving executive who is determined to reach a high management position. She is a thin, seemingly shy person who speaks in a soft voice. Her carefully tailored suits and large, thick glasses give her the appearance of a schoolteacher.

In fact, her early ambition was to be a high school math teacher, and she substituted in an elementary school after the birth of her first daughter, Daphne, in 1966. But after her second daughter was born two years later, she acted against her husband John's wishes and decided to seek a fulltime business career. She wasn't looking for fulfillment or power, she says, so much as "peace of mind from getting out of the house during the day."

She did counseling for an employment agency for two years, and it was there that she heard about opportunities for women in banking. So in 1971 she became a customer representative for Continental Illinois National Bank & Trust Co.'s personal banking division, which services individual customers, rather than business and commercial accounts.

After a few years spent opening accounts and counseling, Mrs. Lowe began to wonder if she would ever go higher in the bank. She was dubious because there was only one female officer in her section of personal banking. And when she asked her supervisor about a promotion, he suggested that she transfer to another area of the bank.

She ignored his suggestion and, instead, took a personnel department test, which indicated she had management talents. As a result, her work was watched more closely, and in mid-1974, at the age of 28, Mrs. Lowe was made assistant sales manager and, later that year, an officer. Early in 1975 she became sales manager.

Mrs. Lowe was Continental Bank's first black woman officer. Now the bank employs about 100 women executives—up from only 30 in 1973—three of whom are black. Altogether, the bank has 1,123 individuals in management.

As sales manager, Mrs. Lowe was in charge of half of the bank's family banking center, which handles all types of customer services. The promotion put her in charge of 30 bankers, most of whom were men. Uncomfortable about the situation, a few of the male veterans complained to her boss. One older woman took early retirement rather than take orders from the new manager. To this day, Mrs. Lowe says she doesn't know whether they resented her because she was black, female or under 30—or all three.

Sometimes, customers also were skeptical of her authority, refusing to talk to her and insisting that they be allowed "to see an officer." One elderly man was finally persuaded to confer with her, and was so pleased with the results that he told her, "You can be my secretary any time." Mrs. Lowe coolly replied, "I don't think you can afford me."

When Continental Bank decided to launch its first branch four blocks from the main office, Mrs. Lowe was tapped to manage the branch. At the time, Illinois law prohibited branch banking except for an additional office offering personal and limited commercial banking services within 1,500 feet of a bank's headquarters. (The law was amended in the summer of 1976 to allow another branch within two miles.)

She took over her new job in February 1976, months before the lobby office opened, to direct the construction, design and equipping of the facility. In the process, Mrs. Lowe learned some lessons about being a woman middle manager. For the first time she had to deal with men in other bank departments, few of whom knew her or had worked with a female executive before. This explains why, she says, "they tended to put my priorities on the back burner. I found I had to prove myself with many of them."

Getting what she wants for her branch also requires Mrs. Lowe to work closely with the three men and one woman who are her fellow executives in personal banking. All of these executives have profit responsibilities and all compete for staff and budget allocations from their boss, vice president Lawrence A. Eldridge.

Two or three times every day, Mrs. Lowe leaves her thickly carpeted, glassed-in office on the branch's mezzanine level for meetings or a working lunch at the main office with the other managers. At these meetings she sometimes finds herself fighting to protect her turf. One dispute concerned dinner plates that the bank gives away as premiums. She argued with her colleagues that she shouldn't have to absorb the marketing expenses when customers with accounts at the main bank pick up free plates at her branch.

But the competition among the personal banking executives is more often friendly and low-keyed, and Mrs. Lowe deliberately tries to encourage bonhomie. Whether it's a marketing strategy conference or an occasional drink after work, Mrs. Lowe prepares diligently, keeping posted on the latest sports scores, even though she hates sports. It's vital for a woman "to work at becoming part of a company's informal social network," she observes.

Her quick adaptation to office politics and her smooth operation of the new office (its deposit volume is running four months ahead of schedule) are winning her praise. Staff morale is high, customers are pleased, "and we're getting a good business there," says John H. Perkins, Continental Bank's president. "It's got to be because she's running the place well."

Challis Lowe pays a price for her success, however. A self-described perfectionist, she spends 12 hours a day at work, leaving for home past 7 p.m., with an attache case full of papers. She's enrolled in a special two-year, masters of business administration program for exeutives at Northwestern University, which she attends one day a week. She also attends a school study group one evening a week. If she has a lot of homework, she gets up at 4 a.m. to study.

Work and school are so time-consuming that she has little opportunity to relax in her apartment, which is in a middle-class, racially mixed neighborhood on Chicago's south side. "I don't do a lot of unwinding, except when I'm sleeping," she' says. Before she went back to school she would unwind by baking bread, kneading the dough "to a pulp."

Her lack of leisure pursuits and the tensions of her job give Mrs. Lowe stomach upsets and an occasional flare-up of colitis, a stress-related inflammation of the colon. Her husband blames the colitis on the fact that she lets pressures "build up to the point where she has to have an (emotional) explosion." After her most recent promotion, he remembers, she tossed and turned a great deal in her sleep, and she was irritable at home for six months.

Another source of tension is Mrs. Lowe's guilt about being constantly away from her daughters, aged eight and 10. She often doesn't see them from one day to the next, especially when her school study group meets until late at night. "As a woman, I feel I should spend more time with them," she says. (It's notable that Mrs. Lowe is the only female officer at Continental Bank with young children.)

John Lowe admits that he resents his wife's extended absences. Mrs. Lowe's career commitment "has shifted a lot of responsibility to me that I probably wouldn't have accepted normally," he says with a sigh. Mr. Lowe is a former television advertising salesman who this year returned to school full-time in an MBA program, leaving Mrs. Lowe as the family's sole breadwinner. He takes the girls to their doctors' appointments and attends their school conferences.

Despite her guilt feelings, Challis Lowe wouldn't think of giving up her management job because, she says, it gives her a deep sense of accomplishment. Her "personal drive," she says, wasn't being "fulfilled" by staying at home.

Her drive is fueled by ambition. With a note of determination in her voice, she declares that her sights "aren't limited to becoming a second vice president." Her race and sex may help more than hinder her futher advancement at Continental Bank, which recently was the target of a sex discrimination suit by Women Employed, an organization of Chicago working women.

But conflicting loyalties between work and home make Mrs. Lowe unsure that she would like to be president of Continental Bank. "The road to the top is filled with more and more commitment to the job and less and less time with your family," she says, her voice growing softer and less steady. Laughing nervously, she adds, "If I spent any more hours away from home, I might not have a family."

Going To Court

Marvin E. Walden is a highly skilled manager for Chrysler Corp. with a doctorate in mathematics. In 1971 his career ran into a wall when his department was disbanded and he was demoted to the position of supervisor.

Richard E. Mathews joined Ford Motor Co.'s assembly line 38 years ago and rose through the ranks to head a sizable staff and to command his own office and secretary. In 1973 he was demoted to the job of engineer.

Edward B. Mazzotta once held a management job as resident engineer at Ford's Dearborn engine plant. In 1974 he was demoted two pay grades and now describes himself as "a paper shuffler."

Like many middle managers in America today, these men feel they have been treated unfairly by their companies. They believe they have been shunted to one side in dead-end jobs to make way for fast-rising, younger men. But these three managers have decided to do something about their grievances: They are suing their companies in court.

An increasing number of managers are hiring lawyers to challenge their companies' personnel policies. Usually older men, they find themselves caught in a middle-management glut due to the over-hiring practices of the 1960s. Often they have been demoted or passed over, and, despite a usually handsome paycheck, they have to do jobs that they feel are below their capabilities.

Even worse, many are being pressured to take early retirement as companies attempt to cut back on the excess of managers. By fighting back in the courts, these middle managers feel they have nothing to lose, says Prof. Eugene E. Jennings, a management expert at Michigan State University. "Today, middle managers are becoming terribly cynical because there's no place for them to go," he says.

In essence, these frustrated employes are challenging the ways in which companies have promoted and developed managers for years. One area under attack is the use by many companies of confidential lists of "high potential" employes as a means of keeping watch on the brightest prospects. This so-called "fast track" is used by companies to move highly motivated people through a series of responsible jobs as quickly as possible. Most companies argue that such a device is necessary to achieve the best possible succession to upper executive ranks.

Now, a growing number of middle managers want to know if they are on their companies' fast tracks. V. Paul Donnelly, a Detroit lawyer who specializes in white-collar age-discrimination cases, believes that some companies' lists may be biased because they consist of the names of only "well-educated, white males under 40 years of age."

Managers also are challenging the way most companies evaluate employes, particularly the performance review. Although the mechanics of such reviews vary widely, they usually involve an annual written appraisal by an immediate supervisor, endorsement by the supervisor's boss and some type of discussion with the employe. "Too often," claims Mr. Donnelly, "performance reviews are used to downgrade older employes who have little, if any, process of appeal within the company."

A major problem in many American businesses is that the way to the top seems just as vague and capricious as ever. In 1973 the American Management Association surveyed 2,600 executives and found that most felt that advancement is the result of a "largely subjective evaluation or arbitrary decision." Middle managers and technical employes added that "who you know" is nearly as important as "what you know."

In a survey held in 1976, Ford found that more than half of its salaried employes felt there is little consistency from supervisor to supervisor in standards used to rate performance at the company. More than half also believed that improved job performance would not help their chance for promotion.

Many companies are clearly worried about this growing disenchantment among middle management, and they are trying to do something about it. In an effort to reduce subjectivity in the appraisal of managers, computer networks are being set up within companies so that the qualifications of all eligible employes can be reviewed when a job falls open.

One notable example of this new approach to promotions is that of Bendix Corp., which is introducing a system whereby an employe sits down with his supervisor and arrives at an agreed-on set of goals for the year. The manager's performance is measured against these objectives. As another example, General Motors Corp. is using the performance review to allow an employe to state his career goals and to work out a plan to correct any deficiencies, such as education, that he might have. "We're trying to get the employes more involved in the process," says Eugene L. Hartwig, GM's assistant corporate counsel.

But in the meantime, more and more companies are being confronted in court by disgruntled middle managers. Here is a look at the three managers introduced at the beginning of this story who believe they have been unfairly treated by their employers, Ford and Chrysler. Both companies decline to comment specifically on any of the individual cases, other than in court papers. A Ford spokesman, in defense of its personnel policies, maintains that it draws on "the ability and experience of each employe." A Chrysler spokesman insists that employes "get promoted solely on the basis of performance."

Each of the men is represented by Mr. Donnelly, the Detroit lawyer. So far he has had only minor successes in suing companies on the basis of age discrimination and breach of employment contract (Ford claims he has yet to win a "big" case). But management consultants believe that as the number of age discrimination suits against companies grows, the likelihood of a landmark case setting an important precedent becomes more likely.

Says Mr. Donnelly of his manager-clients: "Most have their

careers halted for no just reason, and that eats at them. By coming to me, they are trying to recover self-respect and pride."

Marvin E. Walden

In only five years at GM, Marvin E. Walden was promoted to senior mathematician at the company's technical center, receiving several merit pay increases and extensive training at company expense. He felt, however, that his chances of entering management would be better at a company with "less technical depth" in personnel and facilities. "I was young and ambitious, so I sent out resumes to Ford and Chrysler," he says, In mid-1969, he joined Chrysler for a "substantial pay increase."

Within a few months. Mr. Walden became head of a 32-man department assigned to computerize the process of turning clay models of car designs into precisely measured body components. For nearly a year and a half, he ran the department and developed facilities which, he claims, now save Chrysler about $1 million annually. During that time, Mr. Walden says he received a "favorable" oral performance review from the head of Chrysler's technical computer center. He says this was the only performance appraisal he has had in eight years with the company.

With a managerial position that paid about $24,000 a year, Mr. Walden's career seemed "on track." In addition, he was completing his doctorate in mathematics at Detroit's Wayne State University, where he had graduated Phi Beta Kappa with a physics degree and earned a master's degree in math.

His job prospects changed dramatically, however, when his boss was promoted and, according to Mr. Walden, a "personality clash" developed with the new man. In May 1971, Mr. Walden's department was disbanded without warning, and he was demoted to a supervisor without any cut in pay. Chrysler says the move was necessary to eliminate duplication of work with another department; Mr. Walden thinks he was "set up" as part of an inter-departmental political struggle.

"At first I was angry and wanted to quit," says 41-year-old Mr. Walden, "but after sending out hundreds of resumes, I quickly learned I'd have to take a substantial cut in pay." He decided to stay on at Chrysler, hoping that he might eventually be promoted back to his former level. Instead, Mr. Walden says he has been given a series of "make-work, letter-writing assignments, leading nowhere."

In 1975, Mr. Walden was laid off, along with about 20.000 other Chrysler salaried workers, due to the recession. When he returned he found that several younger men had been promoted to positions he thought himself qualified to fill. So Mr. Walden sued his employer, seeking reinstatement to his former management position and $500,000 in damages. "My demotion was without cause, but if they had treated me like a gentleman, I would have saluted and waited for a promotion back to a manager's level." he says. "But there was no internal due process, no mediation procedure."

As part of his suit, Mr. Walden is demanding to see Chrysler's list of "exceptional" employes. Chrysler admits that it centrally compiles such lists to assist it in selecting candidates for internal openings, but the company denies that it uses the list in a discriminatory manner. "One's name on such a list doesn't guarantee advancement," company lawyers say. "There are many, many employes whose names haven't been on such a list who have been advanced much further than most of the employes so listed." Chrysler has been ordered by Wayne County Circuit Court to produce certain details of the list for inspection.

"Usually in Chrysler," contends Mr. Walden, "you get on the list, and you get promoted if you know a director (a management level one step below vice president). It's a 100% sponsor- or godfather-type system and has nothing to do with any kind of scientific management system."

"What results," he feels, "is that many people are under-utilized; yet they continue to pay us high salaries, wasting millions." He says his total economic package, including such benefits as medical insurance, is about $35,000 a year. He lives in a comfortable brick ranch house in the affluent Detroit suburb of Bloomfield Hills, has two cars and sends his three children to private schools. "I've lost a lot of sleep over this," he says. "I started grinding my teeth so much I had to buy a teeth protector." He adds: "It won't be possible for me to take less money and change my life style now."

Richard E. Mathews

"If they thought they were clearing out some deadwood, they picked the wrong man," declares Richard E. Mathews, who has worked for Ford for nearly 38 years. "No one ever told me I didn't do a good job, and I certainly never felt I was ready to retire." But Mr. Mathews asserts that in rough times Ford "makes the mistake of assuming that young is good, older is bad, or now is our chance to weed out the older employes." Mr. Mathews never thought he would be one of those "eased out the door."

In 1939 at the age of 19, Mr. Mathews joined Ford as an assembly-line worker. He left in 1942 to fly B29s during World War II, rising to the rank of captain. He returned to Ford in 1947, and was assigned to testing Ford's German-made trucks. Except for three years on the assembly line, Mr. Mathew's entire career has been in testing and developing products for Ford's foreign affiliates and export markets.

Despite the lack of a college degree, Mr. Mathews rose to the post of supervisor, with as many as 22 engineers and technicians under him. After eight years, he was asked to take a lateral transfer to become supervisor of another department's Latin American section. "I thought the move was made to train younger supervisors and to expand my overall experience," says Mr. Mathews. Two years later, in 1974, however, the department was eliminated, and Mr. Mathews, then 53 years old, was demoted and transferred back to his old department as an engineer.

An indignant Mr. Mathews fired off a letter to chairman Henry Ford II. But the only response was a call from the personnel department saying his complaint wasn't "valid." Mr. Mathews sued, asking for reinstatement to his former position. Ford argues that Mr. Mathews was demoted without any cut in pay at a time when "thousands of employes were being released out-right" due to the recession. Mr. Mathews claims that in his department there was a net gain in personnel of about 15% during the recession.

Although his salary wasn't cut (in 1976, he earned about $45,000, including $10,000 of overtime), he says he "lost prestige, a private office, a secretary and any right to a bonus, which probably would have amounted to about $4,500 in 1976." He declares: "I didn't have any illusions that I could go much higher than one more notch, but the demotion put me further back in the pack for any future advancement."

Sitting in the living room of his Dearborn Heights, Mich., home, not far from Ford's world headquarters, Mr. Mathews says: "I don't disagree with the idea of bringing fresh blood into an organization, but you have to try to hit a happy medium between the young world-beaters and your loyal, experienced people. A lot of the stars burn themselves out at an early age."

Edward B. Mazzotta

In 1953, Edward B. Mazzotta joined Ford as a project engineer designing vehicle components. Eight years later, he left to work for two smaller Detroit-area engineering firms, but rejoined Ford in 1971. Within 15 months, he was promoted two pay grades to resident engineer of the Dearborn engine plant, a $30,000-a-year management job.

"In any corporation, nine times out of ten, you need an angel to watch over you if you're going to get ahead," says the 56-year-old Mr. Mazzotta. "I had an angel, but when a new regime came in to head up the resident engineering staff, my angel got his wings clipped and was forced into early retirement."

What resulted, in Mr. Mazzotta's view, was a "humiliating, systematic step-by-step discrediting" by his new supervisors. Within about three months, Mr. Mazzotta received two poor performance reviews. "These were unwarranted and based on a lack of facts," he claims. "When the reviews were presented to me, I was told to read them and then sign them, but I had no opportunity to discuss them." In March 1974, Mr. Mazzotta, then 53, was demoted two pay grades without a cut in pay and transferred to another department. Now, he says, he's "a paper shuffler, doing nothing that any high school graduate couldn't do," at a salary of about $35,000 a year.

"Some people will tolerate a lot of abuse before they do anything: they'll sit there and take the money. But the desire to feel useful and constructive was too great for me," he says. Mr. Mazzotta says he tried to appeal his case through Ford's personnel department, asking for a promotional transfer, but "it was like going to a priest for confession. Once you've been demoted, it's unlikely you'll ever shake the stigma and be promoted again."

In a lawsuit filed in 1976 in Wayne County Circuit Court, seeking reinstatement and $500,000 in damages, Mr. Mazzotta charges that younger men "with far less experience" have been promoted within the department while several older men "in my age range" have been either demoted or forced into early retirement. Ford says that Mr. Mazzotta's lack of promotion is a function of "few position openings" and of his performance "in relation to others seeking the positions."

The demotion and the decision to sue Ford haven't been easy on Mr. Mazzotta. Eight months after his demotion, he required medical treatment for a duodenal ulcer. At his request, he was interviewed for this story in his hospital room after suffering a heart attack while on the job. Mr. Mazzotta blames his health problems on the way he was treated at Ford.

"You can't eliminate politics from a corporation, but you can try to minimize it," he reasons. "In my case, the performance review was used as a weapon, and I had no way to refute or rebut what was happening to me.

"I don't agree with the idea that a man slows down as he gets older," he says. "If a man is slow at 55, he was slow at 35, and the company has an obligation to tell him of his limited potential then—and not wait 20 years to shelve him or sweep him out the door."

Emphasis on Experience

For the middle-aged executive, it was a nightmare: at age 58, the man was sacked. After years as manufacturing manager of a building materials concern, the official saw his $30,000-a-year job disappear in a corporate reorganization. But much to his surprise, he found a similar job at the same salary in less than six weeks.

"This man was a godsend to his new employers because they were getting into a new field and they needed experience in the business," says Saul Gruner, senior vice president of THinc Career Planning Corp., a New York concern retained by companies to help fired executives find new jobs.

Managers like the manufacturing executive are making a pleasant discovery: After years of the corporate youth cult, the middle-aged manager with specific, hard-won experience is more in demand. Of course, senior people have always been in demand for the few top corporate jobs, but now men and women in their forties and fifties increasingly are being sought for middle-management slots as well.

"We are looking with closer attention at the person in the 45-to-55 age bracket than in the past," says David W. Wallace, chairman and president of Bangor Punta Corp., a diversified Greenwich, Conn., industrial concern. "The emphasis is changing now and there's a greater premium on experience and judgment," he says. Mr. Wallace says that many companies now believe that age brings benefits. "It's why 12-year-old whisky is better than three-year-old whisky," he says.

Signs are that the middle-aged middle manager's lot is improving in areas besides employment. With awareness of the "mid-life crisis" on the rise, some companies are giving more attention to the often-neglected manager who will never be a company president or even a vice president, but who may be on the payroll for another 20 years. To stimulate these employes, a few companies are designing new pay incentives and trying to make the work itself more rewarding.

Certainly, in companies there is a surplus of older, middle managers, many of whom are in dead-end jobs but are unable to find new positions in their high salary brackets. It's also true that some companies have been firing excess managers to cut operating costs. And, of course, countless companies still prefer to hire youth. On the average, it remains easier to find a middle-management job at age 35 than at age 55. But the difference is narrowing.

Boyden Associates, an executive recruiting concern based in New York, says its clients are hiring significantly more executives over age 50 than three years ago and somewhat fewer aged 35 to 40. Handy Associates, another New York search concern, says that several clients recently have specified that they would hire up to age 60. "This was very, very rare five years ago," says Pearl Meyer, executive vice president.

One reason the middle-aged manager has become prized is that his ranks are quite thin. While 3.8 million Americans were born in 1947, only 2.4 million were born in the Depression year of 1932 and thus today 30-year-olds are far more plentiful than 45-year-olds. If companies want experienced talent, they must not only compete for a relatively small number of available 45-year-old managers, but sometimes look closely at the candidate in his 50s as well, recruiters say.

Personnel experts say that although new laws against age discrimination often have generated only lip service, they also have produced some substantive changes. Moreover, pension reform legislation has allowed more executives than in the past to quit their jobs without losing all of their pension rights. This has sometimes made it easier to lure the older executive from one company to another.

But the biggest reason for the change is that many companies want proven experience instead of mere promise. "The image of the 35-year-old hotshot has been somewhat tarnished in the last five years," says Roger M. Kenny, senior vice president of Spencer Stuart & Associates, an executive search concern. Robert Staub, president of Staub, Warmbold & Associates, another recruiter, says one client recently specified a manager of about 50 years of age to replace a 37-year-old official. "The younger man did a super job, but he also alienated a lot of people," Mr. Staub says. "The company wanted somebody with more maturity."

Bangor Punta's Mr. Wallace adds: "In the go-go days of the '60s, a lot of mistakes got covered up by increased profits. But the value of experience is appreciated more in a time when competition is tougher." Besides, starting salaries for young managers have risen so high that "the differential in pay between them and the man who has 20 years of solid experience under his belt isn't that great," Mr. Wallace says. "For $10,000 more, you're just buying a lot more experience."

Even if age itself isn't important, many companies today demand such specific experience that only a middle-aged person is likely to qualify. For instance, American Can Co. says not long ago it hired a 52-year-old manager for a wood pulp operation. "We wanted somebody with woodland experience and mill operations experience, and it's hard to find somebody who has both," says C. Edward Snyder, vice president for employe relations. Chances are a manager with this background won't be in his 30s, he adds.

A Staub, Warmbold client, seeking a technically qualified corporate staff member with experience in Europe, Latin America and Asia, hired a man aged 54. "To have all that experience, the person almost had to be in his late 40s to mid-50s," says Donald Allerton, a Staub, Warmbold vice president.

Now that companies are more willing to hire the middle-aged middle manager, they are finding this is a quick way to buy experience in areas where the company itself is deficient. "If you have a need that suddenly comes on you, you can't start with a beginner," says S. Bruce Smart Jr., president of Continental Group Inc., the diversified container maker.

Mrs. Meyer of Handy Associates, the recruiters, recalls a beverage company that was "delighted" to hire a 56-year-old regional sales manager. "He had years of experience doing similar work and he knew everybody in the region," she says.

Ironically, the expanding company with "whiz kid" top brass often has all the more reason to hire the older executive. Bendix Corp., which recently named a 39-year-old chairman, says it also has hired several managers over 45 in the last few years, including a 53-year-old planning and development executive. In most cases the company was expanding rapidly in a particular activity and wanted a "state-of-the-art expert," a spokesman says.

Small- and medium-sized companies sometimes seek older officals from the corporate giants. "We recently placed a 52-year-old guy who had spent 20-plus years with a multibillion-dollar company," recalls J. Gerald Simmons, president of Handy Associates. "He was a key person in the personnel department, but he would never run it. Now he is vice president of personnel at a smaller company and reports directly to the chief executive officer. He is like a kid at Christmas, and the company figures it is getting 20 years worth of tremendous personnel experience."

Hiring the older official often will help a company keep its young managers, consultants say.

"If you hire somebody of 55, you're telling his subordinates in their 30s that there is still hope for them," says E. Donald Davis, president of THinc Career Planning.

At the same time, middle-aged executives are beginning to benefit from society's growing attention to middle age and its problems. It's notable, for instance, that Gail Sheehy's "Passages," a book which deals with crises of mid-life, was a recent best-seller.

"Companies are definitely more interested in the problems of middle-aged managers," says Patrick J. Montana, president of the National Center for Career Life Planning, a division of the American Management Association that deals with problems of middle age. The onset of middle age, when people are particularly prone to take stock anyway, comes just when many managers find their advancement is slowing significantly, he notes.

Harry Levinson, a clinical psychologist and lecturer at the Harvard Medical School, adds: "For the younger person, there is nothing out there but upward and onward. But when you hit middle age, you become aware of the fact that you are not immortal. When the job adds to this, when it says, yes, you are over the hill, it magnifies the problem." This is one reason that "chronic depression in middle management is much more prevalent than managements realize," adds the pyschologist, who also heads an industrial psychology consulting concern.

Consultants say most companies are unaware of this problem, even though it often leads to poor performance. But a few companies are trying to restructure work and provide new challenges for the older middle manager. Cummins Engine Co. occasionally will assign highly experienced middle managers to short-term duties in new situations, says Ronald Hoge, director of personnel administration. For instance, a 55-year-old official who had spent over 25 years in the company's personnel department was given a four-month assignment to help reorganize the corporate finance department.

Most middle managers are misused, says Roy W. Walters, a Glen Rock, N.J., management consultant. "We often see situations where half or more of the manager's functions should be done by subordinates," he says.

Mr. Walters often encourages companies to push authority further down the hierarchy, a move that can enrich the middle manager's job. For instance, in 1975, the Borg-Warner Chemicals & Plastics U.S.A. division of Borg-Warner Corp. expanded the authority of regional sales managers to offer special prices and authorize returns of merchandise.

"In the past, we had to act like kindergarten kids and get permission for everything," says Russell H. Kendall, a Borg-Warner Chemicals regional sales manager in Indianapolis at the time. "We all took the change as a vote of confidence in us to do our jobs," adds the official, who is now the division's Western

Hemisphere general sales manager. Besides boosting morale, the change made the work much more stimulating, he adds.

Some companies also are giving middle managers greater incentives by relating their pay more closely to performance. For instance, one Southwestern manufacturing company launched a bonus program in 1976 that is linked to results of a manager's division, says James Kuhns, manager of executive compensation for Hewitt Associates, a Deerfield, Ill., consulting concern. The plan, which applies to managers earning more than $35,000 a year, replaces a program for those paid over $45,000 a year that was related only to the overall corporate performance, Mr. Kuhns says. "The idea was to motivate middle managers on things that middle managers can affect," he adds.

But many companies still think very little about motivating the middle manager, especially if he is middle-aged, consultants say. With middle managers, it is often difficult to know what performance to reward and how to measure it, says Reed M. Roberts of Sibson & Co., a management consultant. "Bluntly speaking, for most middle managers, the incentive is to keep your job."

Anguish of the Fired Executive

One sunny afternoon in August 1975, Robert J. Hull, a successful and well-paid national sales manager for Corning Glass Works, was called into his boss's office. There, his career took an unexpected turn. He was fired.

In fact, Mr. Hull was one of 527 middle managers and other salaried employes let go by Corning Glass in what the company called a "reduction in force" to deal with a recession-caused plunge in profits. In a desperate attempt at recovery, the company decided to cast off its unprofitable operations and many of the managers who ran them.

Corning's managers, some of whom had been with the company for over 20 years, were stunned by the swiftness of the action, even though rumors of firings had been floating through the town of Corning for some days. Some recall standing staring in disbelief at their dismissal slips: "I just couldn't believe there wasn't room in the company for someone with the breadth of experience I have," says one. Mr. Hull, a self-confident man, recalls asking himself "why me?" It was particularly hard to accept, he says, because only two months previously he had received a merit raise and had been told "that I'd done an outstanding job."

The firings at Corning Glass, and Mr. Hull's experience of being cast adrift in search of a new job, illustrate the psychological problems that face the middle manager who is fired after years with the same company. Management recruiters point out that a manager who has viewed his career as a lifetime affair with one company is singularly unprepared to find a new employer. Few can remember how to write a resume and, after years of being promoted within a company, most haven't had to think too hard about selling themselves. But, says Max Ulrich, president of Ward Howell Associates, a New York recruiter, "the biggest initial problem is shock."

Life is somewhat less secure for the middle manager these days, as the experience of so many at Corning Glass shows. Many companies once offered an implied promise of a lifetime job for the manager who functioned reasonably well. But with the memory of the recession still fresh, companies are trying to keep their management structure as lean as possible. "The fat days of the 40s, 50s and 60s are gone," says Thomas Hubbard, chairman of THinc Career Planning Corp., a management placement consultant. "They aren't going to carry dear old Joe just because he's been here for 20 years."

A number of middle managers have been put out of work over the past two or three years by industry's increasing tendency to cut back on unprofitable operations rather than to hold onto them in the hopes of a turnaround. Sluggish economic conditions also have been blamed for firings. For example, early in March 1977, Consolidated Edison Co., the New York utility, lopped 211 management-level employes from its payroll. The American Management Association notes that management jobs not directly related to manufacturing, such as in public relations, usually are the first to be pared.

But sometimes, as happened at Corning Glass, which fired 10% of its salaried employes, it makes little difference if the middle managers involved in cutbacks are highly skilled and competent manufacturing men. These managers inevitably are caught up in the corporate panic that usually accompanies falling profits. Thomas MacAvoy, Corning Glass's president, puts it succinctly: "We had businesses that were ineffective. We had to restructure management to make it leaner, and we had to trim off people."

Ironically, Corning Glass has long had the reputation of being the ultimate paternalistic company, possibly due to the fact that the company had a workforce of 7,200 centered around the town of Corning (population, 15,000) in upstate New York. Thus there is a sense of community among employes, who are likely to be next-door neighbors or even close personal friends.

Many families have been working for the Glass Works, as the company is known in Corning, for several generations, including the family of Amory Houghton Jr., the chairman and great-great-grandson of the founder. The Glass Works, says one executive, "always has been a company ... with a very, very high respect for individual workers at all levels."

But the traditional amity between the executive office and workers evaporated in the severe profit plunge that Corning Glass suffered in 1975. Earnings fell by 75% in the first half of 1975 and the company closed the year with earnings of only $1.76 a share, down from $2.73 in 1974. By July 1975, says Mr. Houghton, unit sales were off by 40% and the company was spending more than it was taking in. (In 1976, however, earnings rebounded sharply, spurting 169%, and another 10% gain was scored in 1977.)

The decision was made to cut back immediately on money-draining lines and, by letting skilled managers go, to save $20 million to $25 million a year on personnel costs. Mr. Houghton says he would have liked to have spread the cutbacks out over a period of time, but business had turned sour too quickly.

A list of more than 500 names was drawn up, and rumors of the impending firings quickly spread through the town. On Friday, Aug. 22, the company announced that the firings were coming, but it wasn't until the following Monday that the people involved were told. Former Corning Glass managers recall spending an anxious weekend wondering if their names were on the list. One executive still gets angry when he recalls how his tipsy superior told him at a Friday night cocktail party that Monday would be his last day on the job.

It was at 3 p.m. on that Monday when Mr. Hull got word of the end of his Corning Glass career. Many who had been fired left within minutes, but Mr. Hull stayed on to put his files in order for the man who would have to wind up the business. In fact, he returned several times to help. "Some of my contemporaries thought I was crazy, and maybe I was," he reflects. But, he says, he continued to feel a responsibility to the company.

Mr. Hull was luckier than many of those who had been

fired; he found a new job in three months, just around the corner from Corning. Today he is director of sales for the motor components division of Facet Enterprises Inc. in Elmira, N.Y. But others from the Glass Works went for many months before finding work, and a handful still are searching.

Mr. Hull had joined Corning Glass Works in the middle of 1957 and at the time viewed it as a summer job before returning for his second year at Georgetown University Law School. But he found he liked the business and decided to abandon the law. His first permanent job was at a Corning Glass plant in West Virginia. This was followed by a spell at Corning headquarters, after which he was sent to Chicago as office manager for the Midwest sales operation.

It was while he was in Chicago that Mr. Hull decided to specialize in selling. ("I started selling when I was a kid," he recalls. "I would build model airplanes and take them to school. I would buy them for a dime and sell them for $2.") After Chicago he was sent to Corning's Canadian subsidiary as a manager and salesman for industrial building products. Then followed a period in Atlanta.

In 1972, Mr. Hull moved his wife and four daughters back to Corning, where he was to take over as national sales manager for science-construction products, such as glass acid drains for chemical laboratories. This was all part of a broader business, called chemical processing, whose sagging sales had been giving management sleepless nights for some time.

Mr. Hull says he was well aware of the problems, and even told his family that the gamble of trying to turn the business around might fail. A vice president had assured him, however, that his job would be protected. But, says Mr. Hull, his boss was transferred, and "the whole house of cards fell down."

He recalls driving back to his ranch-style home in Big Flats, N.Y., after the firing and wondering how to break the news to his family. It is, he says, "pretty tough to come home and have to tell your wife and kids, 'well, the game is over.' " But his wife, Lois, was actually glad that the tension and uncertainty were over. Mr. Hull recalls that she simply said "great." Her feeling was that her husband, a highly experienced salesman in his mid-40s, had an excellent chance of finding a better job.

The family's first priority was to put its finances in order. Mr. Hull had left Corning Glass with five months' severence pay and he had been saving hard for a year in anticipation of losing his job. Unnecessary expenses were avoided, and his two younger daughters' piano lessons were canceled. The family weeded out its expendable possessions and held two garage sales and an auction to raise extra funds.

"One of the things you find is that it takes money to go out and look for a job," says Mr. Hull. Companies usually will pay the cost of traveling to an interview, but there are many other costs to be borne. Mr. Hull spent about $1,000 just for phone calls, stamps and stationery.

He says he would have had to spend more if the Glass Works hadn't brought in experts to counsel the fired managers on how to write resumes and to manage interviews. Company recruiters were invited to visit Corning, and they hired a number of the fired managers.

Mr. Hull estimates that he spent 10 hours a day, seven days a week looking for a job. He wrote 800 letters and resumes to companies, trade associations, friends and contacts and executive search firms. Some companies he wrote to hadn't advertised any openings but were simply in an industry that Mr. Hull was interested in. "I found quite often that positions aren't available, but they are there . . . there's an idea in the president's mind for a particular man in a particular job, but it's not posted on the bulletin board."

A well-organized man, he found that 32% of the companies he wrote to didn't bother to reply. So he began experimenting in his approach to companies by sending a resume to one company, a letter to another and a combination of both to others. But the 32% rate held. "I got to the point where I thought, gee, what I ought to do is become a consultant and do this for companies," he says. Probably the main lesson he learned from all this was that getting a new job takes a lot longer than a person at first realizes.

All of his efforts produced interviews with nine companies, from fairly close to his home to as far away as Texas. About half, including Facet, offered him a job. He had a total of eight interviews with Facet, including a talk with the company's president. But, at the same time, he continued to contact other companies. A serious pitfall in job-hunting, he believes, is abandoning the search before an offer is nailed down. Hopes can quickly fall apart, he says.

Mr. Ulrich, the recruiter, agrees with Mr. Hull's pragmatic approach to job-hunting. The key to getting a job, he says, is quickly recovering from the initial shock of being fired and then "positioning yourself to market yourself intelligently." Self-pity, anger or depression are the job-hunter's enemies, he says. "A guy can't be low in morale and have his chin on the floor and go sell somebody on the idea that he's going to be a good financial vice president," he says.

Yet it is easy for the job-seeker to get discouraged, especially after months of hunting. One ex-Corning Glass manager, who is still out of work, describes spending every minute waiting for the phone to ring. "You're very tied down. You can't come and go," he says. When he has to leave home he takes the phone off the hook because "if they think the line is busy, they'll try again." He says, "Every time it rings, I think, 'my God, this may be it.'"

Even Mr. Hull admits to getting frustrated during his search. "You are going to get a lot of form letters back saying 'we have no positions open at this time.' Maybe they'd love to have you, but they aren't going to hire you and put you in a corner," he says.

But Mr. Hull was hired. He has been with Facet for more than a year now and, as he puts it, "it looks like the heart transplant is going to take." Yet he feels no bitterness toward Corning Glass for the disruption in his life. He says he understands why the company felt such drastic measures were necessary. "If I were Amory Houghton, I might have made exactly the same decision he made at the time," he says.

Hard Sell in Detroit

Inside a windowless chamber at Ford Motor Co.'s scientific research laboratory stands a table heaped with futuristic aluminum objects—automobile parts, more or less.

Donald Butler, a Ford auto engineer, circles the table looking skeptical as he sips his morning coffee. But suddenly he puts down his cup, seizes what looks like an internal engine part and begins turning it over in his hands.

"That's nice," he says thoughtfully.

A grin flashes across the anxious face of Martin DiLoreto, who sells aluminum for Reynolds Metals Co.; he has "stirred the imagination" of at least one auto man at this day's session, he hopes. That's a crucial step in the salesman's mission; he wants automakers to convert much of the steel-heavy American automobile to lighter, although costlier, aluminum.

This longtime dream of aluminum companies finally is beginning to come true, with help from the government's push to better fuel economy. As cars have shed weight, their average aluminum content has grown by 19% since 1975 to nearly 100 pounds, pacing the 18% rise of the whole previous decade. With aluminum at last penetrating beyond the usual pistons and trim to bigger-volume hoods, trunk lids and bumpers, aluminum executives happily project that its use in the average car could double or even quadruple between now and 1985.

But behind the scenes in aluminum's hottest market, there's still a painstaking selling job to be done by people like Reynolds' Marty DiLoreto. His maneuvers on the front lines of the auto-materials battle epitomize the problems and pressures that arise as any material invades a new market.

Aluminum makers really have been courting the auto industry since 1950, when David Reynolds, now chairman of the company that bears his family name, garnered the industry's first big order for use in the automatic transmission. (So eager was he to close that legendary deal that he rushed from his family to visit Detroit at Christmas time, at the bidding of General Motors Corp.)

Richmond-based Reynolds is the nation's number two aluminum producer, but years of such cultivation—including serveral jet trips the chairman makes each year to chat with auto moguls—have made it number one in Detroit. The company provides nearly half of what the "Big Three" U.S. primary aluminum makers supply directly to automakers, compared with about a third for bigger Aluminum Co. of America and under a fifth for third-ranked Kaiser Aluminum & Chemical Corp.

Yet passenger-car uses for aluminum have been held to just 9% of total aluminum industry shipments by one big bugaboo: cost. And the metal's price per pound, roughly three times that of steel, is still a sensitive subject in the flurry of visits and phone calls Mr. DiLoreto makes each week from Reynolds' aluminum-curtained sales office building near Detroit. He meets resistance even though a pound of lighter aluminum can go further than a pound of heavier steel, narrowing the cost gap.

When it comes to the cost battle between competing materials, asserts Mr. DiLoreto, "Everybody turns into a whore," meaning that the price, not the quality, becomes paramount. And so he must build his pitch around a more esoteric ingredient: lightness.

Armed with movies and reams of statistics on aluminum's weight and strength, he goes about, as he puts it, "Preaching the gospel of fuel economy." Automakers got religion on this subject at the time of the 1973 Arab oil embargo, and their interest rose when Congress told them two years later to about double gasoline mileage by 1985. President Carter's energy program could help, too.

Marty DiLoreto is an earnest, nattily dressed man of 41 who has an engineering degree, a master's in business administration earned at night school, and prior experience at packaging. His father was an imigrant Italian welder in an auto plant.

All his hustle—such as the early morning arrivals at the office when he has to ask the security guards to turn off the night burglar alarms—gets put to the test in selling the auto market. The steel salesmen—the competition—already "are in the door, so they have more contacts," says an auto engineer.

The aluminum salesmen have to nose around auto research labs and stamping plants, looking for clues to products that might be redesigned in aluminum, and even carrying magnets to identify steel parts they might supplant. "We're selling all the people all the time for all the parts," says Mr. DiLoreto.

The auto makers, it seems, are slow to change. Consider Mr. DiLoreto's biggest sale, the aluminum bumper on the 1977 Ford Pinto. "It wasn't like selling a vacuum cleaner," he says. "It took three years."

The selling began back in 1972, when Ford wasn't projecting any increase in its use of aluminum. Mr. DiLoreto's pitches were falling on deaf ears. Reynolds technicians drew up dozens of designs for auto bumpers; Ford engineers countered by arguing the light metal looked "yellow" beside the usual chrome-plated steel.

So Reynolds polled auto dealers and announced that 99% of them couldn't identify an aluminum bumper when they saw one. "All this time we were working on paper, and looking at the Chevrolet Vega bumper" that GM already had switched to aluminum, recalls Mr. DiLoreto.

The turning point came when Reynolds put its craftsmen to work to make a sample bumper that auto engineers could bang on to test its strength. First, they scrambled to invent an alloy that would be lighter, stronger and, most significantly, 10% to 12% less costly. A meeting was scheduled at Ford between top auto materials experts and Reynolds officials.

The Reynolds team plopped its bumper on the top Ford man's desk. He heaved it up—and found it so unexpectedly light that he teetered off balance for a moment.

Ford ordered testing to begin in earnest. But aluminum's

struggle wasn't over yet. Ford ordered aluminum bumpers in August 1975—and cancelled the order two months later, after its own disgruntled bumper-making unit raced to design a competing part in thinner steel.

The order finally returned to Reynolds after Thanksgiving. Mr. DiLoreto had argued convincingly that still-lighter aluminum eventually would be needed to meet the Pinto's reduced weight target for 1978; thus automakers could cut tooling costs by using the same metal in both years.

That sale got Mr. DiLoreto promoted from district sales manager to automotive market manager, and soon thereafter he decided to buy a new automobile—another black Ford Grand Torino. "I'm very associated with Ford," he says with a smile.

Most of his annual pay—which industry people say probably is "in the high 20s"—comes from salary rather than commissions, but that doesn't diminish his zest. Now he discerns that some formerly suspicious auto engineers are thinking aluminum —a critical transition, since once an auto man is won over, he may plant the seed of many future aluminum sales.

An encouraging word came one recent day when Mr. DiLoreto and a colleague called on Chrysler Corp., lugging along two previously spurned car parts in a brief case. "We're so anxious to save weight," confided F.R. Winders, Chrysler's chief engineer for materials, as he tapped his fingers on a fabricated aluminum wheel. "We may just pay the price."

A switch to such wheels today would bring a weight saving of about 50 pounds per car—along with a cost increase of anywhere from $30 to $60, industry sources estimate. Auto makers tentatively have planned this switch for some 1979 model year cars, they say.

Most auto industry experts agree that materials such as aluminum, plastics and lightened thin steels are going to keep edging out the heavyweights like cast iron and steel. (Acknowledging the pattern, Motor Trend magazine even switched its 1977 Car of the Year trophy to aluminum from steel.)

But it's still uncertain who will win biggest in the battle of the lightweights. "Aluminum will run fast early," opines Arvid

Jouppi, vice president and auto industry analyst for Colin, Hochstin Co., a Wall Street institutional brokerage house. But Mr. Jouppi thinks lightweight steel may make a comeback in a few years. Mr. Jouppi also foresees more inroads by plastics, which are even lighter than aluminum and are being promoted by Du Pont Co., Dow Chemical Co. and Union Carbide Corp.

The range of possibilities shows in a 1976 study done for the government by International Research and Technology Corp., a unit of General Research Corp. It predicted that auto makeup surely will change from 1975, when the average car was 2.9% aluminum, 3.5% plastic and 61% steel. By 1990, the study said, aluminum's share could rise to anywhere between 10% and 24% and plastic's share to between 8% and 17%, while steel's share could fall to between 46% and 54%.

Reynolds has been hustling for its share of that market— even to the extent of getting into the auto parts business itself a few years back, when GM suddenly decided it needed light-weight aluminum bumpers on two Chevrolet models. Reynolds threw up an $8 million plant to supply them in what it calls a "miraculous" 44 weeks. By contrast, Alcoa has resisted making actual auto parts, preferring to remain "a raw materials supplier."

The bumper plant speedup shows how auto companies can make extreme and costly demands on suppliers. For the supplier, reliability is crucial. "The cardinal sin is to shut down an assembly line," says Mr. DiLoreto.

For instance, when the bumper plant ran into startup delays, Reynolds undertook special measures to meet its commitments. "About once a week we flew racks of bumpers to San Jose, Calif., from Grand Rapids, Mich.," says Mr. DiLoreto. Reynolds picked up the bill for the difference between air fare and train fare.

Pricing often comes under pressure as a material worms its way into a new market, and aluminum is no exception. One high-level auto marketing strategist for a major aluminum maker says, "In the early stages of developing a market, you don't really know what your costs are." At the same time, he concedes, "You're much more sensitive to competition, not only with other aluminum companies, but with plastics and steel."

That sensitivity shows in the laggard pace of aluminum price rises for auto material in recent years. Since early 1974, the list price of aluminum sheets used for auto body panels has gone up 50% while prices for soft-alloys used in many other consumer goods have zoomed by 72%.

The overall auto market pricing situation seems to be improving, however. Some molten-metal contracts were made in years past at loss leader prices that "hurt our profitability," says Mr. Reynolds. But now, he says, sales of auto market mill products produce a profit "comparable" to that on other fabricated items.

The aluminum business in general is continuing to recover, and the automakers probably won't be pinched for aluminum supplies soon. But in some auto executive suites there is growing concern about longer-term aluminum supplies.

Increases in the rate of domestic consumption of the metal are expected to outpace capacity growth at least through 1980. Mr. Reynolds says auto makers have been "very cooperative recently" in giving advance notice of their needs. He says the auto market eventually could take "a good portion" of a proposed 10% addition to capacity at Reynolds smelters.

Selling in such a competitive market takes social savvy as well as aggressive salesmanship. Despite a modest entertainment budget, Marty DiLoreto takes customers to lunch "once or twice a week."

With his recent promotion, he's also hoping to obtain membership in the exclusive Orchard Lake Country Club. There, "You're able to get the ear of the right people so you can tell your story," says one Reynolds aluminum salesman whose membership helps solve an identity problem in Detroit. His name is John Steel.

Hustling For Banking Business

Richard Antonucci was just lifting a chunk of honey-laden baklava to his mouth when his dinner partner suddenly peeled off his jacket and bounded onto the stage usually occupied by belly dancers at the Grecian Gardens restaurant.

Mr. Antonucci watched dumbfounded as the man and the restaurant owner, their hands clasped firmly together, dipped their knees and stomped out an impromptu kalamatiano, a Greek folk dance.

"That's the guy you want me to do my banking with?" Mr. Antonucci asked his other dinner partner, a friend who owned a local construction company. The two men had a good laugh about it.

But two months later, Mr. Antonucci, owner of a candy brokerage concern that has annual sales of $20 million, yanked his accounts out of the Cleveland bank that had had them for 22 years and opened new accounts with Christ G. Spillas, amateur folk dancer and manager of a branch office of National City Bank of Cleveland on the southwest edge of the city.

Mr. Spillas's impromptu turn on the Grecian Gardens stage hardly fits the banker image. But at National City's 50 branches the role of manager is considerably broader than sitting at a desk making sure all the tellers get to work on time and occasionally okaying a car loan for a walk-in customer. Here, the branch managers double as loan officers, which means that much of their time is spent out of the office, hustling loan business from as many merchants and small manufacturers as they can find in their branch territories.

Cleveland isn't exactly a Sun Belt boom town with new businesses coming in every month. Yet its many small and medium-sized manufacturers, tool-and-diemakers, steel distributors and construction firms do provide a certain stability year after year. About five years ago, National City Bank, the city's second largest, began an aggressive campaign to use its branch managers in soliciting loan business from these middle-tier companies with $1 million to $25 million a year in sales.

"We've got to keep our own customers and get some of the competition's," comments David H. Mortensen, regional manager of National City's western branches, including the one Mr. Spillas runs.

This intensive spadework has begun to pay off in a big way, partly because of a sharp change in the banking climate. The nation's largest corporatons in recent years have begun to rely more and more on internally generated cash and the sale of commercial paper at rates lower than commercial-bank rates. Their bank borrowings have shrunk drastically, and this has left the banks loaded with money to lend. But at National City, the smaller business borrowers who don't have recourse to the commercial-paper market have more than taken up the slack.

Despite fierce competition from the bigger banks, which frequently shade the prime rate for big corporate customers, loan volume at the Cleveland bank has moved up smartly. Claude M. Blair, chairman and chief executive of National City, attributes much of this showing to the "aggressive work" of his branch managers in changing the composition of the bank's business-loan portfolio to include more medium-sized companies.

Firms with lines of credit of $100,000 or more make up 95% of the bank's current business-loan volume, and the number of borrowers in this category rose to 220 in June from 185 a year earlier. Many of the new borrowers are medium-sized companies added through the branch managers' contacts.

Conditions were vastly different in 1972, when the branch managers' campaign first started. Then, the bigger corporations were sopping up all the bank loans they could get. But, Christ Spillas says, "regardless of whether or not the bank is flourishing, my relationship to it is to get as much business as I possibly can."

Mr Spillas, 39, tall and soft-spoken, with a healthy tan, says he devotes 80% of his time to what the bank categorizes as "middle-market customers," mostly companies with five to 50 employes. Much of his time is spent behind the wheel of his avocado Oldsmobile Toronado calling on about 30 companies a month. He splits those contacts evenly between existing customers and a "prospect" list, most of whom have accounts at other Cleveland banks.

Capturing loan business from competitors requires patience and persistence. "There are certain allegiances a customer builds with his old banker," says John Tijanich, another National City branch manager. "But the day will come when he's upset and unhappy with his bank. That's when I hope he comes to me."

That's how Mr. Antonucci, the candy broker, came to be a National City customer. Mr. Antonucci's business, E. Pellegatti Co., often buys production overruns from candy manufacturers. That requires immediate payment in cash, usually for more money than Mr. Antonucci has on hand. To finance such purchases, he had applied for a line of revolving credit with a Cleveland bank where he had had accounts for more than two decades.

"Every time I'd call about the credit line, the bank kept telling me the papers were downtown and under consideration," the candy broker recalls. He mentioned his frustration to Mr. Spillas, who had come to call two months after their dinner at the Grecian Gardens. Mr. Spillas asked to have a look at Mr. Antonucci's personal and company financial statements. Two hours later he offered Mr. Antonucci a $25,000 line of credit. Recently, it was increased to $100,000. Subsequently this enabled Mr. Antonucci to buy a candy brokerage concern in western Pennsylvania.

What of the rival branch manager? "I never heard from him," Mr. Antonucci says. "He's only three minutes from here, and he's never been in this office. Not that I want him to hold my hand, but you'd think he'd stop by once in 22 years."

Mr. Antonucci's decision to change banks after a single personal visit is a rarity. "A lot of times it's frustrating calling for years without its bearing any fruit," Mr. Spillas says. The Leonard C. Richters of the world, however, ease the frustration.

Mr. Richter is president of Western Reserve Insurance Agency Inc., Ohio's largest individually owned agency, with $3.6 million in premium volume in 1976. Mr. Spillas had called on Mr. Richter at his Colonial-style office in suburban Parma semiannually since January 1971. Because Mr. Richter's accounts were with another Cleveland bank that did business with his agency, however, nothing came of the calls until December 1976, when the insurance agent decided to form a finance company strictly for use by his customers to pay their premiums.

Mr. Richter says he was "hungry for advice" on how to capitalize his new company. His bank's branch manager, however, "didn't bother to come out of his office" to discuss the matter. Along came Mr. Spillas for his seasonal visit. He suggested that Mr. Richter finance the finance company with a $38,000 secured loan at 0.5 percentage point above the prime rate, using stock from the insurance man's personal portfolio as collateral, rather than restrict the new company's growth to Western Reserve's excess cash.

"A half percent over prime. That made me feel like General Motors," Mr. Richter says.

Making local companies feel like corporate giants through personal attention to their banking needs is paying off throughout National City's branches. Among Cleveland's five major banks, National City has increased its market share of commercial and industrial loans in the past 18 months to 17.2% from 14.2%, notes Mr. Blair, the chairman. "That means taking somebody else's share of the pie," he says.

Sales calls don't end once a branch manager has gained a new customer. "I don't want to lose them the same way I got them," Mr. Spillas says. Besides, happy customers tend to talk to friends about the personal attention they get from their banker. Mr. Spillas estimates that more than half of his new loan accounts in the past three years were referred by bank customers.

Referrals also spare Mr. Spillas the discomfort of going unannounced to the office of a company president he has never met to try to sell the bank's services. But he says he rarely feels awkward anymore going on the one or two cold calls he makes each month. "It's not like I'm selling pots and pans or encyclopedias or even a computer service. Most people are happy to see a banker," he says.

On a recent cold call to a local trucking company, for example, Mr. Spillas had barely given his business card to a secretary when the company's owner came out and ushered him into his office. Although the trucker said he was happy with his present bank, he listened attentively as Mr. Spillas offered National City's services for a second opinion on any future investment decisions he might be considering—the same pitch that finally brought Mr. Richter's business to National City.

The task of establishing a trusting banker-borrower relationship isn't easy, even with a referral from a satisfied customer. Mr. Antonucci says he was leery of disclosing his financial statements to someone he hardly knew for fear Mr. Spillas would reveal their contents to other clients. Sensing Mr. Antonucci's reticence, the banker met the confidentiality issue head-on, saying, "If I told everybody else's business, do you think I'd get the referrals I get?"

Part III:

The Venturers

A Simply Splendid Business

Fayetteville, N.Y., a suburb of Syracuse has its share of businesses. It has a Sears Roebuck store, a Household Finance office, a Chevrolet dealership. And it has Simply Splendid Studio Inc.

If Simply Splendid isn't exactly a household name around the country, it isn't that well known around Fayetteville, either. It is an unusual kind of women's clothing store, and it has been in town just two years, occupying a Civil War-era clapboard house on a side street near a shopping center.

Its owner is Joan Massey, a 50-year-old divorcee who has been running a nursery school in nearby De Witt for over 20 years. Mrs. Massey has no illusions about the school ever being very profitable, but she has great plans for Simply Splendid. It could blossom, she is convinced, into a large company with nationwide sales.

Every year, thousands of people go into business for themselves. Some, like Mrs. Massey, have hopes of turning what they believe is a new idea into a major enterprise. Most, however, would be content to earn a decent living while enjoying the benefits of being their own boss. In either case, starting up and succeeding in a small business is far from an impossible dream. Of the more than 10 million non-farm businesses operating in the U.S., 95% are considered small businesses by the Small Business Administration and account for about 43% of the gross national product.

But these statistics hardly give a clue to the tremendous effort involved in getting a new enterprise off the ground. Nor do they hint at the odds that are against keeping it going for any length of time. "Though the survival-probability rates are fragmented or dated, the evidence indicates that the risks have multiplied and the chances of making the grade have not brightened," said Bette Blondin and Rowena Wyant in a recent report for Dun & Bradstreet, the diversified publishing and marketing services concern.

Difficulties of raising capital, a lack of adequate information, government red tape and problems of day-to-day management all seem to conspire against the entrepreneur. "Whether boom or recession, nine out of ten failures are traceable to managerial inexperience or ineptitude," says Dun & Bradstreet. The obstacles are such that it takes great initiative to strike out on one's own. "You definitely have to be the entrepreneurial type, compulsive, tenacious and a little on the weird side," says Joan Massey.

"Weird" isn't an adjective that those who know her would apply to Mrs. Massey. But they insist she has the other qualities. "Joan is go, go, go," says Miles E. McNeal, a retired partner of Ernst & Ernst, the big accounting firm, who lives in Syracuse. Even so, Simply Splendid has gone through difficult times, and its future is still very much in doubt. A look at Mrs. Massey's experience shows why.

Five years ago she came up with a new idea in women's clothing that seemed to bridge the gap between home sewing and ready-to-wear garments. In part she was motivated by her own experience in buying clothes. At a shade under five feet, two inches, Mrs. Massey found that little girls' dresses were about the only clothes that came close to fitting her.

She decided to ask other women at a New York State fair if they had similar problems. Of the 2,500 women she asked, 54% said they couldn't buy proper-fitting clothes. And 98% of the women who said they bought dress patterns admitted that they didn't know how to alter them for a proper fit. Mrs. Massey also learned that there was a shortage of quality fabrics available for those who sew at home in the Syracuse area.

Her idea has been to provide a selection of fabrics and classic clothing styles to enable customers to "play designer" and create their own coordinated wardrobes. At Simply Splendid they try on sample garments in the shop to get the correct size. At the same time they decide on the style of neckline and sleeve they want and choose the fabric from large swatches.

Using its own patterns, Simply Splendid then makes up a package that includes parts of the garment pre-cut to size, the necessary decorations and instructions for sewing the garment. If the customer wants, the store will put the garment together, but that increases the price by 50%. "We're selling a service," not just clothes, says Mrs. Massey.

To many people, Mrs. Massey's approach has merit. "It's a good enough idea that if she doesn't make it, someone else will," says Dick Davis, vice president of Monarch Fabrics, a New York wholesaler. Marjorie Dorr, a customer for two years, finds her trips to Simply Splendid a better way to shop than wading through clothing racks in a department store. "What you are getting for the same price is quality," she says. "In a department store you find something for $100 and the seams are falling out of it."

Unlike the typical tale of a small business, Simply Splendid didn't get its start in a garage. That's because the garage and basement in Mrs. Massey's home in De Witt already housed her nursery school. So the showroom of the clothing business was tucked into a first-floor bedroom. To reach it, customers had to walk through another room, adapted as a production area. Closets in the bedroom served as display racks. An adjacent bathroom was pressed into service as a dressing room.

Most of 1973 was spent in researching the kind of product the company would offer and in developing patterns. Nursery-school mothers were recruited as advisers and models, and local seamstresses were hired to begin cutting the cloth from the patterns. By the end of 1973 the company was able to begin test-selling its product.

As sales increased, three full-time employes were taken on and a part-time bookkeeper. Costs were still relatively low, and Mrs. Massey was able to finance the business out of her own savings and her nursery-school earnings.

In November 1975 Mrs. Massey took over the mortgage on a $26,000, run-down, eight room house in Fayetteville and put $20,000 into turning it into a store and production area. This was partly paid for out of $27,000 in bank loans and partly with a $13,000 loan from her parents.

There was much that she didn't count on. She expected, for example, to find plenty of information about setting up and running a business such as hers. "I don't believe what's not available," she says. "I have encountered so many pitfalls along the way that could have been avoided if I had had professional services which most small businesses are in no position to afford. There is no organization you can go to. No road maps." Tracking down the information she needed was, she says, "like a detective story."

Others report similar experiences. "I'm taken aback at the lack of resources that exist for entrepreneurs in what is supposed to be a free-enterprise society," says Beatrice A. Fitzpatrick, executive director of the American Woman's Economic Development Corp., a quasi-federal agency that aids businesses run by women.

Mrs. Massey did go to to the Small Business Administration for advice and was impressed by what she describes as the agency's "super" brochures. But in terms of the direct assistance she needed at the start, the SBA wasn't much help, she says. For example, the agency offers the services of SCORE, its Service Corps of Retired Executives who counsel small businesses. But the retired executive sent by the agency to help Simply Splendid was the former vice president of a major soft-drink company. "He told me that he knew as much about small business as he did about flying to the moon," Mrs. Massey recalls.

She also found little encouragement at the New York State Department of Commerce. The department did send along a business consultant. But he disappeared after a few months, the victim of a budgetary cutback.

So Mrs. Massey had to develop her own group of experts by asking for advice wherever she could. Her advisers ranged from Hovey Larrison, president of his own advertising agency (who came up with the Simply Splendid Studio name) to Robert Pietrafesa, president of Learbury Clothes in Syracuse, whose children had attended Mrs. Massey's nursery school.

"I've never seen so many people volunteer for work," says Mike Kisselstein, branch manager for Lincoln First Bank in De Witt, who provided financial advice. One reason was Mrs. Massey's persuasiveness, he says. Another was the vicarious experience of trying to make a new business succeed. "I suspect all of us would have liked to have done what Joan is doing," Mr. Kisselstein says.

Sometimes, though, the help proved costly. Once, an adviser, without consulting Mrs. Massey, changed the quality of paper to be used in a catalog. Mrs. Massey was shocked to discover that the change increased the catalog's cost to $1,500 from the $875 that had been budgeted. She also regrets spending $1,500 on a consultant who failed to find a source of capital.

But much of her free help did pay dividends. Fred F. Hoyt, the 81-year-old retired treasurer of Carrier Corp., plunged into putting Simply Splendid's bookkeeping in order (he says he was "looking for something to do"). He found that the company's bookkeeper, whose only previous experience was keeping the books in her husband's drugstore, was putting down orders as sales. He also discovered there was no system of cost control. "Generally the small business owner is irked by figure work," he says. "That happened here. You've got to know what costs are, but Joan didn't know what the cost of selling garments was." It has only been recently, in fact, that Simply Splendid has had a workable cost-control system.

One of the big boosts for Simply Splendid came from Mr. Pietrafesa of Learbury Clothes, who, among other things, asked his cutting-room foreman, Leonard Annesi, to look at Simply Splendid's production problems. "We probably cut her piece goods consumption by 30% or more by teaching her to cut more efficiently," Mr. Pietrafesa says.

Mr. Annesi also converted Simply Splendid's patterns from flimsy paper to paper a tenth of an inch thick. "They used to pin needles through paper on every pattern," he says. "With the hard paper it was easier to fit the patterns to the material and easier to trace without pinning or anything. Before that they were wasting a half yard per unit. In the course of a year that adds up to thousands of dollars."

But the biggest problem for Simply Splendid, in common with other fledgling businesses, is the lack of working capital. About a year ago Mrs. Massey was forced to borrow $2,500 from a friend to meet her payroll, which now has grown to five full-time employes, four part-timers and 10 seamstresses, who are paid on a piecework basis. And she was only able to buy her fabric for this fall because of timely investments, in return for stock, of $10,000 by Phyllis Sherwood, a local businesswoman, and of $5,000 by Mrs. Massey's mother.

Mrs. Massey still isn't taking any salary from Simply Splendid. Last year she put up her house in De Witt as collateral on a $28,000 bank loan, plowing some of the money into the business and using the balance for living expenses. She still has $6,000 of this left in her personal bank account and, she says, if she runs short of money she might sell her house. "I'd do that if I had to," she says.

Part of the problem is that Simply Splendid is growing so quickly. In May, the last month of its 1977 fiscal year, the company recorded a profit of just $214, for the first time. Sales for the 1978 fiscal year are expected to be 40% higher than the previous year's sales of $91,000.

Until recently, Simply Splendid's fabric orders weren't big enough for Mrs. Massey to worry about asking for credit. But now that the company is thinking in terms of orders of several thousand dollars rather than several hundred, credit is essential. "But the minute you put in a $4,000 order, you'd be amazed how much trouble it is to get credit," she says. Recently, Simply Splendid went to two factoring concerns (which provide ready cash by buying accounts receivable from manufacturers) but was turned down flat. The reaction of one was that the company appeared to be in bankruptcy on paper, says Mrs. Massey.

"If I had $100,000 sitting around, this would be a whole different ballgame," Mrs. Massey says. But her efforts to raise large amounts of capital have come to nothing, in part because she has little knowledge of money management. "Her understanding of financial statements is zero," says one man who has worked with her.

One solution, she says, would be to find a partner, "someone with capital, a feel for business and with skills I don't have." Right now she can't even afford to hire a business manager to take over daily operations. "I'd like to unload some responsibility so I can sleep nights," she says. As it is she devotes seven days a week to Simply Splendid. (The running of the nursery school is now delegated to others.)

Even so, Mrs. Massey is attempting to cut herself loose from the running of the Fayetteville store to concentrate on the company's future. One possible direction, she says, is a nationwide franchise operation. Another is to become the research and design arm of a large company that would distribute the product.

But she realizes that this is all a pipe dream until "we get our act together in Fayetteville." Mr. McNeal, the former Ernst & Ernst partner, observes that she clearly isn't about to settle for running a small clothing store. "She has big ideas, and knowing Joan I wouldn't bet against her," he says. And Frank J. Cleary, president of a graphic design concern in Fayetteville and one of Mrs. Massey's earliest advisers, notes, "I think she's at this point because of her drive. Without that energy, this thing would have blown away some time ago."

Building a Better Bulb

In the late 1960s, when investors were going wild over the promising high-technology companies that were springing up around the country, five young scientists decided to go into business together.

They dreamed of forming a high-powered company to manufacture a unique invention and of financing their venture with a $1 million public offering. Within a few years, they believed, sales would be booming. They would all be rich and they would be able to write the story of how they did it. They even had the name of the book picked out: "Another Xerox."

The book is unwritten. For by the time the company, which they named Fusion Systems Corp., actually got into business with a device to produce ultraviolet light, the financial winds had shifted. The firm is still private. The $1 million is nowhere in sight. And instead of becoming wealthy overnight, the founders are earning less than they would have if they had kept their old jobs.

"I never believed that starting off on your own would turn out to be so tough," says Marshal Greenblatt, one of the founders. "It seemed so easy back in 1968."

Young high-technology companies like Fusion Systems share an impressive past. Fledgling firms have been responsible for such advances as the light bulb, the air brake, the plain-paper copier and instant photography. A number of today's most successful companies in such fast-growing fields as computers, technical instruments and electronics were started in garage shops by scientists, inventors or engineers who were gambling their futures on unproven technology. And yet their example is becoming increasingly difficult to follow.

Most analysts agree that the birthrate of small technical firms is rapidly declining. "The situation is a disaster," says Richard S. Morse, a former lecturer at the Massachusetts Institute of Technology, who has co-authored a federal study of new technical enterprises. "New high-technology growth companies are not being organized in sufficient numbers to provide the jobs and the technically advanced products ... which will be needed in the decades ahead," the study concludes.

A number of hurdles confront the aspiring young scientific company. The flow of investment dollars has been diverted from the risky to the more established. Equity financing has nearly dried up. And most Small Business Administration loans are going to retail and service firms.

Inflation is another major barrier. It's estimated that today it would require $10 million to launch a company such as Intel Corp., the semiconductor concern that was founded a decade ago for $3 million. Data General Corp., the minicomputer maker, opened its doors in the 1960s, for about $800,000; today's cost would be about $5 million.

University research, which once nourished small technical companies, also has been cut back as budgets have been trimmed. And Washington's military procurement policies now emphasize competitive bidding on research and development contracts, effectively shutting out fledgling firms.

Even in the best of times, of course, high-technology companies have had a troubled infancy. Their failure rate tends to be higher than average because their founders lack specific training in sales and accounting and, more important, are unused to thinking in terms of profit. "They're more concerned with the cerebral than the marketable," says William Zucker, a management professor at the University of Pennsylvania's Wharton School.

That was certainly the case with Fusion Systems. In fact, it took the five founders (four of whom have doctorates) nearly two years of meeting at night and on weekends in each other's homes just to come up with a product. And even then they didn't have any specific market in mind.

At the time, four of the men, Mr. Greenblatt, Bernard J. Eastlund, Michael G. Ury and Leslie S. Levine, were working for various government laboratories. The fifth, Donald M. Spero, was on the faculty of the University of Maryland. The five had known each other at college and had all gone into nuclear-fusion research.

It was this research that led to their unearthing of an experiment that was conducted in the 1950s: Microwaves had been pumped into a hot gas in an effort to produce a nuclear reaction, but ultraviolet light was generated instead. "Our breakthrough was in seeing that experiment as an ultraviolet success instead of a fusion failure," says Mr. Spero.

So the idea was born of making a lamp that would produce ultraviolet light by energizing gas with microwaves rather than with electric current, as in other ultraviolet devices. The plan was to design a small lamp containing various gases through which microwaves would be beamed, much in the fashion of a microwave oven. The extremely hot gas molecules would then give off ultraviolet rays. Such a lamp would be more efficient and longer-lasting than the existing electric device and could be switched on and off instantly, the scientists believed.

They now realize that at the time they were far more interested in inventing the lamp than in trying to sell it. They were vaguely aware that ultraviolet lamps were needed to make industrial solvents, such as carbon tetrachloride, and to make vitamin D and certain kinds of nylon. The lamps also are used by doctors to treat skin diseases, such as psoriasis.

In 1971, the five men formed Fusion Systems with about $10,000 of their savings. Mr. Spero left his job at the University of Maryland to become the company's president and only full-time employe. Because he was the only bachelor in the group, it was felt that he could best afford to take the risks of a struggling young concern.

The company office was an eight-by-fourteen-foot room in a Rockville office building. The room was jammed with so much scientific equipment that Mr. Spero had to sit on the sink to eat lunch or to make notes. The equipment included two 20-

kilowatt arc welders to supply power to huge electric magnets. The arc welders drew so much current that they had to be operated at night so as not to blow the building's main fuses.

Because the room was so crowded, Mr. Spero usually worked with the door open, and other tenants in the building would often drop by to ask what he was doing with all that exotic-looking machinery. "They never believed me when I told them I was making lightbulbs," he says.

In about four months, Mr. Spero had the equipment adjusted well enough so that it could be turned on without clouds of smoke billowing out of the office. A few months later the first actual lamp, a 300-pound behemoth, was ready for testing. It didn't work.

A year of development followed. Mr. Spero and his colleagues, who were still working part-time for the company, fiddled with the microwave equipment, adjusted circuits and tested different bulb sizes and a variety of gases. "We put everything in those lamps except peanut butter," Mr. Spero recalls.

While the others worked on the lamp, Mr. Greenblatt, then a specialist in computer analysis of nuclear weapons at the Naval Research Laboratory, began his sales career. "I couldn't have sold a fan on a summer day," he says. "But nobody else wanted to be our vice president for marketing. So I was elected."

One of his first moves was to write letters to the research directors of 40 companies extolling the virtues of an ultraviolet lamp that still didn't exist. He got no responses. Then he spent about a fourth of the company's advertising budget on a $500 advertisement in The Wall Street Journal. Again, nothing.

Gradually, Mr. Greenblatt realized that the original markets the founders had dreamed of, from industrial solvents to the bleaching of cloth to treatment for psoriasis, had little need for what was certain to be an expensive device. But he did learn that ultraviolet light was beginning to make rapid strides in the printing industry as a way of drying ink on nonabsorbent surfaces, such as plastic, slick paper and metal.

Traditionally, these printed surfaces have been dried by

passing them through ovens or under heat lamps to evaporate the solvent from the ink. But because the solvents escape into the atmosphere, this process has run afoul of antipollution laws. Also, the natural gas used to fire the ovens is both expensive and in short supply. By comparison, ultraviolet devices consume less energy and are used with solvent-less inks that solidify when exposed to the rays.

But finding a printing concern willing to take a chance on an undeveloped product proved enormously difficult. Mr. Greenblatt threw himself into the printing business. For two years he took time off to visit printing trade shows and conferences while on many of his business trips for the naval laboratory.

Mr. Greenblatt says he would leave for a laboratory meeting a day early and return a day late, using the extra time to tout the lamp to prospective buyers. "I might have been fired if the guys at work had suspected what I was really up to," he says. "But they were all convinced I was merely visiting a mistress, so they never said a word."

Meanwhile, the company was desperately in need of funds. The original $10,000 investment had barely been enough to pay a few months' rent and to buy the equipment. To keep the company afloat until a major backer could be found, the partners scraped up another $16,000. When this was gone they managed to coax an additional $31,000 from relatives and friends, giving them both stock and convertible notes in return. Finally, Mr. Greenblatt had to use his house as collateral to make a series of loans to the company, totaling about $17,000. "I really began to wonder if we were going to make it," says Mr. Spero.

Then the company made its first sales of three lamps (all three buyers asked Fusion to keep the sales confidential). Because Fusion hadn't actually produced a lamp at the time, it set the price at $2,500 apiece. It discovered a few months later that the lamps cost $7,500 each to build.

The company was rescued from its financial plight by American Research & Development Corp., a division of Textron Inc. ARD is a venture capital firm that invests in young, struggling companies in the hope of making long-term capital gains. ARD's most notable success was the $70,000 it invested in Digital Equipment Corp. in 1957. Fifteen years later, when ARD distributed its Digital stock to its shareholders, the investment was worth $309 million.

When Fusion was introduced to ARD through a professional "finder," it looked like an unusually risky investment, says James F. Morgan, an ARD vice president. "They were too smart, there were too many of them and they were shooting at the wrong market without a product and no business experience. And yet the more we talked, the better they looked." In December 1973, ARD decided to put $700,000 into Fusion in return for a 56% interest in the company. As a result, the four other founders were able to give up their government jobs and work full-time for Fusion. (Mr. Levine, however, has since gone back to government service.)

But ARD's money didn't immediately bring results. Fusion struggled along, managing to sell only a handful of units. After 18 months, more than half of the ARD capital was gone and the partners were becoming despondent.

In 1975 Mr. Spero went on a skiing vacation in Colorado. It was, he says, almost as an afterthought that he decided to drop in at Adolph Coors Co.'s huge brewery in Golden, Colo., to make a pitch for the Fusion lamp. It was to result in a much-needed break for the company.

Coors, which makes more than three billion cans a year at its brewery, had been experimenting with ultraviolet printing (using electrically powered lamps) and agreed to test the Fusion equipment. A Fusion lamp ran an entire 21-day production cycle at the Coors plant, and Coors immediately made a $250,000 order. (By now the lamp unit was down to the size of a typewriter, weighing 27 pounds, with a 10-inch-long bulb. The power-supply unit was also the size of a typewriter and weighed 90 pounds. The cost of the entire system: $5,150.)

The order put Fusion on the road to solvency. By the end of 1977, all but one of the 19 can lines at Coors were scheduled to be using Fusion lamps.

Anheuser-Busch Inc. also is buying the lamps for printing some of its Budweiser cans. And Fusion is selling other lamps for large commercial presses and for applying non-wax coatings to floor tiles. As a result, Fusion's sales reached an estimated $1.5 million in 1977, up from $1.2 million in 1976. The company occupies considerably more spacious quarters in Rockville and has 12 production employes.

But the wealth the founders dreamed of remains elusive. Although they pay themselves an average of more than $30,000 a year, up from $15,000 two years ago, they earn considerably less than many of their former colleagues in government laboratories. They also have gone from the frontiers of nuclear research to the more mundane problems of the quality of printing on such containers as cans and cottage cheese cartons.

The struggles of the young company have put a tremendous strain on the scientists' families. Mr. Greenblatt's third child had just been born when he quit his government job and went to work for Fusion. "I was very frightened," says his wife, Marion. "I really got to hate the company for making Ben work 70-hour weeks," says Sherry Eastlund. "Then I realized that Ben *was* the company, and laid down some rules, like he can only work three nights a week."

Fusion's founders now realize that in their inexperience they did everything backwards. "We should have looked at the market first to see what sort of products people needed," says Mr. Spero. Yet despite all of these trials, Mr. Spero declares, "We love it." He says, "Ten years ago, all this would have seemed very boring to me. Today I can't think of anything I find more challenging."

Rules, Red Tape and Regulations

John A. Newton had a piece of machinery that didn't produce anything. Now, thanks to government bureaucracy, he has two.

One machine is a $1,200 pollution-control pump that hums away at Mr. Newton's iron foundry in Cleveland. The other is an identical pump that is a backup required by the Ohio Environmental Protection Agency. "Normally, you wouldn't have a spare, $1,200 pump on hand. But they insisted on it," Mr. Newton says.

The spare pump symbolizes for Mr. Newton the endless rules, red tape and regulations that confront his company, Meech Foundry, every day. They consume his time, drain his capital and, he says, drive him crazy with local, state and federal rules about noise, dirty air, pensions, operating permits, labor negotiations and hiring and firing.

Mr. Newton's anger is shared by the 9.7 million other owners of small businesses in the U.S. "Red tape, paper work and proliferating government regulations are suffocating the small businessman," says James D. McKevitt, the Washington counsel of the National Federation of Independent Business. The small entrepreneur, he says, "can't afford to hire full-time lawyers and CPAs to find out what is required of him. He is his own boss, and time spent filling out forms is time taken away from his business."

But government is not entirely unsympathetic to these problems. President Carter, himself a former small businessman, has vowed to cut much of this red tape. The process already has begun at the Occupational Safety and Health Administration, or OSHA, which has won a reputation for onerous and petty rules. In recent months the agnecy has cut back sharply on routine job-safety paper work required of smaller companies.

But the process of reform can only go so far, warns Herbert Kaufman, a senior fellow at the Brookings Institution in Washington. The majority of people want the protection provided by government rules, and red tape is the price you have to pay. "The dangers in industry are great and growing every day. Nobody ever eliminates them, but maybe we can contain the rate of growth of such hazards," he notes.

Mr. Kaufman also points out that much government regulation springs from social legislation, such as unemployment and disability insurance and Social Security. "Look at workmen's compensation: In previous days, a worker was out of a job and had medical bills and no income," he says.

For the small businessman, though, that's little consolation. Society's demands are often the small entrepreneur's nightmare. Take taxes. The average small business in Cleveland files about 110 tax-related documents a year; it files corporate income tax once a year, personal-property tax twice a year, federal unemployment tax four times a year, state tax 12 times a year and payroll tax 52 times a year. In between, it files franchise taxes, real-estate taxes, city taxes, state unemployment taxes and many others.

Paper work costs small businesses a staggering $15 billion to $20 billion a year, according to a recent report by the Commission on Federal Paperwork. And much of the federal government's own $30 billion-a-year paper-work bill is spent on regulating small businesses.

Of course, the taxpayer and consumer ultimately bear the cost. "Customers don't see the $10 in a television, the $100 in an automobile, the half-cent in a soft drink or the four cents in a supermarket chicken," the paper work commission noted.

John Newton has been tangling with government rules for years, and he believes that his loathing of bureaucracy is shared by many a small homebuilder, retailer and factory owner. "I'm not alone. There are a lot of guys out there like me," he says.

"Our problems aren't being heard. But we don't have time to go to Washington and do a lot of rah rah."

An engineer by training, 61-year-old Mr. Newton spent 20 years working for other companies, including Chrysler Corp. and Thompson Products Co., now TRW Inc. Yet he always wanted to be his own boss. In the 1950s and 1960s, he helped convert a small screw-machine company into a prosperous concern making precision parts for the auto industry. He sold the company to Buckeye International Inc., Columbus, Ohio, in 1972. Shortly afterwards he bought Meech Foundry, which makes iron castings for hoists, motors, pumps, and other types of machinery. As Meech prospered, Mr. Newton bought Atlas Foundry and Zoller Casting, which now are Meech subsidiaries. The combined annual sales are $3.5 million and there are 125 employes.

As president and sole owner of Meech, Mr. Newton runs a one-man show. "I look at the bank manager or the attorney sitting at his desk all day: I couldn't do it. It's stimulating to be active and coping with every changing problem," he says. This may be why the blunt and articulate Mr. Newton gets frustrated every time a government rule crops up to take the decision-making away from him.

He can even calculate the cost of coping with rules and paper work. In 1976, Meech paid $16,000 to outside lawyers, accountants and consultants. In 1977, the figure jumped to $18,000 to $20,000. Often the costs are subtle and indirect. Mr. Newton says the company has been losing revenues of about $1,000 a month simply because he hasn't had time to set price increases on some product lines.

Much of the paper work is handled by Milly Lusk, Mr. Newton's energetic bookkeeper. She has to fill out surveys, including the U.S. Census Bureau's annual survey of shipments and unfilled orders, which is chock-full of questions that Meech Foundry has trouble in answering. The questions require details about iron production for inplant use and the types of iron used in various products.

On other surveys, Mrs. Lusk says, the questions are so rarefied that she simply guesses the answers. It is, she declares, "a pain."

Mr. Newton is far more vehement about workmen's compensation, which he calls "a cancer of industry if ever I saw one." He holds this strong view because every one of his 35 employes at the Atlas subsidiary, in addition to regular wages, is collecting partial-disability payments for on-the-job injuries and illnesses, a far higher rate than at Mr. Newton's two other foundries. "And all of them are working a full day," he scowls.

Although the awards were made to the Atlas employes by the compensation bureau, Mr. Newton has to bear the cost in the form of insurance premiums levied by the state for every $100 paid out in wages. Because the awards against its Atlas subsidiary have been so high, Meech must pay out $17.96 for every $100 in wages, compared with the average rate of only $9 for foundries in Ohio.

Meech hires an actuarial firm to fight dubious claims filed by employes, but Mr. Newton insists that "for the most part there is a compromise settlement and you get nicked." As a result, he says, Meech pays "close to $100,000 a year in workmen's compensation" on a payroll of $1 million.

Mr. Newton also has to fight unemployment-compensation claims. As with workmen's compensation, Meech has to make unemployment-insurance payments into a state fund based on the level of successful claims by employes.

As one example, the company has had to spend considerable time and money fighting the claims of an employe who was fired in April after a three-week unexcused absence. The man applied for $56-a-week unemployment payments, or half of his weekly wage. Ohio officials ultimately denied the claim, but not until the company had filed documents and depositions to justify the firing. Meech has fought six similar cases this year and has won them all. The paper work involved, says Mr. Newton, has been tremendous.

But even problems like these pale when compared with pollution-control regulations. Neither Meech nor its Zoller subsidiary had pollution-control equipment when Mr. Newton took over. Now the Meech foundry is having to install a $200,000 "wet scrubber" to remove dirt particles as they escape from the furnace.

Mr. Newton says he objects to this $200,000 outlay purely on practical grounds. He is, he says, a very small polluter with a very big antipollution bill. "I think it's unduly restrictive for a small foundry. It takes time and money that could be used to provide more capacity and more jobs. Unproductive time and money are being spent," he complains.

Some of the unproductive time, for example, was spent looking for money to pay for the equipment. Mr. Newton tried unsuccessfully for months to float a pollution-control bond issue through local banks and investment bankers. Finally, National City Bank of Cleveland loaned him the money at 1% above the prime lending rate. But it isn't even a corporate loan because Mr. Newton's signature on it means he is personally liable for the debt.

But if some rules are forced on Mr. Newton, others, more loosely regulated, get short shrift. "Here's an OSHA list of things we should be doing," he says as he slaps on his desk a yellow sheet containing 13 regulations.

"We don't do any of it," Mr. Newton admits. "If I did everything the government asked me to do, I wouldn't be in business. I couldn't afford it."

Steven R. Wessell, vice president and general manager of Meech (and Mr. Newton's son-in-law), handles day-to-day compliance with OSHA standards. "We have ear muffs, dust masks, safety glasses and shields, but once you have bought new equipment, you never see it again," says Mr. Wessell. The company spends about $4,200 a year on safety gear, but much of it goes unused or is lost or stolen. "We spend $200 a year on safety glasses. If I went out there in the plant today and collected what's left, there wouldn't be $30 worth," Mr. Wessell says.

Even hiring a new employe isn't necessarily a straightforward procedure. Several months ago, Mr. Newton hired Terrance J. O'Shea as plant superintendent at Meech's Cleveland iron foundry. But because Mr. O'Shea is an Englishman living in Ontario, Canada, Meech has been caught up in a maze of regulations that have prevented the new employe from coming to the U.S. to work.

Mr. Newton says that of more than a dozen people who applied for the job, Mr. O'Shea was the one who impressed him the most. He thought it would be a fairly simple matter to obtain a work visa after filing two documents with the U.S. Immigration Service. "But when I called Immigration, they referred me to the Ohio Bureau of Employment Services," Mr. Newton says.

Meech has had to prove to the bureau that it had tried to hire an American for the job and to explain why the other candidates were unsatisfactory. It then had to advertise the job twice in a newspaper. No candidates were suitable, so the bureau put the position in its state-wide job bank for 30 days. Because still there were no suitable applicants, Mr. O'Shea's application was sent to Columbus, the state capital, and then to the Labor Department's regional office in Chicago for review.

It is only now, after all of these efforts have been exhausted, that the documents are finally in the hands of the Immigration Department, but it may be another three months before they are approved. "I feel I should have the freedom of choice, provided I'm not employing a thief, a rapist or a fugitive from justice," says Mr. Newton angrily. "I can accept Immigration wanting to make a check, but this other jazz is bureaucratic and unnecessary."

Because of his feelings about bureaucracy, Mr. Newton admits that he delights in brushing the government aside whenever he can. A few months ago the United Steelworkers of America won the right to bargain for employes at the Zoller subsidiary. Both the union and the Federal Mediation and Conciliation Service asked that mediators be allowed to attend bargaining sessions.

Mr. Newton refused. "I told the union I wouldn't bargain with the federal mediator in attendance," he recalls with satisfaction. "This is my business, not theirs, and I feel strongly that there is too much government interference in business."

Capital For Small Concerns

The 1975 recession was rough on small businessmen in Lancaster, a city of 58,000 in southeastern Pennsylvania. Sales dropped and available cash was scarce. Frank Filling badly needed money for operations and for a major purchase for his men's clothing and dry-cleaning business ("Filling Cleaners for Fussy Folks"). But a loan seemed out of the question.

The small company already had outstanding about $121,000 in mortgages and $65,000 in short-term bank debt. "We had exhausted our ability to borrow money to expand," says Mr. Filling. "We decided that we couldn't borrow any more on the basis of the value of our existing assets."

Then Mr. Filling had an idea. He went to a private appraiser and had all of his company's property revalued. He found that inflation had vastly increased the value of the company's real estate and equipment over its book value. As a result, the company was able to get a $200,000 long-term loan and a line of bank credit.

Small businessmen like Mr. Filling are finding that if they can produce the collateral, banks increasingly are eager to do business with them. Although it is still difficult to obtain venture capital to launch a new business, the established concern is finding more financing avenues for expansion and for dealing with cash shortages.

The willingness of many banks to offer small-business loans is welcome financial relief for many hard-pressed concerns. Inflation has pushed many businesses into higher tax brackets, which means they have reduced retained earnings to spend on expansion. Inflation also means that they have to spend more money on building inventories. In addition, the collection time for accounts receivable has slowed considerably.

Many of the nation's smaller banks have decided to seek small-business loans aggressively. Among them is Fulton Bank, Filling Cleaners' bank since the 1930s. "That's the name of the game here in Lancaster," says James K. Sperry, the bank's executive vice president. Small-business loans in 1977 rose 20% to 25% from a year ago, he says.

One of the first concerns in the U.S. to court small businessmen was Southeast Banking Corp., a Miami bank-holding company, which began offering term loans a few years ago. Term loans, as opposed to seasonal loans, run for more than a year, often for several years, and are repaid in installments. "Many banks have missed a fine opportunity in not developing term lending," says Jack Eachon Jr., the bank's senior vice president and a former Small Business Administration official.

In fact, Southeast Banking is now so wedded to the idea of small businessmen as customers that it has started seminars for businessmen. "We begin at the beginning, how you organize a business, and go on from there," says Mr. Eachon.

This is a sharp departure from banks' traditional view of small-business loans. Commercial banks long held the view that business loans should be short-term and self-liquidating. A store, for example, might borrow in the fall to stock up for Christmas. But in January, with its merchandise sold, the store would repay the loan. Smaller banks did long-term business with small companies usually on the basis of commercial mortgage loans. These usually are based on the appraised value of a building or of a factory's equipment and may run for as long as 20 years.

But in recent years, the smaller banks have begun to follow the example of large banks, which began offering term loans to their largest customers several years ago. Now many small banks are offering loans of more than a year to their small-business customers and are finding these loans to be a robust part of their business.

"We seldom make seasonal loans any more," says Mr. Sperry of Fulton Bank. "We've found they often aren't fitted to a business's needs. Normally we make a term loan of up to five years and sometimes seven."

The banks have been encouraged to do more for small businessmen by the American Bankers Association. John Clark, director of the ABA's correspondent banking division, notes that more than 12,000 of the association's 15,000 members are "community banks," which are really small businesses themselves. This, he says, gives them a good deal of understanding of small businessmen's problems, and, he says, "they usually know the borrower."

The ABA also has been working closely with the Small Business Administration in promoting the agency's loan program. In most cases the SBA doesn't make a direct loan but guarantees up to 90% of a loan made by a private lender. The loans often can be for as long as 10 years without collateral and for 20 years with collateral, such as real estate.

However, the agency has been widely criticized for the amount of red tape involved in obtaining a guaranteed loan. SBA financing director Anthony Armstrong defends the tough rules as necessary. "Under the law we must examine each case to determine whether it's reasonably safe for the government," he says. Despite the agency's caution, the cumulative loss on the loan-guarantee program has been 3.12% of the loans approved, compared with about 1% for regular commercial bank loans.

The SBA also is criticized for spreading its guarantees too thinly. There are an estimated 10 million small businesses in the U.S., but in the fiscal year ended September 30, 1977, the agency's busiest year since it was founded in 1953, it approved only 27,510 loans for a total of $2.8 billion.

But for small businessmen unable to offer collateral, a direct bank loan is no easier to get than an SBA-guaranteed loan. That's because banks usually demand specific collateral for term loans. Even a company like Filling Cleaners that has been doing business with Fulton Bank for so many years must be able to provide such assets as property or equipment.

That is why Mr. Filling's discovery of inflation financing was so important in establishing collateral for a much-needed loan. A look at the growth of his small company shows why, in 1975, he was in the position, familiar to all small businessmen, of having a business in need of funds to maintain its growth.

Mr. Filling, who is 60, runs a business that, like many small enterprises, is family-owned. His brothers, William and Albert, manage parts of the business, and a third brother, Richard, was active in the firm until this year when he became chairman of the Pennsylvania Republican Party. The company, which had sales in 1976 of $1.3 million and has 81 employes, has always expanded carefully and slowly, unlike many established small firms that try to grow too fast and then find, too late, that they are not generating enough income to take care of cash needs. "In the $2 range (the cost of dry cleaning a garment) it takes an awful lot of sales to get money to expand," Mr. Filling says.

Mr. Filling's father was a clothing manufacturer in Lancaster until he lost practically everything during the Depression. He was able, however, to buy a candy store in the nearby town of Millersville and to put a dry-cleaning machine and a press in the basement. On the side, he made suits for $25.

Just before World War II, Mr. Filling's father mortgaged the family's home to buy a defunct nightclub in Lancaster for $10,000. After the war, it was converted into a dry-cleaning business: The cocktail lounge became the office, the dining room was for the spotting and finishing equipment and for the clothing racks. As long as the family stayed exclusively in dry cleaning its money needs were fairly small, mainly short-term bank notes to tide it over temporary emergencies.

But in the years after the war, the Filling cleaning outlets grew to three and the family decided to begin selling men's clothes in one of them, in a working-class neighborhood of Lancaster. "When my father died in 1951 we decided to build up the shop into a really good traditional menswear store. Lancaster didn't have one then," Mr. Filling says.

The clothing store and cleaning outlet was in a remodeled row house. As neighboring houses became available, Filling Cleaners took them over with bank mortgages and slowly expanded the shop. The firm's rising income was enough to pay off existing mortgages and to obtain new mortgage loans. The rising property values helped to build the firm's net worth.

But by the early 1970s the company's cleaning equipment was operating at less than capacity, and it became clear that the company couldn't continue to prosper with such a heavy reliance on dry cleaning. The sluggish U.S. economy in recent years has badly hurt the dry cleaning industry, as has the development of fabrics that are easier to care for. A spokesman for the International Fabricare Institute, the dry-cleaning trade group, estimates that "30% of our plants" have gone out of business in the past seven years.

Through the Fabricare Institute Mr. Filling heard that the Cincinnati-based owner of 100 cleaning stores in Ohio and Indiana was starting a new business to rent clean uniforms to people such as factory workers and gas station attendants. "It seemed an ideal way to use our idle cleaning capacity," Mr. Filling says. In 1971, Filling Cleaners became the Pennsylvania licensee of the uniform concern, Apparelmaster Inc. Mr. Filling was able to obtain short-term bank loans, and Apparelmaster helped arrange credit terms with suppliers.

But as the business grew, Filling Cleaners needed capital to build its uniform inventory. Each customer's employe needs 11 uniforms, one to wear, five being cleaned, and five more for the week. The company also had various other cash needs. "We had some pretty bad times around here in 1974 and 1975, just like the rest of the country," Mr. Filling says.

The inflation financing through Fulton Bank helped the company recover. "We have always been careful not to borrow beyond the value of our existing property. We always want to feel that we're able to handle what we take on," declares Mr. Filling.

But this has hardly been the end of the company's financing needs. Filling Cleaners must stock between $6,000 and $7,000 in spare machine parts, because "we can't afford to have a machine down while we wait for parts." Occasionally the company must obtain short-term bank loans to buy more parts.

Short-term loans also are required occasionally to tide the

firm over its cash-flow problems. This is partly because of the large number of charge accounts. In the dry-cleaning and menswear part of the business, outstanding charges often are as high as $85,000 to $95,000. "We've had to work harder to get customers to pay their bills. We recently put in a 1% charge on overdue accounts," Mr. Filling says. In addition, Apparelmaster charges are about $24,000 a month.

Trade credit also has tightened up. "Clothing suppliers are insisting that we order earlier and pay faster. Everyone has the same sort of problem," he says. And he adds, "There was a time when I could pay all my bills just as soon as they arrived. Now I pay them when they're due. I wish I could still do it the old way."

At present, the company has a mortgage debt of $181,000 and a $10,000 short-term note. Its debt service is less than $2,000 a month, which, Mr. Filling says, can easily be handled out of earnings.

Filling Cleaners now is considering opening a second menswear store in Lancaster. But, says Mr. Filling, "If we do expand, we'll do it the way we have in the past, carefully, making sure that we can handle it."

Back From Bankruptcy

The year 1973 was a good one for Henry Kissinger, the Oakland Athletics and corporate profits generally, but it was a bad one for Doyle Hayt. That was the year his company, Forms Corp. of America, a maker of business forms in Spring Grove, Illinois, a suburb of Chicago, filed for protection under Chapter 11 of the federal bankruptcy code.

"It was the most frustrating, agonizing period of my life," says the 43-year-old businessman, whose good looks and accentless voice could be those of a television-news anchorman. "For the first time, I was forced to admit to myself and others that I'd come up against a situation I couldn't handle successfully."

Mr. Hayt (pronounced "Hyatt") can look back on the experience with equanimity, because Forms Corp. has emerged from bankruptcy to become solidly and increasingly profitable. But some aftereffects still linger.

"I think I'm a quite different person than I used to be," he says. "Realizing that I'm not superman has helped me set more realistic goals in both my business and personal lives."

Forms Corp.'s survival of its plunge into bankruptcy is fairly unusual in American business, but bankruptcy itself certainly isn't. Federal court records show that the company was one of 17,490 that sought protection under the various sections of the bankruptcy law in the fiscal year ended June 30, 1973. Harsher business conditions pushed that figure to a record 35,201 in fiscal 1976. The total declined to 31,151 in fiscal 1977.

Large companies bite the dust from time to time (one recent casualty was W. T. Grant Co., a national retailer), but for the most part, bankruptcy in the U.S. is a small-business phenomenon. Experts say that the smaller and newer a company is, the more likely it is to fail. More than half the firms that go out of business annually have been in existence for five years or less; the vast majority have annual sales of under $1 million.

The reasons for this situation are simple: Small businesses typically lack the capital and management know-how to cope with the adverse developments that all concerns face. However, a further search almost always reveals causes that stem from the nature of the people who go into business for themselves.

"An entrepreneur is an optimist by definition, and overoptimism is what does companies in," asserts Kenneth Eaton, head of Associated Business Consultants, a Chicago management-consulting firm. He explains: "When things are going well, the average businessman assumes they will continue to go well. When a problem arises, he assumes it will go away quickly by itself. By the time he wakes up to the fact that he really has a problem, it's often too late to do anything about it."

Whatever the cause of a business failure, the result usually is disastrous for all concerned. The great majority of companies that seek refuge in the courts are so far past saving that their assets must be liquidated and the proceeds distributed among their creditors. Even creditors of companies with impressive balance sheets don't often fare well in such proceedings because a firm's inventories, equipment and furniture are worth far less at auction than they are as part of a going concern.

Creditors of a liquidated business are lucky to recover 10 cents on each dollar owed them. The owner of a bankrupt corporation loses whatever he has put into his company. The owner of a bankrupt unincorporated concern (most small businesses are not incorporated) fares even worse. Because he is, in fact, the company, he faces seizure of his personal assets.

And yet for some companies bankruptcy doesn't necessarily mean sudden death. Chapter 11 of the bankruptcy act provides that if a firm can obtain the approval of the court and of the majority of its creditors, it can discharge its debts at less than full value and begin to operate afresh, the theory being that a live company is potentially worth more to its creditors than a dead one. Roughly 10% of all companies going into bankruptcy take this route, and about half of these, like Mr. Hayt's Forms Corp., obtain the required approvals.

But even when Chapter 11 status is granted, later success doesn't usually materialize. No figures on this are available, but experts say that only about a quarter of all businesses that go through the process survive for five more years.

This low salvage rate is due in part to the difficulties that bankrupt companies have in obtaining financing and credit from suppliers, but it also stems from the stigma and emotional trauma that attach to the process. "Most guys are so down and defeated by bankruptcy in any form that they simply can't function again as businessmen," observes Alex Dolnick, a Chicago bankruptcy lawyer who has practiced for 46 years.

Malcolm Gaynor, another veteran Chicago bankruptcy attorney, agrees. "In a society that worships success, failure is regarded as something of a disease, and people avoid it like it's catching," he says. "A lot of men who have been through bankruptcy don't want to be reminded of it. I see former clients at parties occasionally, and some of them act like they don't know me."

These feelings are well known to Doyle Hayt. "One of the hardest things about going bankrupt was facing people with whom I'd done business," he says. "Fortunately, most of them were pretty good about it, and that helped me get back on the track. They knew my record in the industry was a good one, and they encouraged me to believe I could be successful again."

Indeed, before his troubles with Forms Corp., Mr. Hayt was the very model of the small-town-boy-made-good. His business career began at age 16, when he went to work as a part-time apprentice printer for a publishing company in Parsons, Kans., where he grew up. By the time he was 21 he was production manager of the firm, and two years later he and two friends each put up $3,000 to strike out on their own.

Their company, Va-Co-Hy Business Forms Inc. (taken from two letters of each partner's name), started life with a single press in a storefront office in Girard, a nearby southeast Kansas town of 2,600 people. Within a half-dozen years the company had sales of more than $3 million, occupied a shiny new plant and employed more than 200 people, making it Girard's largest employer.

Things were so good that in 1963 Mr. Hayt helped start another company, Mid-America Business Forms Inc., in Ft. Scott, Kans., north of Girard. That concern, too, was a quick success.

By 1969, Va-Co-Hy's sales had reached $5.5 million, Mid-America's totaled about $2 million, and both were showing healthy profits. They had become the regular recipients of take-over offers from larger companies, and that year Mr. Hayt and his partners decided the time was ripe to sell.

Va-Co-Hy was purchased by Livingston Oil Co. of Tulsa, Okla. (later LVO Corp.), for stock worth about $1.75 million. Mid-America fetched stock worth $500,000 from Ennis Business Forms Inc. of Ennis, Tex. Mr. Hayt owned 45% of Va-Co-Hy and 27% of Mid-America when the transactions were made, so his share came to more than $900,000.

Mr. Hayt now believes that he probably should have hung on to the two companies, but the money was just too tempting. "Did you ever want to be a millionaire?" he asks. "Well I did, and I saw my chance to do it, even if the million was only paper (stock). That was my way of showing the world I was a success."

Mr. Hayt stayed on with LVO as president of Va-Co-Hy, but after being his own boss he chafed under the demands placed on an executive of a larger company. "The political games and the infighting weren't for me," he says. "I couldn't function in that environment."

So he began looking around for a way to get back into business for himself. It turned up in 1971. Pfieffer Business Forms Inc., a six-year-old firm in Spring Grove, Ill., was in trouble and was looking for a buyer. The company had lost $151,000 on sales of almost $1.5 million the year before, but its "growth pattern and assets looked good to me when I talked to the owners," Mr. Hayt says.

He recalls, "They'd recently acquired some assets of another forms outfit, and I figured that the additional sales would put the company into the black. I met with Pfieffer's creditors, and they said they'd go along with me if I took over, so I went ahead. The problems were there for anyone to see, but I guess I didn't want to see them. I thought I'd be a hero and turn the place around."

So Mr. Hayt sold his LVO and Ennis holdings for about $400,000, less than half their worth when he got them, and put $100,000 of the proceeds into Pfieffer, changing its name to Forms Corp. From the first, things went badly.

"I found an organization that was totally sick," he says. "Morale was low from the janitor on up. Orders that looked good on paper were losers in practice. There was no cost-accounting system, so it was impossible to tell which parts of the business were profitable and which weren't. I was running around in circles trying to get a handle on things."

Mr. Hayt attempted to remedy the situation the following year by buying some assets and the sales organization of Workman Business Forms, a Chicago firm. This boosted sales, but the difficulties of integrating the new concern with his already tangled company raised costs even higher. The company's losses, which had been trimmed to $135,000 in 1971, climbed to $260,000 the next year, even though sales rose to $1.9 million.

By mid-1973, things were so bad that Mr. Hayt called in an attorney and an accountant to sort them out. "We had a meeting, and the lawyer said to me, 'Doyle, you're bankrupt.' I said, 'Who, me? No way. I'll work things out.' He explained Chapter 11 to me and recommended I try it. He said that if I didn't, my employes would lose their jobs, my creditors would get practically nothing, and I'd be out in the cold.

"I hated the idea at first, but the more I thought about it the more reasonable and honorable it seemed," he says. He hired a law firm that specializes in bankruptcy and paid the $15,000 lawyer's retainer by selling his company's accounts receivable to a finance company. (The legal fees and court costs eventually came to $50,000.) On June 6, 1973, Forms Corp. filed for Chapter 11 bankruptcy in federal court in Chicago.

When the company went to court it had unsecured business debts of about $718,000, federal and state employes' withholding-tax liabilities of about $160,000 and a negative net worth of $878,000. By the middle of 1974, it had obtained creditors' approval of a plan to pay them a total of about $179,000, or 25 cents on the dollar, out of future profits. .

The profits have been forthcoming. After a loss of $671,000 in 1973, the year in which the company took all of its losses stemming from the bankruptcy, the company has recorded four straight profitable years. In the fiscal year ended May 31, 1977, it earned $260,000 on sales of $3.7 million and its net worth stood at $537,000. It has discharged its tax liabilities in full and has made plans to begin repaying creditors. Employment at the company's 35,000-square-foot plant in Spring Grove has grown to 75 from 45 since the bankruptcy.

Although some businessmen are depressed by the act of filing for bankruptcy, Mr. Hayt was elated. "It was like a giant rock had been taken off my shoulders," he says. His lawyers saw to it that angry creditors would no longer harass him over the telephone (one had even turned up at his office to shout at him). "I could start doing things to get the company straight again," he says. "Everything we did from that day on was new and clean. I fired my psychiatrist, stopped taking pills for my nerves and started gaining back the weight I'd lost."

Mr. Hayt says that the company's recovery was helped considerably by a piece of business it had landed the week before it applied for Chapter 11. Its Workman unit had been making forms for Allstate Insurance Co., in nearby Northbrook, Ill., for several years, and it had just won a contract that would increase its sales to the big insurer.

"The day we filed, I arranged a meeting with the Allstate people and laid everything out for them," he says. "They were great. They said they had confidence in us and would go ahead as if nothing had happened." Forms Corp.'s annual sales to Allstate have grown from $400,000 in 1973 to an estimated $1.2 million in fiscal 1977.

Mr. Hayt has taken other steps to restore his company to profitability. He has hired management-consulting firms to institute cost-accounting and materials-control systems, has bought a couple of trucks to speed deliveries to customers and has hired new financial and sales officers.

He also has reviewed every sales account to make sure it is producing profits as well as volume. "We don't bid on business just to bid anymore; we try to make sure that everything that goes through our shop makes money for us," he says. "We're concentrating on getting business in the Chicago area, where we can service our customers personally and quickly. That's the only way a company our size can compete with the majors in a market like we're in."

As Mr. Hayt's efforts have shown results, Forms Corp. has been able to shed some of the disabilities that go with bankruptcy. Suppliers, for instance, no longer demand cash on delivery, and an expensive line of credit with a commercial lending firm has been shifted to a bank offering far lower rates of interest.

Mr. Hayt also has benefited from the resurgence, increasing his salary from the company to $60,000 a year from the $30,000 he was making during his time of troubles. "Best of all, I have a company that's worth something again, and my suppliers have a good customer," he says. "I wouldn't recommend the experience (of bankruptcy), but it's a lot better than the alternative."

Dealing With Minority Firms

Archie Williams has had his share of rejections in trying to solicit business for his small electronics firm. Many of his letters to large companies have gone unanswered. He has flown to meet purchasing managers only to be treated, he feels, with condescension. And he believes he misses out on the contracts that often result from businessmen meeting each other socially. The reason, he says, is that he is black.

Mr. Williams says he can't be blamed if he frequently feels insecure, because as the black owner of a small business he must depend on the white business community for survival. "I deal constantly with the possibility that racism might cost me my business," he says.

Despite his fears, his nine-year-old company, Freedom Electronics & Engineering Inc., is gradually making its way. His firm, which helps put together transformers, cables and printed circuit boards for large electronics and computer firms, has emerged from years of losses, and in 1976 it made a profit of $148,000 on sales of $1.9 million.

Similar success stories are convincing a growing number of business experts that in order for a minority-owned business to prosper, the once-popular notion of marketing primarily to the minority community has to be abandoned. Minority businesses "should be out in the white community" pushing products and services, argues William Zucker, professor of management at the University of Pennsylvania's Wharton School, who has counseled minority firms. Nonwhite urban communities "don't have the resources" to support many sizable businesses, he says.

The government also is urging nonwhites to venture into

the larger business community. The Commerce Department's Office of Minority Business Enterprise is working hard to have minority entrepreneurs steered "into larger businesses where there's opportunity for greater profit," says a spokesman. The office, which dispenses $35 million annually to organizations that assist minority business people, such as the Urban League and the National Business League, believes that manufacturing, particularly in the areas of energy and electronics, is particularly promising.

Statistics are scarce, but there are indications that nonwhite entrepreneurs are taking this advice. The latest available statistics on minority businesses, compiled by the Census Bureau in 1972, showed that of the nearly 400,000 minority-owned firms in the U.S., about half were owned by blacks. And the greatest growth in the kinds of businesses being started by nonwhites was in manufacturing.

A number of large companies are making an effort to ease this entry into the marketplace. At least half of the nation's 500 largest companies as well as hundreds of small publicly held concerns have started programs to do more business with minority-owned firms. The amount spent on purchases from such firms in 1977 exceeded $1 billion, compared with only $87 million five years earlier, says Thomas I. Ahert, executive director of the National Minority Purchasing Council, a trade group. For example, about 65% of Freedom Electronics' business comes from the minority purchasing efforts of Digital Equipment Corp., the minicomputer maker in Maynard, Mass.

As well as being minority-owned, Freedom Electronics also is an employer of minorities. The company is based in a window-less former supermarket in a rundown black and Puerto Rican neighborhood in Boston's Dorchester section. All but four of its 52 employes are black or Spanish-speaking. The birthdays of Martin Luther King and Malcolm X are company holidays.

But Mr. Williams, who is 43, believes that race also has cost the company business. He cites examples of purchasing managers buying from their neighbors or from social contacts, whereas he lives in the black Roxbury section of Boston and rarely meets white businessmen socially. He also knows of white purchasing officials who are afraid to venture into the declining neighborhood around the Freedom Electronics plant to discuss business.

He doesn't hear racial slurs against his company directly, but the firm's manufacturer's representative, who is white, does. "I've been called everything from a carpetbagger to a nigger-lover" by purchasing officials for representing Freedom Electronics and several other minority firms, says Gerald McGonagle, an independent representative from Waltham, Mass. Purchasing officials "are against Archie Williams and they don't even know Archie Williams," he says.

But this view of the white community as being biased against black-owned enterprises is challenged by some. What might appear to be racism, some people in industry contend, is often caution, based on business factors. "Most companies want (minority firms) to be fully competitive in all areas," says Donald Leroy, Gillette Co.'s purchasing director and the head of the New England chapter of the National Minority Purchasing Council. But competition is often difficult, he says, because "most minority suppliers are new" and may be unable initially to offer the lowest prices or the fastest delivery.

Mr. Williams knows well the difficulties of trying to market in both the white and black communities, because he has tried both approaches. In the mid-1960s, when he was a Boston lawyer and civil-rights activist, he became convinced that black-owned businesses offered the best hope for solving the employment and economic problems of black urban areas.

The most attractive market, he felt, was the "golden electronic circle" of computer and other high-technology businesses on Route 128, which rings Boston. After research at the Harvard Business School library and talks with the school's students, he settled on trying to form a sub-assembly electronics firm. Such firms perform relatively simple tasks, such as putting screws into plugs, preparing wire for soldering and soldering electronic components onto printed circuit boards.

Mr. Williams visited some of the larger firms around Boston, such as Raytheon Co., Digital Equipment Corp., Polaroid Corp. and others, to line up possible backers and customers. He usually began by seeing public-relations people, but because of growing interest in black-owned businesses he invariably got appointments with executives.

At Raytheon he met with Thomas Phillips, who was then president, and now is chairman, of the big maker of consumer and aerospace products. The executive clearly was impressed because he agreed to put up $5,000 of Raytheon money to help get Mr. Williams's business started. He also set up a luncheon at a private Boston club to introduce Mr. Williams to other executives.

At Digital Equipment, Mr. Williams did even better. The company agreed to provide enough sub-assembly work to employ 10 people for more than a year. He was also able to obtain a $20,000 personal bank loan. And in August 1968 he opened Freedom Electronics in a rented garage a few blocks from the present plant. He chose the name Freedom, he says, because "to be self-reliant is to be somewhat free."

The fledgling firm's capital requirements were small because it bought used equipment and built its own work benches. Help in training the employes was volunteered by a group of engineers from Digital Equipment. Mr. Williams says that the employes began with simple tasks, such as turning a screw, and gradually moved into more complex tasks.

His success in putting together Freedom Electronics convinced him to try a second business that would both employ and sell to blacks. "I figured that black people had to eat," he says in explaining his decision to open two supermarkets in black neighborhoods.

"I was one of the best money-getters around," says Mr. Williams, and indeed there seemed to be no limit to what he was able to raise. He bought two supermarkets in late 1968 and in early 1969 from Purity Supreme Inc., a food chain in North Billerica, Mass., by obtaining a $253,000 note from the company and a $500,000 mortgage from John Hancock Mutual Life Insurance Co. He also obtained $250,000 in special loans designated for minorities from the Episcopal Church.

After the stores opened, he obtained a $50,000 loan from First National Bank of Boston and a $300,000 Small Business Administration loan. This money went into the supermarkets and into several other business ventures that Mr. Williams was involved in, including a shoe-importing business and a tool-and-die operation.

Although Mr. Williams had occasional doubts about all the money he was borrowing and about his ability to stay on top of his ventures, "my ego told me I was doing wonderful things," he says.

But the supermarkets failed, partly because they were in an economically depressed neighborhood. There were dozens of burglaries and an armed robbery in which two security guards were killed. The stores, says Mr. Williams, were "financially exposed" because he had been unable to get insurance to cover theft.

Mr. Williams also realizes that he had hired too large an administrative staff that was draining the venture by more than $100,000 annually. And the largely black staff wasn't experienced enough in the intricacies of running a food operation, which forced up overtime costs.

The experience illustrates what Mr. Zucker of the University of Pennsylvania calls the "double whammy" that many nonwhite businessmen are exposed to. They generally have less managerial experience than their white counterparts and are more prone to go into business on borrowed funds, he says. When the minority business also is confined to a nonwhite community, the businessman is inevitably "a dead duck," he says. The percentage of nonwhite businesses that fail isn't known, but Mr. Zucker and others speculate that the rate is higher than for businesses owned by whites.

A low-capital, manufacturing business is preferable for the novice black entrepreneur, Mr. Williams says. It isn't "subject to robbery," and it can be started without incurring major debts. He notes that he is still working out arrangements for settling the thousands of dollars of personal debts resulting from the failure of his supermarkets. In the meantime he is paying himself only $15,000 a year.

Some other tough lessons came out of the supermarket experience. Mr. Williams says that although he isn't by nature "an excessive detail kind of guy," he has learned to handle personally much of his electronic company's accounting to keep closer tabs on internal expenses. He also keeps Freedom Electronics' labor force lean because "you have to concentrate on profitability before you can consider the social aspects."

But the company does have a very liberal employment policy. It will hire applicants with criminal records and those who have been on welfare for a long time, people who often are rejected by larger concerns. When employes run into problems in paying their rent, Freedom Electronics will advance them up to $300 in wages, and if they or their families get into legal difficulties, Mr. Williams will act as their lawyer. To keep down absenteeism, a major problem, employes can choose flexible working hours.

A much greater problem, however, is getting orders. At present, the company has about 15 corporate customers, but only Digital Equipment regularly provides what Mr. Williams considers sizable orders. "If I had five customers like Digital Equipment, my sales figure would be in the neighborhood of $10 million, which would allow me to hire 250 or 300 people," he says.

Despite corporate minority purchasing programs, there is no record of how many minority-owned firms are actually helped. This leads some critics to feel that the dollar-amount of the aid is misleading. "The amount of (white) business going to minority businesses is insignificant," possibly under 1% of all corporate purchases, maintains Eugene Baker, president of the National Association of Black Manufacturers, a trade group. Companies, he says, "can always say how much they're spending but they can't pinpoint where the money is going." He speculates that the money is spread too thinly to have much impact.

Mr. Williams notes that, as one example, he has been able

to obtain only about $600 of business from Gillette over the past nine years, even though the big Boston company currently earmarks more than $2 million annually to be spent with minority businesses. He says he's particularly bitter over an unsuccessful bid that Freedom Electronics made two years ago for a contract to repair Gillette hair dryers. Gillette gave the contract to a more experienced appliance repair firm (not minority owned) even though Mr. Williams contends that the work would have been "less complex by a factor of 100 than everything else we do."

Gillette acknowledges that there are deficiencies in its minority purchasing program. "I think we should be doing more for Archie," says Mr. Leroy, Gillette's purchasing director. But he bristles at the suggestion that Gillette may be partially responsible for Freedom Electronics' failure to grow faster. The small firm "still has to cut it on its own," he says.

There may be other reasons for Freedom Electronics' failure to grow more quickly. Mr. McGonagle, the company's independent representative, observes that because of the heavy reliance on Digital Equipment as a customer, the firm has "acquired some bad habits." For example, its prices to Digital Equipment aren't necessarily competitive, he says.

Recently, Mr. McGonagle helped Freedom Electronics obtain an order from Raytheon. But it was awarded only after Raytheon had allowed the firm to submit a second bid more competitive than the first.

Recipe for the Restaurant Business

Bob Dallas is in the Gatsby Room attending to customers, while in the Sting Room, singing waiters and waitresses belt out Broadway show tunes.

Robert (Pop) Dallas is greeting two young women at the door ("Such lovely girls—why wasn't I born 40 years later?").

Elizabeth (Mom) Dallas, a plump, tiny woman, is in the kitchen sauteing shrimp and mushrooms and keeping an eye on a simmering pot of clam bisque.

Here at the Sting Restaurant, life is a 16-hour-day, six-day-a-week whirl for the Dallas family. The three-year-old restaurant consumes their time and energies as they try to balance reasonable prices with fresh food and homemade dishes while competing with the quick-frozen economics of the chain restaurants springing up around them. Within a short distance of the Sting, located in the affluent Philadelphia suburb of King of Prussia, can be found such corporately owned dining spots as Stouffer's, Victoria Station, the Joshua Tree, Howard Johnson's, the Dutch Pantry and Valle's Steak House.

The Dallas family is only too aware of the inroads that the chains are making in the restaurant business. Chains now run 24% of all U.S. restaurants, compared with 10% a decade ago, and by 1982 they are expected to account for as much as 35%, according to the National Restaurant Association. Partly as a result, it's estimated that nearly 40% of independently owned restaurants close down or change hands in their first year. "When we move into a neighborhood, local independents lose business," says Frederick Rufe, an executive of Marriott Corp., which owns the Joshua Tree chain.

Despite the enormously high risks, every year more people

decide to open their own restaurants. Some view it as a glamorous way to make a living. Others want creativity while being their own boss. "We're all shooting for the rainbow," says Bob Dallas.

But it's becoming much tougher to shoot for. "Small businessmen can't get into the restaurant business as easily as they once could," says Thomas Haas of Nation's Restaurant News. Mr. Haas estimates that the minimum investment necessary to start up a restaurant now exceeds $100,000.

Many new restaurants are seriously under-capitalized, which is one reason why they fail, says Graeme Cooper of Laventhol & Horwath, an accounting firm specializing in the restaurant industry. Unable to secure bank financing, they are forced to skimp on advertising or to make do with outmoded kitchen equipment or a dining room that's too small, he says.

Many restaurateurs, industry experts say, are just plain poor managers. "Some people figure that their wife makes great apple pie or meat loaf so they ought to be in the restaurant business," says Mr. Haas. "What it really takes these days is a sharp businessman."

Of course, survival also means serving good food. And some restaurant experts believe that the future of the independent restaurant depends on emphasizing fresh ingredients and refusing to follow the chains into the ways of microwave ovens and chef-less kitchens.

Despite the chains' growth, some industry observers are optimistic about the future of the independent restaurant. "No one has been able to start a major chain of Italian or Greek dinner restaurants," says Steven Vanelli, a vice president of the investment research firm of Davis, Skaggs & Co. A well-run independent, he says, also has the advantage of being able to adapt its menu to local tastes.

But many independent restaurants feel they must also compete with the chains' costly emphasis on ambience: olde English pubs, German beer halls and cowboy motifs. "It would take too many years for us to make a splash just with good food," says the stocky, 39-year-old Mr. Dallas.

So Mr. Dallas has given the Sting a 1930s theme. The Sting Room has a working fireplace, a dance floor, stage (where the singing waiters entertain) and a picture of Al Jolson on the wall. The Gatsby Room has chandeliers, along with velvet drapes and hunting scenes on the walls, and the Speakeasy Room at the back has a bar, and a TV set is fixed on the wall. Even the menu is spiced with the unusual: A sandwich, for instance, is called a Stingwich.

But the Sting also manages to serve up food that many diners agree is a good deal better in quality than that served up by most chains. It serves Italian dishes, homemade sauces and soups and prepares topgrade prime ribs and steaks, unlike some of the neighboring restaurants that use tenderized, lower quality beef.

Most of the Sting's food is fresh, although recently, to cut costs, it has turned to frozen flounder and is using some frozen vegetables. "Food at the Sting is good quality and well prepared, even though not gourmet," says A. O. Schaeffer, president of a local advertising agency.

The Sting also manages to keep its prices competitive with the chains. It is able to do this mainly because the chef is Mr. Dallas's mother, and she cheerfully spends all day directing a kitchen staff of four and whipping up her sauces and soups from scratch. And the host is Mr. Dallas's father. Both parents, known as Mom and Pop by the staff of 50, work without pay and live on Mr. (Pop) Dallas's pension from his 25 years as a high-school teacher and football coach.

By comparison, many restaurants the size of the Sting have to pay a trained, competent chef as much as $25,000 a year. There's also a shortage of chefs because, says Mr. Haas of Nation's Restaurant News, "most people in the U.S. don't like the idea of sweating over a stove all day long, and being a chef isn't looked upon as a profession in this country."

Even with this free help, the Sting's lack of capital is evident: The vestibule has a plywood floor because Mr. Dallas doesn't have the money to spend on a proper ramp; the restaurant uses vinyl tablecloths; the kitchen is small and antiquated and has an inadequate oven; the storage space is so cramped that Mr. Dallas can't take full advantage of volume discounts on such foods as shrimp and fish.

The Sting (its name comes from the stinger cocktail) didn't have this money problem at first. It was financed by two wealthy businessmen, who, with Mr. Dallas as a partner, bought an old gabled house beside the Pennsylvania Turnpike that had previously housed two unsuccessful restaurants. The partners remodeled the house and gave it a new bar. Mr. Dallas, who had previously run a steakhouse, a bar that featured rock-and-roll entertainment and a businessman's dinner club in downtown Philadelphia, became manager of the Sting.

But the partners quickly fell out and Mr. Dallas was dismissed. He brought a legal action against the other two owners and in the settlement that was reached in 1976 he became the sole operator of the Sting. Under the agreement, he gave up his part ownership of the property and agreed to pay $3,000 a month rent. He also assumed liabilities of $140,000, mainly in suppliers' unpaid bills.

Mr. Dallas recently managed to obtain a $50,000 bank loan to consolidate some of the money he still owes to about 40 suppliers (many of these firms are refusing to make further deliveries until their bills are paid). Even so, through sheer hard work he has reduced the debt to $90,000. Profits are running at about 6% of revenues, which in the first six months of 1977 were $356,000, compared with about $300,000 a year earlier. Despite his long hours, Mr. Dallas draws a salary of only $300 a week, although he is able to charge his car to the restaurant's operations.

Running the Sting on a shoestring means having to keep a constant watch on food discounts. Mr. Dallas buys fish from a roadside market in Delaware, and every Friday he arrives at a produce market in Philadelphia at 6:30 a.m. to buy cut-price vegetables that are being cleared out for the weekend. He also has to keep an eye on waste, such as a waitress serving more than one container of cream with coffee. "These containers go for 2½ cents each. A lot of small things add up to big dollars of waste," he says.

The long hours involved in running the Sting are taking their toll on Mr. Dallas. He recently began treatment for high blood pressure, and he has gone on a diet. Last spring he began closing the restaurant one day a week because, he says, his relationship with his wife, Toni, and his six children was becoming "strained." Mrs. Dallas admits that she has to spend a great deal of time on her own, although she does work as a part-time waitress in the restaurant of the local J. C. Penney store. "It wouldn't do me any good to be a clinging vine," she says.

Mrs. (Mom) Dallas, who has been cooking in restaurants for the past 11 years, spends long hours at the Sting. She usually arrives at 9 a.m. and doesn't leave until 10 at night.

Her first job in the morning is to get the chili and soups ready for lunch. Her lunchtime usually is spent operating the sandwich counter. She often eats her own lunch standing up in the kitchen stirring the sauces and gravies that the four cooks will use to prepare various dishes later in the day.

On a recent day she could be found in the kitchen sauteing shrimp and mushrooms for a sauce to go with flounder and at the same time keeping an eye on a pot of chopped clams being cooked for clam bisque. Mrs. Dallas, who has been cooking since she was 10, "just pours" wine into her sauces. "I don't have to measure," she says.

Three times a week she must find time to prepare a large batch of lasagna, and twice a week she makes stuffing for chicken breasts. "I try to get a lot of my cooking done early in the morning or right after lunch because there are often no free burners on the range at night."

The cramped kitchen and the inadequate appliances are two of Mrs. Dallas's frustrations. Another is the high staff turnover, which means she often has inexpert kitchen help. Recently a new helper overcooked and ruined the asparagus. But Mr. Dallas says he's afraid to hire culinary school graduates "because they all want to be chef."

Most of the chain restaurants only want young inexperienced (and, thus, low-paid) people. Marriott doesn't have any chefs in its Joshua Tree restaurants. "The kids we employ in the kitchen know only what's on the recipe card," says Mr. Rufe, the Marriott executive.

Marriott now has nine Joshua Trees and plans to open six more next year. All of the restaurants receive their food, both in frozen and fresh form, from the Marriott central commissary in Washington. In this way Marriott can invest most of its capital in a restaurant's decor. For example, the Joshua Tree that recently opened about a mile from the Sting cost about $1 million, much of which was spent on creating a decor with a Western theme, complete with spurs and leather saddles.

Because of the chains' food economics, Mr. Dallas sometimes finds himself challenged on food prices. He is delaying making a much-needed increase in the price of sirloin steak and crab legs because the new Joshua Tree is selling these entrees at a lower price and even is offering unlimited wine with meals.

Mr. Dallas works hard to create an image as an alternative to the chains rather than as a competitor. When he drops in for a drink at the Stouffer's and Sheraton hotels on either side of the Sting he makes a practice of leaving $5 tips for bartenders. "I want them to remember to recommend the Sting when conventioneers want a change from hotel cooking," he says.

Still, Mr. Dallas worries that the competition is getting tougher. "Sometimes I feel I'm in the middle of a cattleyard and I have to be careful or I'll get trampled," he says. But, he insists, "even with all the problems I have, I can meet the chain restaurants toe to toe. They're tops in efficiency, but the chains don't make Mom's gravy."

Part IV:

Managing To Succeed In a Variety of Situations

Coping With Life In Iran

One high-level executive for General Motors got a real taste of Iranian life when some GM people in Tehran gave a dinner party for him. There was no *shish kebab* for the visiting vice president from Detroit. There were no other broiled local delicacies either.

What there was—a sudden cutoff of the power flowing into the GM-Iran car plant—left the plant's kitchen unable to boil an egg. The party fare was reduced to drinks and cold hors d'oeuvres; the auto mogul boarded his midnight plane to India a hungry man.

"And this was the big boss," says Louis H. Wilking, shaking his head mournfully. In the three years he has spent managing GM operations in Tehran, including the dinner-less dinner party, this Cincinnatian has found that one dependable rule overseas is Murphy's Law: If something can go wrong, it will.

Mr. Wilking, who is heading for South Africa to direct GM operations there, is part of an expatriate army working abroad. Many of these Americans have followed new oil wealth to the Middle East; for instance, their numbers in Saudi Arabia and Iran, the two leading Mideast oil exporters, have quadrupled to 30,000 in five years. There are oil-well drillers, bank managers, accountants, engineers, teachers, miners, salesmen and managers.

But there is also a high attrition rate, for, as Mr. Wilking's executive experience shows, it isn't easy to transplant a U.S. way of life. Among new tasks that he has had to learn are those of handyman, barterer and highly skilled driver.

Most Iranian drivers are male, and they enjoy displaying their macho on the road. During one 300-mile car trip through the mountains to Tehran, Mr. Wilking counted 22 accidents. "It was unbelievable," he says. "Cars and trucks over the cliff, head on into each other, people passing everywhere, trucks and buses coming at you on your side of the road." GM's parts department doesn't mind; one study showed that out of 1,000 cars sold in Iran, 200 needed new left front fenders within three months.

But the energy shortages are maddening. Mr. Wilking counted 15 power failures within 12 months. He had a reason to count them. Each idled the GM plant and its 2,200 workers. Indeed, power outages are part of the reason Iran figures that its car plants run at just 51% of capacity. The basic trouble is that the local energy plants aren't being expanded fast enough to meet soaring demand. GM may take scant comfort in a recent move by the Ministry of Energy to schedule rotating blackouts, so each district gets just one a month.

The cultural complexities may be just as unnerving. In Kuwait on a business trip, Mr. Wilking ran afoul of one Mideast custom by forgetting that a guest shouldn't admire anything lest his host feel obliged to make a gift of it. The GM man told his host at an all-male cocktail party that he intended to buy an Arab robe as a souvenir. The robe-clad host promptly stripped off his garments and handed them to Mr. Wilking, who recalls, "That left him standing in pale-yellow long johns."

Clearly, the go-go U.S. businessman must change his style in Iran, where meetings begin with endless cups of tea, where 120-degree summer temperatures discourage frenetic activity, and where bargaining dominates business talk. Mr. Wilking doesn't even speak Iran's language, called Farsi. It's a strange climate for American women, too. Allah said women should be submissive. One American woman in a Persian Gulf city had her undergarments painted black for showing too much leg.

Religion is taken seriously. One doesn't joke about Islam as one might about the Christian missionary in the cannibal pot. A cocktail-party host must stock up on fruit juice; the orthodox Moslem doesn't drink. (In Iran, ordinary Scotch sells for over $15 a bottle, but at least it's available. Nearby Saudi Arabia is dry, leading some expatriates to install stills in their kitchens.)

New chores cropped up in Iran for Mr. Wilking, his enthusiastic wife, Dorothy, and their three teen-agers. The family had a swimming pool, like many families of U.S. executives. But they cleaned it themselves. Common laborers couldn't be found, what with many better-paying factory jobs going begging.

Once, city crews installed curbs on the unpaved road in front of the Wilkings' residence, piled up gravel in the middle of the road, and then left for good. With visitors expected one evening, the Wilkings decided to make the road passable themselves. GM's top man in Iran could be seen swinging a shovel along with the rest of the family.

"Some people back home seem to think that if you are working abroad, you are living in the Taj Mahal with 14 servants. Ha!" Mr. Wilking says. "Most of the time you are your own electrician, plumber, carpenter and mechanic. There's always something broken down and nobody but you to fix it."

Living costs are so steep in Iran that sometimes a loyal company man resists paying them even when his employer will pick up part of the tab. Mr. Wilking could get a GM housing allowance if his rent exceeded a certain portion of his salary, which is estimated at between $60,000 and $70,000. But when one landlord increased his monthly house rent overnight to $4,500 from $1,800, he quickly moved to an apartment with rent at $2,200 monthly. (The move wasn't all for love of GM. Notice of the rent rise had come just after the dining-room ceiling collapsed, giving 40 dinner guests a clear view of the stars.)

A help-thy-neighbor spirit is developing among Americans abroad. A man who likes to tinker with autos may find himself tuning up a neighbor's car. Mr. Wilking, who isn't the handiest man on the block, did have all those GM employes working for him. But he felt they couldn't properly be pressed into service for personal odd jobs.

One exception came when he had a GM engineer as a house guest, and the furnace gave out. The day was cold, for Tehran has a winter. Both men took apart the furnace and cleaned it before discovering it was simply out of oil. A fuel-delivery man had pumped a truckload of fuel into a nearby pipe that led blindly into the ground.

Mr. Wilking earns a comfortable salary by U.S. standards, but it wouldn't go far if his purchases were confined to Western items, many of which must be imported. A spot check turns up steak at $7 a pound, a bottle of Heinz ketchup at $3.40, two rolls of toilet paper at $1.16, a teenager's denim suit at $110, and a double room in a good hotel at $90 a night.

Hotels once were used by GM as a place to accommodate its newcomers. But as Iran's current economic boom developed, there was no room for them. So the auto maker bought a cluster of apartments for workers doing short hitches. It then began to worry about how they would be furnished, in a city where it may take an expedition into a dozen stores to locate a certain size screw.

"I took the job," Dorothy Wilking says. "There was no one else to do it." She personally selected every carpet, piece of furniture, painting, door lock and pillow case. When a cleaning team couldn't be located, the executive's wife got out her own scrub pail.

The executive abroad may find a spouse either a help or a hindrance. Many wives, of course, aren't too happy to leave American suburbia for a hacienda in Bolivia, a compound in Malaysia or a villa in Iran. By contrast, Mrs. Wilking was eagerly poring over maps from the night in 1971 when she learned that her family would be moving from Detroit overseas, first to Australia.

She is an avid joiner of women's clubs, PTAs and hospital volunteer groups. "There is always something to do," she says. "Ultimately, I might get tired of living abroad. But I don't see that day, yet."

A housewife's lot abroad has a flavor all its own. In Iran, petty thievery is common, and the housewife learns early to tip the municipal garbage man if she doesn't want trash dumped "accidentally" all over her yard. It's different from Saudi Arabia, where there is virtually no thievery; a second-time thief may have a hand lopped off as punishment.

There are more serious crimes. Mr. Wilking won't discuss the safety precautions he has taken against the groups of anti-government guerrillas that exist in Iran and have murdered several Americans on Tehran's streets. But Mr. Wilking drives an old, inconspicuous auto instead of one of GM's newer models. And he staggers his work schedule to avoid any easily recognizable routine.

There are bonuses in exotic vacations. Last year, the Wilkings vacationed in Bangkok, Singapore and Bali. And there are aggravations in taxation. Mr. Wilking becomes nearly apoplectic in discussing the impact on expatriates of the new U.S. tax law, which among other things tightens Washington's tax treatment of Americans abroad. The law maddens him even more than the experience he once had of paying taxes in three countries in a single year.

GM currently has a program to pick up the difference between an employe's tax bill and what he would pay in the U.S. But that policy may become uneconomic some years hence because of a pyramiding effect. Each reimbursement for taxes becomes taxable too, lifting the American into ever-higher tax brackets. "How long can any American company go along with such a system?" Mr. Wilking asks. "Ultimately you reach a point where the man becomes too expensive to keep overseas. What is worse, all the added costs may be pricing you out of the market," where many foreign nations compete.

The Wilkings also worry that their youngest child, Steven, may be losing touch with his American roots. Now 16, he has spent most of his formative years abroad. The two older children, Michael and Luann, were already Americanized teenagers when they moved abroad.

In Melbourne, Luann had rebelled against the uniforms and wide-brimmed straw hats that girls at her new Australian school had to wear. "I'm not going to that Mickey Mouse school," she asserted. But she did go, and grew to like the place and her classmates.

The Tehran American School is thoroughly Americanized, with a jean-clad student body that takes classes ranging from football to drama. Now, with school in South Africa facing Steven, the Wilkings wonder whether he should go to a U.S. boarding school to renew ties to his homeland or continue living with his parents in a foreign land.

"We're going to let Steve make up his own mind on this," Mrs. Wilking says.

Mr. Wilking's parents were grocery-store owners. He got an accounting degree from Xavier University, and spent a year in Korea as an artillery officer. He then married and rose through the ranks in GM's accounting and finance departments. Moving abroad, he became financial adviser to GM's Australian subsidiary, treasurer of GM-South Africa, then managing director of GM-Iran. Now returning to South Africa to head company operations there, Mr. Wilking talks like a good company man: "I have never yet turned down a GM assignment when asked to undertake it."

Women of the World

When an American banker named Fredrica Challandes-Angelini recently went to Saudi Arabia to negotiate a loan, her first problem was getting a foot in the door. Literally.

Saudi Arabia generally doesn't allow unaccompanied women into the country—no matter who they are. So Miss Challandes-Angelini took a transit visa—indicating that she was only stopping at the airport before her flight carried her to another destination—and, when no one was looking, she walked out the airport door.

"Once in the country, I had no problems whatsoever," says Miss Challandes-Angelini, who is an assistant vice president with Amex Bank Ltd., a London-based subsidiary of American Express Co. "I suppose that if your company has sent you there and you act in a competent manner, they'll accept you." When the time came for her to leave, her Saudi customers took care of the exit formalities.

The experience may have been awkward, but it wasn't unusual. It reflects a new development affecting even the most socially restrained parts of the world: Female managers are beginning to move into international business.

"Starting in mid-1976, more women began appearing," says Mary R. Gibbons, a vice president of Morgan Guaranty Trust Co., who arrived in London in 1974 and was the first woman in a prominent British banking post.

"Before, I virtually never spoke to a female on the other end of the line" when calling on business matters, she says. "Now, there will be women, and they will be the people to speak to."

In many ways, that's a predictable extension of the women's movement in the U.S. As more American companies have admitted women to management—either because of enlightened corporate attitudes or the threat of lawsuits—some women naturally have moved into companies' international operations.

Companies have acted cautiously, however. When one big American bank considered assigning its first woman overseas, the decision was deemed so sensitive that it "went all the way to the top," an officer says. The move has worked out well enough that the bank has since sent several women to foreign branches.

Most companies publicly acclaim the wisdom of their decisions to post women overseas, and some prominently feature women managers in advertising campaigns. Henri Debuisser, executive director, personnel and organization, of Rank Xerox Ltd., says: "We have some very capable women executives, both in headquarters and in our marketing operations in Europe. They are well accepted, and we would very much like to see more women of similar caliber in our national and international managements."

However, many observers privately say women often are expected to be of higher caliber than men in similar positions. "She has to be exceptional, outstanding, dynamic, flexible, venturesome—a bundle all rolled into one—before they hire her," says Charles Mannel, director of the career services center at a leading business training ground, the American Graduate School of International Management in Glendale, Ariz.

Moreover, there still aren't many women in foreign posts. U.S.-based companies—which by most accounts are leading the trend—are only beginning to send women abroad, and most of these women are in what one describes as "lower-middle-management positions." Much of the activity has been concentrated in a few fields, such as banking, which generally have led in promoting women at home. It's all so new that neither women's groups nor international organizations have data on the number of women in international management.

The trend is almost sure to accelerate, though, because

more women are preparing for international careers. Mr. Mannel says his school has had a "phenomenal" growth in women's enrollment; women now account for about one-third of the total, up from one-fourth a year ago and from only about 2% in 1964.

Despite all that, the feeling persists in many corporate circles that women can't operate effectively in many foreign economies. Some companies are reluctant to send women overseas for fear of losing business. "Maybe you could put a woman in London," says a male manager with a big American electronics company. "But in the Middle East? Forget it."

However, some big banks and companies are sending women to the Mideast—and to Africa, South America and other areas (including much of Europe) generally considered to be male domains. And many women are finding—as Miss Challandes-Angelini's experience suggests—that many presumed barriers to women are more apparent than real. They also are discovering that many of the real barriers aren't quite so formidable when a woman has the backing of a big bank or corporation.

"It's like driving around in a Rolls-Royce," says Yvette M. Newbold, an attorney with Rank Xerox, which is 51%-owned by Xerox Corp. "If you are working for a big and fairly glamorous multinational, it has got to count more than your sex."

Kimberly Albright, who is with Citibank's merchant banking operation in London, probably would agree. She has helped put together loans in Morocco, Turkey, Jordan and Iran, among other places, and says the people there "seem to accept the fact that they are dealing with Citibank and that I will deal with them." She adds that one "revelation" in her travels has been that some clients—such as the financial director of a government-owned development bank in Morocco—have themselves turned out to be women.

Miss Albright says she likes the fact that Citibank "actually will try these things out and test the hypothesis" that women can't work in such parts of the world. She adds, "I think the hypothesis tends not to be true."

Although women sometimes do run into unpleasant situations, Morgan Guaranty's Miss Gibbons, who is involved in syndicating Eurodollar loans, says, "Obviously, there are going to be a few people you're never going to get along with, but I don't think the ratio is any different than for a man in the same position."

Miss Gibbons traveled the globe in 1977; she visited 13 countries on three continents—and she says her work experience has been "very successful." Among other things, she helped coordinate a $1.2 billion loan to Mexico—an effort that took her to negotiations from London to Frankfurt to New York to Mexico City to Paris. "I believe anyone I come in contact with feels Morgan Guaranty wouldn't put me in the position if I weren't qualified," Miss Gibbons says.

Not all the stories are happy ones, however. One woman banker in Europe requested and received a transfer back to the U.S. because, a colleague says, "The pressures had become too much for her mentally—she had met resistance everywhere." Another woman quit her banking job in Canada because she was convinced that she wasn't being promoted as rapidly as her male associates.

Women often run into difficulties abroad because, except in the Communist bloc, they generally are even more of an oddity in most foreign countries than they are in the U.S. Many female managers are blazing trails—and doing so in countries where the women's movement hasn't had much visibility.

"Companies here haven't gotten to the stage, which they have in the States, of saying, 'We must look at ourselves under a microscope in this context and see if we are discriminating,' " says Anne Mackie, a commissioner with the U.K.'s Equal Opportunities Commission. "They still are at the stage of saying, 'We know some (sex discrimination) legislation has been passed, but we aren't discriminating at the present moment.' "

The state of things was illustrated in a recent study by the International Labor Organization—a Geneva-based agency of the United Nations—of female employment in Britain, France, Belgium and Sweden. It found that women's work "generally remains rooted in traditional spheres of feminine activity" and said the recent increase in the numbers of working women "hasn't to any significant extent broadened their range of employment opportunities."

That's partly true in the U.S., of course, but many American women say the climate is worse abroad. "I couldn't believe the atmosphere when I came to London," says one woman lawyer with a major American bank.

"It's considered much more radical than in the U.S. to voice opinions about women's rights or even to do something as commonplace as calling yourself Ms,' " says Fredrica Challandes-Angelini. "Things I might say in the U.S., I wouldn't say here."

Some of the problems are cultural. One woman still smarts over an angry session with a male manager from one of her bank's African operations. The African had flown to London to help draft a corporate position for negotiations with a customer. He apparently hadn't been told that his co-worker would be a woman.

"From the minute I entered the room, he began fighting with me—fighting everything I said, in the rudest possible way," the woman recalls. "We couldn't get anywhere—he just didn't want to deal with me. Finally, I said, 'Hey, we're supposed to be on the same side.' "

And finally, after a full hour of arguing, the African "came around," the woman says, and the two got down to business. She thinks the problem was "completely because I am a woman." She explains: "From where he came from in Africa, he had never—absolutely never—had to deal with a woman in business."

Such a cultural lapse isn't all that surprising—just as it isn't very surprising that many women say they have found it difficult to work in male-oriented Japan.

But less predictably, women say the same thing about some West European men, such as the West Germans and French. "They're so chivalrous and so charming to women," one woman says of the French, "but doing business with them is very difficult. It seems to be a totally sexual kind of thing."

And London's financial district—known as the City—gets low marks from many women. "The City is the last bastion," says Mrs. Newbold of Rank Xerox. When she worked for a law firm there, she says, "I had my bum pinched more times than when I was on the Italian Riviera."

By contrast, women working in communist-bloc countries say they are taken seriously and treated well. Anna Ksiezopolska, an American who is Rank Xerox's sales manager for Hungary, says she has had "absolutely no difficulty" there. Working in Eastern Europe, she says, is "easier for a woman than it is in the West." (It isn't easy for an East European woman, however. "As far as work goes, she is treated as an equal," Miss Ksiezopolska says. "But she has two jobs—she is still a housewife.")

Sandra Beers, a second vice president in Chase Manhattan Bank's Moscow office, says the reaction of many customers there has been, "It's about time we saw American women coming over and handling our accounts." Miss Beers is the second woman to work for Chase in Moscow; she previously had traveled for the bank in Eastern Europe.

Some places unaccustomed to native businesswomen are willing to accept foreign ones. Miss Challandes-Angelini has worked in the Ivory Coast, Gabon and Cameroon, and she says those African countries are "really quite pleasant and straightforward" in accepting Western businesswomen.

Women still have a long way to go, of course. As is true in the U.S., most women overseas aren't in top—or even upper-middle—management ranks. Miss Challendes-Angelini thinks "the real test" of corporate attitudes is "whether they'll put a woman in charge."

Many women think that eventually they will get top posts —and they are making long-range career plans. Citibank's Miss Albright, for instance, says she expects to spend "two or three years" in her London post, then perhaps serve in another foreign assignment. "In my mind, the Eurodollar markets still are growing at a tremendous pace, as the oil countries develop," she says. "To me as a merchant banker, that's where the action is."

Battling The Time Zones

Ah, those wily Arabs. Always looking to get the edge on a person.

Take the matter of selling their oil. Frequently an American oil-company executive arrives after an overnight flight to find that his Arab hosts have scheduled bargaining sessions to begin immediately.

"I'm sure they think it's to their advantage to bargain while you're experiencing jet lag," says Paul Macht, a vice president of Sun Oil Trading Co., Radnor, Pa. "The Libyans are notorious for it," Mr. Macht says that on one occasion, Algerian bargainers got an American company to pay 15 cents a barrel more than it should have paid because the American crude oil buyer was hampered by jet lag.

Jet lag, or, scientifically speaking, the disruption of circadian (daily) rhythms, is by now a recognized syndrome that tourists, business executives and government officials alike know they must confront when flying across more than a few time zones. In fact, some think that the subject has gotten altogether too much attention.

"I've listened to so many people talk about jet lag; I think it's a fixation," says Willard R. Gallagher, vice president, international, for Textron Inc. "Enough people spend enough time talking about jet lag so that it becomes a condition of their flying."

However, even Mr. Gallagher, when traveling to Europe, takes care on his first day abroad to do only "routine" work, "with no big decisions." Jet lag, in fact, is a bit like a hangover; everybody has his or her formula for dealing with it. Television journalist Barbara Walters strives always to sleep on planes, wearing "booties" so her feet won't get cold. Some travelers take a dose of Valium or Seconal before embarking. Others make a point of jogging or playing tennis when they arrive.

One executive never adjusts his watch. "I try to fool my body that I'm still in Boston," he says. Another, who travels to London, relies on hot baths to recover, "The English have these great big tubs where you can soak," he says. "Loose trousers" while traveling is another man's remedy. Fly Concorde, say others.

Loy Weston, president of Heublein (Japan) Ltd., often drinks only water on a flight, and abstains from food. "It lets your metabolism adjust faster," he says. "I learned that from (South African golfer) Gary Player." Then there is the defiant approach; a St. Louis executive says he refreshes himself on a flight by "drinking a hell of a lot of champagne," and rests later. And an oilman comments, "I just let my body hate me."

None of the palliatives, say scientists, can overcome the inexorable laws of the circadian rhythms. The most familiar rhythm is sleep and wakefulness. But the body has many biological "clocks," some daily, some on other schedules. Body temperature, the digestive process, the liver, and secretion of hormones such as adrenalin all have their own timetables. Some rhythms are "cued" by external signals like the dark-light cycle; others are cued internally.

The diverse rhythms normally function synchronously, like a well-rehearsed orchestra. But rapid passage through several time zones shatters the harmony. And the different rhythms take differing times to adjust. So complex is the problem, it seems unlikely that medical science will devise an effective treatment soon to stave off or redress jet lag.

"I fell into a dreamy sleep in front of our chairman," says Thomas Hague, area director, Asia, for Borg-Warner Corp., based in Tokyo, recalling the end of one trans-Pacific flight. Joseph C. Bates, vice president, international, for Aluminum Co. of America, once ordered some new business cards directly after returning from an Australian trip, and misspelled his own name in giving instructions to the printer (he left out the "s" in Bates).

Harry Weinberg, New York-based president of a Tiger International Corp. unit, once plunged into negotiations in London just after arrival. Suddenly, he recalls, "I found I couldn't concentrate any more, I stopped the negotiations and said, 'I can't go on.'"

Every traveler has a jet-lag story. In view of that, surprisingly few companies queried in a Wall Street Journal roundup have formal policies on the subject. One that does is International Business Machines Corp., which operates in 127 nations outside the U.S.

IBM directs employes who are crossing four to seven time zones, or spending 10 to 15 hours aloft, not to conduct business on the day of arrival. If the trip involves eight or more time zones, or if travel time exceeds 15 hours, employes are asked to split the trip by taking a one-night stopover, or to schedule a full day of rest after arrival before conducting business.

Some concerns, such as Alcoa, follow the less formal policy of informing their executives of the hazards of jet lag, and advising how to minimize it. Alcoa has circulated a booklet called "Human Factors in Long-Distance Flights," prepared in cooperation with the Flight Safety Foundation and the Federal Aviation Administration; the booklet recommends rest periods after a flight similar to the IBM rules.

Companies "should have official policies," says Walter S. Mukash, Westinghouse Electric Co.'s area director for Eastern Europe. But Mr. Mukash confesses that he conducts his day "as though it was a normal day" when he arrives in Moscow after passing through eight time zones. That reflects the pattern at most companies: The decision of how to deal with jet lag is left up to the individual.

"Everybody's expected to use good judgment," says Ben Murphy, a vice president of Tyler Corp., Dallas. Many travelers take the course chosen by Paul F. Cornelsen, executive vice president of Ralston Purina Co., who tries to schedule his trips so as to arrive on a weekend and rest before going to work Monday.

"I may drag a little the second day, but I won't be a zombie," says Mr. Cornelsen.

Joseph Abeles, president of Kawecki Berylco Industries Inc., Reading, Pa., says he is "completely against going over on a night flight and then going straight to a morning meeting; you give away a big negotiating advantage by doing that, like giving up 20 to 25 pounds in a prize fight."

It may not be just the Arabs who are alert to capitalizing on the other fellow's jet lag. A pamphlet produced by Aer Lingus, the Irish airline, says that North American executives traveling in Europe often "seek to keep negotiations going as late as possible; the North American's afternoon coincides with a European's evening and time of declining efficiency."

Jet lag is one thing; simple fatigue is another; and the special discomforts of confinement in an airplane create yet another problem. Many a traveler's jet lag precautions seem to embrace all three problems.

Travelers who shun alcohol, for instance, are taking note of the unnaturally low humidity of airplane cabins, and of alcohol's tendency to hasten the body's excretion of water. A common recommendation of frequent travelers is to drink a lot of nonalcoholic beverages to replenish body liquids.

Sleeping en route is another preoccupation. A British Foreign Office official says he always takes his daughter's sleeping bag on trips and stretches out on the floor of a VC-10 to rest. Oliver M. Langenberg, a vice president at A. G. Edwards & Sons Inc., St. Louis, says, "Even though I don't smoke, I always head for the smoking section because it'll have fewer people." There he looks for three adjacent seats that aren't occupied and uses them as a bed.

Exercise en route seems to help, too. A United Airlines official says, "We recommend that the pilots do deep knee bends on the plane." This helps to fend off "the tendency of the blood to settle in the legs." Some executives say they do light isometric exercises in their airplane seats, or just walk around the plane.

One way of combatting jet lag is to act as though no time changes are occurring. A U.S. Air Force physician says many

crews on long trips—for instance, touring bases in the Pacific—
"just stay on their own time cycle." They leave their watches
unchanged and eat or sleep according to the time at home.

This seems to have some benefit. A British diplomat says he
often remains on London time when visiting Washington. "It's
doable for two days, provided you give up all social life," he
says. After that it is difficult. "It becomes incredibly dull—
you're really not doing anything but going to meetings."

The businessman normally can't require others to adjust to
his timetable. But J. Peter Grace, president of W. R. Grace &
Co., says, "I just stay on New York time in Europe. I go to bed
about 3 in the morning, and get up about 11 or 12." But sometimes even Mr. Grace gets dragooned into morning meetings
there. "I dig my fingernails into my palms so hard they almost
bleed, to avoid falling asleep," he confides.

Any number of important people, including Presidents of
the U.S. and Secretaries of State, operate by paying little or no
attention to jet lag. Lyndon Johnson went around the world in
four and a half days in 1967, and Henry Kissinger repeatedly
plunged into sensitive negotiations after hurtling through many
time zones.

Many people in the private sector also give the back of the
hand to their biological clocks. "When you land, go directly to
work," says Mike Wallace, the TV interviewer. "In other words,
hit the ground running." Dr. William Kelley, assistant medical
director for Standard Oil Co. of California, says, "Our people
. . . have got to charge, charge, charge once they get there."

Alcoa's Mr. Bates points out that taking a rest after arriving
overseas can get expensive if several executives are traveling together. "You can't tie up such high-priced talent as this," he
says. And Lawrence Klamon, senior vice president of Fuqua Industries Inc., Atlanta, says, "If your particular method of fighting jet lag is to lie on the beach at Malibu for three days, that's
going to raise eyebrows."

Dr. William Lukash, physician to Presidents Ford and Carter, says, "it always amazes me" how alert officials remain during long journeys. He attributes it to a sense of excitement that

keeps them energetic. Similarly, Alan J. Dalby, vice president, international, for Smith Kline & French Laboratories, says he has few problems on an outgoing flight, "Because I'm more excited and my adrenalin is pumping."

But when Mr. Dalby gets home he feels the ill effects. So does Stanley L. Lopata, chairman and chief executive officer of Carboline Co., St. Louis, who says it takes him "ten days to two weeks" to shake the effects of jet lag after coming home from an overseas trip.

"The adrenalin is flowing" while on a trip, says Frank M. Warren, executive vice president of Raymond International Inc., Houston. "It suppresses the effects of fatigue on the body. . . . It's like an athlete in a game. He may get wounded, but he'll forget it and go on playing. But he may not be able to walk after the game. It's the same sort of thing."

"You have to realize some of these executives keep weird hours," points out Perry Harmon, an official of Hames Corp., Winston-Salem, N.C. "They work 12- or 16-hour days, sleep maybe five, six hours. When they take off on a plane, what's jet lag to them? Getting up at 7:30 in the morning, instead of 5:00 a.m.?"

Medical opinion on jet lag, perhaps reflecting fragmentary research, isn't firm. For instance, a Lockheed Corp. physician says, "It really takes up to five days for a traveler to become fully acclimated."

A possibly definitive experiment on jet lag is being carried out by scientists from the universities of Chicago and Brussels. Five Belgian students (all male, to avoid complications of the menstrual cycle) were flown across the Atlantic; then scientists monitored numerous body functions.

Analysis of the tests is due this spring. More than 500,000 "determinations" were made, including the taking of blood samples as often as every 15 minutes. Dr. Samuel Refetoff, the Chicago endocrinologist heading the experiment, cites one early finding: Production of the hormone cortisone, which helps the body resist stress, took about 10 days to adjust its daily cycle from Brussels time to Chicago time.

When In Rome

The Japanese executive sucks in air through his teeth and exclaims, "Sa! That will be *very* difficult!"

What he really means is just plain "no." But the Japanese consider an absolute "no" to be offensive and usually seek a euphemistic term. That's why, in Japan, the "difficult" really may be impossible. The American on the other side of the negotiating table knows none of this and presses ahead to resolve the "difficulty." The Japanese finds this inexplicable persistence to be abnormally pushy. The atmosphere deteriorates and, sure enough, the big deal falls through.

The film that portrays this situation is part of a popular course at New York University's Graduate School of Business Administration—one of the many increasingly well-attended courses in international business offered around the country. As American business involvement abroad has expanded, avoiding the pitfalls of overseas work has become an important management problem. Dozens of times every day, as airplanes touch down in Kuala Lumpur, Buenos Aires and Dar es Salaam, nervous American executives wonder, how on earth do I get things done in this place?

To help its graduates escape this sense of panic, NYU's business school has nearly tripled its international business faculty since 1970. Enrollments in the department have more than tripled since then, says Ingo Walter, the school's associate dean. But course offerings aren't limited to young MBA candidates. NYU and other institutions offer international business evening courses for working businessmen who aren't seeking degrees.

In a typical approach for such courses, NYU's Prof. Ashok Kapoor stresses the need to understand how perceptions of the same event will differ from one country to another. He cites a senior American executive who was irked when an Asian businessman suggested changing the date of the American's visit 10 days before the event. The American thought he was receiving shabby treatment. In fact, the Asian executive considered the meeting so important that he had consulted with a religious adviser who urged a more auspicious date for the talks. Anyone familiar with the local scene would have grasped the significance of the change, which the Asian meant as a compliment, Prof. Kapoor says.

In another case, American executives negotiating a contract in the Middle East found there wasn't time to have their revised negotiating proposal typed, submitted a hand-written version and thought nothing of it. But the Arabs across the bargaining table considered the gesture so bizarre that they began to analyze it intensely, seeking significant messages. Some concluded the Americans were trying to imply that they considered the whole contract unimportant, says Prof. Kapoor, a young specialist in international business who was educated at India's Delhi University and at the University of North Carolina.

Prof. Kapoor says a common frustration many Americans feel overseas involves dealing with strikingly different concepts of time. "What will take a week here will take a month there," he adds. In many Third World countries especially, anywhere from 50% to 80% of the time spent talking with businessmen will be spent discussing anything but business.

But while the American often views this personal chit-chat as a waste of time, it can be crucial to business, Prof. Kapoor says. "The American may want to separate his professional life from his personal life, but in many countries business is almost an indirect outcome of the personal relationship—you do business with your friends," he says.

Prof. Kapoor also urges students to watch for significant unspoken signals. In many rigidly hierarchical societies, the order in which a group of people walk through a door may be a dead giveaway to the pecking order among them. But the comparatively egalitarian American may miss this entirely, Prof. Kapoor says.

To help students deal with the crucial Japanese business world, Prof. Kapoor and others use a movie called "Doing Business in Japan," produced by the nonprofit Business Council for International Understanding. The film shows how blunders and misinterpretations on both sides ruin negotiations between an American and a Japanese company. For instance, when the Americans make one proposal, the Japanese react with complete silence, giving them time to reflect—a sign of interest. But the Americans think the silence shows *lack* of interest in the proposal and take offense.

On many campuses across the country, students want to learn how to operate abroad. In the last few years, the University of South Carolina, the University of Denver and others have started or greatly expanded international business programs. The growing American Graduate School of International Management in Glendale, Ariz., is devoted entirely to preparing students for world business careers.

In an international advertising course at the Arizona school, students develop a complete mock advertising campaign to sell a product like Kentucky Fried Chicken or frozen orange juice abroad. Often traveling to the country involved, the students conduct their own market research, develop art work and even write jingles in a foreign language, says William Voris, president of the institution.

Reflecting interest in world business, enrollment at the Glendale campus has risen to 850 from 300 ten years ago, Mr. Voris says. Applications have doubled to 4,000 last year from 2,000 a decade ago, he adds. "The school is really the child of the times," he says.

The Four-Day Week: Changing Times

South Padre Island, a Texas resort area, was nearly deserted when Terry and Vicki Shea and their two sons arrived for a winter weekend. They had driven 300 miles to the national seashore from their San Antonio home on a Thursday night. They had the whole place to themselves the next day, but by noon Saturday hordes of sunseekers were swarming over the beach. "I enjoyed Friday much more than Saturday," says Mr. Shea, who is director of research for United Services Automobile Association, an insurance company.

Ralph and Cindee Hurlburt also have their Fridays off, but instead of relaxing like the Sheas, they "moonlight" in an effort to build their hobby, raising quarter horses, into a business. It's a tough grind, but they figure it will be worth it if it allows them to escape their tedious and tiring regular jobs on the assembly line of a frozen-food plant in Fairmont, Minn.

What Mr. Shea and the Hurlburts have in common is that their Fridays are free regularly, and so are their Saturdays and Sundays. They are among an estimated 1.2 million Americans for whom the four-day work-week, with all of its attendant problems and pleasures, has become a reality. This represents about 2% of the full-time work force, and the number seems sure to mount steadily in the near future.

In the fall of 1976, the United Auto Workers Union's settlements with the auto and farm-implement industries gave 852,-000 workers 12 extra paid days off over the next two years; the union says it sees this provision as the opening wedge in its drive to make the four-day, 32-hour week standard in those industries. The United Steelworkers Union says it will follow the UAW's lead and give a shorter workweek high priority in its talks with the steel industry.

During the 1977 energy crisis, President Carter suggested that government agencies and private industry temporarily make the switch to a four-day week to cut consumption of dwindling natural-gas supplies. But federal law requires payment of overtime for more than an eight-hour day to U.S. government workers and companies with federal contracts of more than $10,000. And Mr. Carter stopped short of requesting Congress to suspend overtime provisions of these laws.

Even before the energy crisis, a bill was introduced in Congress that would allow several hundred thousand federal workers to try out both the four-day week and flexible daily starting and quitting times over a three-year period. If the experiment works, the scheduling options could be offered to all of the government's 2.8 million employes. The bill's chances for passage are considered good.

A sizable number of firms—perhaps 10,000 in all—have adopted the four-day week hoping that it would reduce absenteeism, boost productivity and improve employe morale. Interest in the short week was high in the early 1970s, but lagged during the 1974-75 recession. Now it is reviving again.

"I pretty well think the idea is here to stay," says Kenneth E. Wheeler, a Lowell, Mass., management consultant who advises companies on rearranged workweeks. Mr. Wheeler says his firm has been contacted by "a lot of companies," including several Fortune 500 concerns.

He and other experts foresee many social consequences as the four-day week or similiar reshufflings in standard work time come into vogue. Everything from consumer spending habits to school hours and family relationships could be affected.

For example, people may decide to live in barracks-like dwellings in the city during the week, commuting on weekends to their distant "real" homes near, say, a favorite fishing hole. "You might get some very interesting patterns," says John D. Owen, professor of economics at Wayne State University in Detroit. "The second-home movement would get a tremendous boost from the four-day workweek," he says.

Getting away for the weekend—and going farther away—will become more common. Longer weekends will "produce an even greater exodus from urban places into outdoor settings," taxing the resources of already overburdened national parks and forests, says Tony A. Mobley, dean of Indiana University's school of health, public education and recreation. He also thinks that such recreational facilities as private campgrounds and amusement parks will burgeon.

With fewer or rearranged working hours, men will be at home more. Their presence may strengthen solid marriages and weaken troubled ones, authorities say. Men with working wives may assume more parenting and household-maintenance chores.

Economists think that moonlighting will increase to perhaps double its current rate. Government figures place the incidence of moonlighting at 5% now, but some experts say the real figure probably is much higher. Many wage earners will need a second job to pay for expensive recreational pursuits, such as owning a boat or traveling abroad. "How do you afford the leisure time? I think that is a matter of concern to all jobholders," says Frank H. Cassell, professor of industrial relations at Northwestern University's graduate school of management.

The demand for extra income is likely to be especially acute among young blue-collar workers who, like the Hurlburts, are in their late twenties. Younger employes, lacking seniority and purchasing power, are "still trying to make it," observes Brian E. Moore, associate professor of management at the University of Texas's school of business.

The dual pattern of more blue-collar moonlighting and more leisure for executives and professionals comes across strongly in closer examinations of how the four-day week has changed the lives of the Sheas and the Hurlburts.

Terry Shea didn't know that USAA was on an unusual schedule when he applied. But he soon felt the effects of working a four-day, 40-hour week (with a half-hour off for lunch), an arrangement most companies on short weeks use.

The 10-hour day was two hours longer than he was used to, so he found himself worn out by the end of the day. He began drinking lots of water to stay awake until quitting time (he dislikes coffee), gave up serving on church committees that met weekday evenings and started going to bed at 10 o'clock.

Another disadvantage is that like many managers on a four-day week, Mr. Shea doesn't get to take full advantage of long weekends. One or two Fridays a month, the 35-year-old executive is at his desk for a half-day. "You don't work by the clock if you're in management," explains Mr. Shea, a large, square-jawed man who earns more than $30,000 a year. Freed of jangling phones, demanding subordinates and long meetings, he uses these Friday mornings to write reports.

On the plus side, Fridays off have given the Sheas their first opportunity to be alone since their children were born. One recent Friday, Mr. Shea left his modern, sprawling office building around 1 p.m. and met his wife for a leisurely lunch and an afternoon of shopping at a suburban mall. (Seven-year-old Tim was in school, and Mrs. Shea dropped off four-year-old Kevin at a day-care center.)

While these excursions mean spending more money, they're also helping to strengthen the Sheas' marriage. "I probably know her a little better as a person," Mr. Shea says. "It's easy to regard your wife only as a mother and housekeeper."

Mr. Shea's sons reap the benefits of his extra time off as well. Frequently, Mr. Shea spends Fridays mowing the lawn, running errands and fixing up his house. (He built a sidewalk recently and is considering constructing a waterfall in his backyard.) This frees him on Saturday to coach Tim's football team or to draw posters with Kevin. "I get to play with my Dad more," Tim says with a grin.

The Shea family has taken five weekend trips in the year and a half they have been in Texas, driving to Mexico, Dallas and the Gulf Coast. They never took any short trips when they lived in Bloomington, Ill., where Mr. Shea worked for State

Farm Mutual Automobile Insurance Co. A weekend in the mountains near El Paso is being planned. "That's something you really couldn't do if you just had Saturday and Sunday," Mr. Shea observes. El Paso is 600 miles from San Antonio.

Terry Shea finds that the longer weekend means he's more rested and relaxed on Monday mornings. He hasn't missed a day of work since joining USAA, although this may be attributable as much to the mild Texas climate as to the four-day week.

Still, Mr. Shea remembers that at State Farm, he used to stay home several days a year because he was feeling lethargic or depressed about his job. When such feelings occur now, he can hold out "because I know that Friday is coming," he says. "Before, I couldn't hold out until Saturday."

Exhaustion and lethargy are bigger problems for blue-collar employes on four-day-week routines. Compared to management or clerical types, they often hold more physically taxing jobs, and their work environment is not as pleasant. Certainly this is true for Armour & Co. workers Cindee and Ralph Hurlburt.

Nearly every work day, Ralph Hurlburt shovels five tons of ground beef from a grinding machine to a metal hopper. He earns $4.06 an hour, tossing meat from 6:30 a.m. to 5 p.m., with a 30-minute lunch break. Even though Mr. Hurlburt used to work a seven-day week as a farm manager, he says that at Armour, he's "ready to drop by the end of the day." He also has developed an arm injury from the strain.

Cindee Hurlburt's $3.73-an-hour job is less strenuous but equally boring. The easy-going, soft-spoken woman usually stands for an entire 10-hour shift, fingering pieces of cooked chicken to see if the bones have been entirely removed.

Her tasks vary on some days. On a recent afternoon in the noisy, chilly plant (where the temperature hovers around 50 degrees), Mrs. Hurlburt carries 15-pound trays laden with wrapped ham sandwiches over to shipping cartons and then loads them. Closing time approaches; she pauses to flex her shoulder and complain, "Oooh, my whole side aches."

Some of her co-workers, mostly middle-aged women,

grumble that if their union asked them, they would vote to abolish the four-day week. The 140 members of the Teamsters local originally approved the shorter week in 1971. But Mrs. Hurlburt doesn't mind the long hours. "If I have to work, I want to get it all done in four days," she says.

More important, the compressed work-week permits the couple to raise and train quarter horses on their five-acre farm. It's an expensive hobby that they hope to turn into a full-time occupation someday. Feeding, grooming and exercising their six horses take up nearly all their spare time and cash.

On weekday evenings, Mr. Hurlburt does chores in the two barns while his wife prepares dinner and helps their seven-year-old son, Robbi, with his homework. Robbi is in bed by 7 o'clock, and his parents usually fall asleep an hour later. "We don't have enough time to argue with each other," Mr. Hurlburt says.

Between January and October, the Hurlburts spend numerous weekends displaying their animals at shows in Minnesota, Iowa and Wisconsin. They went away seven times for the entire three-day weekend during the summer of 1976, but usually limit their trips to two days during the school year. Their regular attendance at such shows, where they compete against full-time trainers, is helping to build their stable's reputation.

Armour laid them off for 18 months between the fall of 1974 and the spring of 1976. (Mr. Hurlburt had previously worked there for one month and Mrs. Hurlburt for four years.) When they were called back, she was employed as a store clerk and he as a truck driver. At the time, they considered giving up the food-plant jobs—not only because of the fatigue, but also because they feared future layoffs.

Then they realized that the four-day schedule would help them move closer to their dream of a horse-training business. The rearranged hours represent something else that's just as important to them: personal independence, or "more of your own time," as Mr. Hurlburt puts it. His wife adds: "You feel freer when you don't have to go out and work at a job on Fridays."

The Four-Day Week: "One Big Happy Family"

As a company that operates a small, nonunionized manufacturing plant in a tight labor market, C. A. Norgren Co. is nothing if not pragmatic. To recruit skilled workers away from its unionized competition, it has had to offer special benefits and an especially pleasant work environment.

"We try to be one big happy family," says C. Neil Norgren, president of the maker of accessory equipment for pneumatic machinery.

Norgren was among the first companies to institute an employe profit-sharing plan. Its plant, situated at the base of the Rockies in the affluent Denver suburb of Littleton, Colo., bears little resemblance to the grimy factories in the industrialized East and Midwest: A flock of Canadian geese inhabits the landscaped grounds, and floor-to-ceiling windows open onto dramatic mountain vistas. The top brass maintain friendly, informal relations with the workers; once a year they even take their turn dishing out food in the employe cafeteria.

Thus, it came as no real surprise in 1970 when Norgren became one of the first companies in the U.S. to schedule most of its 700 employes on a four-day workweek. Though Norgren had special reasons for moving early to adopt the innovative work schedule, the benefits and headaches it encountered in making the changeover are now being shared by an increasing number of U.S. concerns.

Some 10,000 companies nationwide are operating on the four-day week or some other form of revised scheduling, according to Riva Poor, a Cambridge, Mass., management consultant who advises companies on such matters. They range in size from Pacific Southwest Airlines in California and Equitable Life Assurance Society of the U.S. in New York to a 20-employe leather-crafts company in upstate New York. While these companies are only a fraction of the employers in the U.S., the number represents a big increase over the estimated 3,000 firms that used the four-day week in 1973 and the fewer than 100 that did so in 1970.

"The four-day week is a growing phenomenon," says James A. Wilson, professor of business adminstration at the University of Pittsburgh. "I think we'll see many conversions to the four-day week within the next 10 years."

In the early 1970s, the impetus for switching to the four-day week came mainly from companies who saw it as a way to reduce absenteeism and turnover, attract employes in tight labor markets and improve efficiency. Typically, companies switched from five eight-hour days a week to four 10-hour days.

Recently, however, the United Auto Workers union has been pressing to make a four-day, 32-hour week an industry standard. Its reasons are twofold: to increase leisure time for union members who have jobs and to create new jobs for members who are out of work. Indeed, if there were no operating efficiencies generated by a changeover, the auto industry would need 25% more employes working 32 hours a week to do the amount of work presently being done by the 40-hour-a-week work force.

"What the big unions are pushing for today is work-sharing," Prof. Wilson says. "It's an effort to create more jobs in this time of high unemployment."

A retrospective look at Norgren's decision to switch to the four-day week reveals that it was motivated both by a concern for efficiency and the management's desire to "spread work around" in a recessionary economy.

In early 1970, Norgren was anticipating a downturn in business as a result of the impending recession. Moving from a five-day, 40-hour week to a four-day, 37-hour week "was a natural way to reduce total hours worked without laying off any employes," says Robert Felt, senior vice president for finance. After some grumbling, employes agreed to accept the new fringe benefit (they continued to get paid for 40 hours' work) rather than a pay increase. "We didn't have much of a choice, but everything worked out well," one plant supervisor says.

Besides generating loads of favorable publicity for the company, the popular new schedule became an effective weapon in Norgren's sucessful battles against organizing drives by national unions, including the UAW.

It also helped the company to compete for labor against such nearby unionized concerns as Gates Rubber Co. and Samsonite Corp. "We wanted the same skilled people—tool and die makers, machinists and such—but we just couldn't match the pay increases the big companies were giving," Mr. Felt recalls.

The idea of moving to a four-day week originated with Mr. Norgren, whose late father founded the company in 1926. (The firm was sold by the Norgren family for more than $13 million in 1973 to Great Britain's Imperial Metal Industries Ltd., but Mr. Norgren still serves as chief executive.) "I honestly don't remember where I got the idea," Mr. Norgren says, but after reading Riva Poor's book, "Four Days, Forty Hours," he appointed a task force to study the idea, and if possible put it to work at Norgren.

"We worried about all sorts of things," he recalls. The key goal, he says, was to maintain productivity levels and, "with luck," improve them. "We worried about employe fatigue, made models of all kinds of scheduling and wondered how customers would react. We also worried about the social impact on workers with families."

In August 1970, five months after the study began and after consultations with employes, a six-month trial of the plan began. Paid holidays were reduced to five a year from eight, the number of breaks and their length were cut, and the new schedule went into effect.

That schedule, concedes John Karpan, vice president for industrial relations, is "incredibly complex." Most office employes and about half of the factory workers were put on the standard day shift, which runs from 7 a.m. to 5 p.m., Monday through Thursday, with a half-hour off for lunch. The standard night shift, also Monday through Thursday, goes from 5 p.m. to 3 a.m., with a half-hour for lunch. On Thursday, the work day is reduced by an hour for day-shifters and by two hours for night workers.

Because part of the reason for the changeover was to reduce production during the 1970 recession, the factory remained closed Friday through Sunday except to fill emergency orders. But when orders picked up, additional day and night shifts were added on Wednesday through Saturday. And the hundred or so employes in the capital-intensive casting and plastic molding operations went on three-day-a-week, 12-hour shifts that enabled them to operate equipment around the clock six days a week.

Despite the upheaval, workers responded favorably. "It's noisy, boring work," says a factory worker over the din in Norgren's 139,000-square-foot plant. "Once you're here, you may as well keep going an extra couple of hours and get a three-day weekend." A company study found that the only employes who didn't like the new schedule were working mothers who couldn't see their children off to school because of the early starting hours.

Some companies whose workers are on a four-day week have foremen and supervisors work five-day shifts, to help insure continuity in the production process. At Norgren, however, everyone works four days. With different shifts, managers would resent the workers' long weekends, Mr. Karpan explains.

The changeover at Norgren resulted in some initial loss of productivity. "It was pretty disorganized with people not used to the schedule," says George Loury, vice president for production. But in about two months, when the schedule became routine, productivity per hour returned to normal. Eventually, it even improved because of operating efficiencies such as shorter breaks and fewer cleanup and start-up periods.

There were some snafus, of course. Customer service suffered at first because order takers who were on duty Fridays weren't around on Mondays to follow through on orders. "We were dropping the ball too many times," says Phillip Thompson, vice president for marketing. The solution: Order takers were scheduled Tuesday through Friday one week and Monday through Thursday the next. This assured continuity, and gave the workers alternating two-day and four-day weekends.

Also, with the shipping department closed on Fridays, some customers complained about delays in their shipments. "We corrected that quickly," Mr. Thompson says, by reassigning people on Fridays. He notes that Norgren's air filters, regulators, lubricators and valves are crucial equipment in many factories where air-powered tools are used. (Norgren's products also go into air-powered wrenches used at gas stations, and into dentists' high-speed drills.)

But for the most part, the new schedule had its desired effect. Costly employe turnover dropped to 16% annually— "about a third of the normal rate in our business," Mr. Karpan says. In addition, he says the company has found recruiting, especially for skilled craftsmen, a lot easier. Indeed, Norgren received over 2,100 unsolicited job applications the first week after the changeover. And absenteeism fell to 4.1% last year from about 7% before the change. "There's less malingering in general," Mr. Karpan concludes.

The fear the workers would be unduly tired from the long hours proved unfounded. "Oh, there was some complaining at first," Mr. Loury says. "But we've measured their efficiency and it holds up pretty well over the course of the shift." He adds that Norgren hasn't seen an increase in its accident rate, "and that's the first place fatigue would have shown up."

Finally, the four-day week served the company well in its fight against unionization. The International Association of Machinists "has been trying to organize us since 1946," says Mr. Norgren, whose father was known locally as an ardent right-to-work advocate. Since 1970, the United Rubber Workers and the UAW have also tried to organize the plant. All include the popularity of the four-day week among reasons for their failure.

"I helped handbill the gates of the plant there," says Richard Beasley, a UAW organizer. "The guys were worried that if they got a union in, they'd lose the four-day week."

The four-day week may not be for everyone, but consultant Riva Poor says many companies can benefit by juggling schedules. Specifically, she cites manufacturers in tight labor markets and those that can't afford to expand downtown production facilities because real-estate values are so high. The latter, she says, can enhance production simply by rearranging scheduling. Other potential beneficiaries include employers in service fields that have peaks and valleys in demand during the workday, such as police and fire departments and hospitals.

And Mr. Norgren, pointing to the Rocky Mountain view from his office, thinks a pleasant locale is necessary, so that employes can take advantage of the added day of leisure. "People who move to Colorado want to enjoy it here," he says. "That makes the extra day off so much more important."

The Early Bird

In his Air Force days in Nome, Alaska, John Kern came close to winning a sleeping contest. He spent 17 hours in the sack but finished second to another airman who put in 19 hours conked out in the land of the midnight sun.

Today, Mr. Kern, now personnel manager at Prudential Insurance Co. of America's Western office in Los Angeles, finds it impossible to sleep past 6 a.m. even on work-free weekends.

This is not because he is "slept-out" nor because of any lingering effects of overindulgence in sleep during his youth—in fact, he spent his childhood summers in Nebraska, where his grandmother would roust him out of bed at 4 a.m. to milk the cows—but because of habit patterns established during the week, when he gets to work before daybreak.

Mr. Kern is up at 3:45 every morning. From his home in the Torrance section of Los Angeles, he drives to an all-night doughnut stand for a breakfast of black coffee. When he arrives at his office at 5:15, he is already one-up on nearly everybody else in town: He has beaten the legendary L.A. rush-hour traffic. By 6, he is on the phone with Prudential's Newark, N.J., headquarters. "There's a three-hour time difference, but the people there are still fresh at that time," he says. Thanks to his early start, Mr. Kern also finds that he doesn't need to take work home anymore because he finishes it at the office.

The alarm rings even earlier for Robert Hyland, CBS regional vice president in charge of radio station KMOX in St. Louis, who gets up at 2:15 in order to get to work at 3:30, fully five hours before his fellow executives. He says he prefers to start early "because I work more effectively in the morning and I like to have my evenings free for my family."

Benjamin Franklin, of course, said it all long ago with his dictum: "He that riseth late must trot all day" as well as "Early to bed and early to rise, etc., etc., etc." But a surprising number of executives are discovering fresh reasons to join the dawn patrol. Not only do they beat the commuter rush, but also they can get more work done in the hours before the telephone starts to ring and the normal distractions of the day begin to crowd in on them.

One of the early birds is President Carter. Although he has no commuting problem and by comparison with Messrs. Kern and Hyland might even appear to be a slugabed, Mr. Carter gets up at 6:30 and starts work at 7, an hour before his staff is officially supposed to report.

The hour between 7 and 8 is "his private time," a White House spokeswoman says. She says Mr. Carter uses the period to read four newspapers besides memos and other documents. When the President took office last January, he had to tell his eager staffers to leave him alone during this hour so he could read in peace.

Another early riser is Robert Abboud, chairman of First National Bank of Chicago and its parent, First Chicago Corp. He makes a travesty out of the phrase "bankers' hours." Rising a 5:15 at his farm in Barrington Hills, he is picked up at 6 by a chauffeured limousine. The next hour in the car is spent reading newspapers and reports and dictating memos to his secretary. Mr. Abboud explains that the hour in the car is the only time he can get a lot of reading and writing done.

"I'm the boss, so I am the center of attention at every meeting I attend, and it's very difficult to get away and do the studious kind of work I need to do," Mr. Abboud says. Three members of Mr. Abboud's staff are more affected by their boss's schedule than President Carter's White House aides are by his. They have to be in at 7 a.m. when he arrives.

J. Robert Harman, Jr., senior vice president in charge of executive recruitment for Booz, Allen & Hamilton, Inc., a Chicago-based management-consulting firm, says the majority of corporate chief executives he deals with get to work early. He contends that there is a "high correlation between executive success and early arrival at the office," and he says he uses arrival time as one criterion in judging an executive's qualifications.

Not all early risers are completely utilitarian about their work habits. Irving R. Burling, president and chief executive officer of Lutheran Mutual Life Insurance Co. in Waverly, Iowa, doesn't have to fight traffic, and the business atmosphere of Waverly (pop. 7,205) is a good deal less pressured than, say, midtown Manhattan. But Mr. Burling is up every workday at 5:30 a.m. to read the Bible and other religious material. At 6:30, he jogs and jumps rope, and at 7 he's in the office, reading memos and insurance-related articles.

Mr. Burling's wife benefits from his early-morning regimen because he always serves her breakfast in bed, often returning from the office to perform this service.

Conrad Balentine, president and chief executive officer of Franklin Electric Co., in Bluffton, Ind., gets to work before any of his office cohorts so he can find out what's really going on in his manufacturing plant. "It often happens that a guy in the office will gloss over something that happened on the factory floor," he explains. So at 7 every workday Mr. Balentine walks through the plant talking with workers and their supervisors, 30 minutes to an hour before his white-collar colleagues have arrived.

"It's surprising how much information there is on the factory floor," he says. "I don't have to rely on information that has been filtered three or four times."

Early rising permits a few especially industrious executives to carry on two careers at the same time. The late Douglas Southall Freeman, editor of the Richmond (Va.) News Leader for 34 years, rose at 4 every morning to write biographies and histories. Over the years he turned out 17 volumes, including a four-volume Pulitzer Prize-winning biography of Robert E. Lee, three volumes on "Lee's Lieutenants" and a seven-volume biography of George Washington.

Early workers generally explain their proclivity by saying that they are "morning people" or that they like to be alone for a while each day. But not everyone can get up with the birds and do effective work. John Palmer, professor of physiology at the University of Massachusetts, says the population can be divided roughly into early birds and night owls, with some variations in between.

He says a person's efficiency tends to follow his daily curve of body temperature—low early in the day and peaking in late or mid-afternoon. "Early birds get warmer quicker and cool off earlier," he says. He also says early birds tend to be introverted, while night owls are more likely to be gregarious extroverts.

As for himself, Prof. Palmer says he "tends to be terribly efficient" at 5 a.m. when he writes books and articles at home. He gets to his office at 7, two hours earlier than he has to.

There are some indications that the standard American office schedule begins a little too late. According to Bernard Keppler, president of Interflex, Inc., a New York firm that helps companies design flexible work schedules, about two-thirds of employes who work under "Flexitime" choose to start work earlier rather than later. He says they do it because they want a couple of hours in the afternoon to shop or work around their homes, as well as to avoid the peak commuting hours. It's mainly the younger employes who tend to choose a later starting time, usually because of mid-week evening social engagements, he says.

Even confirmed early birds aren't always too alert when the alarm goes off. Take the case of Jay H. Tolson, chairman and president of Fischer & Porter Co. which makes process control systems in Hersham, Pa. His normal wake-up time is 4:30, and he gets to work by 5:30. One day, however, his two-year-old daughter was playing with his clock and set the alarm back two hours. Mr. Tolson awoke as usual in the dark, drove to work oblivious of the hour and didn't recognize his mistake until he looked at the office clock.

Just the same, Mr. Tolson says, "The world is a very pleasant place in the morning even if most people think it's still the middle of the night."

Performance Pays

The nation's employers are searching for ways to restore the golden allure of the merit pay raise.

Its attraction was dimmed in recent years, they complain, when companies felt compelled to protect the incomes of all employes against the surging cost of living. White-collar employes, outstanding or average, came to expect a sizable automatic pay boost each year; little was left in company budgets for special raises to reward top performers.

Now, employers are regaining their determination to tie pay to performance. More managements are "focusing attention on allocating salary dollars where they can do the most good," says James A. Kuhns, manager of executive compensation for the Deerfield, Ill., consulting firm of Hewitt Associates.

If these efforts succeed, some employes will no longer get merit raises. But those who do may win fatter increases than ever before.

Some samples of current approaches:

Many employers are measuring employe performance more realistically. The Continental Group, the big container maker, has abandoned a merit-pay system that consisted of "a write-up from the manager stating why an increase was justified," says Charles Gadsden, a vice president. Instead, evaluators use standard benchmarks for judging quality and quantity of performance as well as special criteria significant for a particular job; a salesman, for example, may be rewarded for opening an important new account or selling more products with high profit margins. Under the new system, marginal-to-unsatisfactory performers won't get any merit raises while "truly outstanding" workers may earn a 12% pay boost.

Performance-related goals are being set in advance for many jobs. A company intent on improving product quality may tell a foreman that half of any year-end bonus will be based on his department's quality-control record. Some corporations, such as General Electric Co., establish goals for hiring and promoting minorities and women; they appraise managers partly on their success in meeting these objectives.

At International Multifoods Corp. in Minneapolis, employes and managers mutually set goals each year; the final results help determine merit pay raises. Without such a system, says Ron Pilenzo, the company's director of corporate compensation and management development, "no supervisor can tell Suzie Smith or Pete Jones why one employe got more money than another."

Some companies are instituting onetime bonuses for superior performance, without building those sums permanently into their payrolls. Pitney-Bowes, for example, the business-equipment maker, established what Raymond Sasso, compensation manager, calls "an extra carrot for truly outstanding performance." About 2,000 employes are eligible for once-a-year lump-sum payments ranging up to 15% of base pay.

About 140 Pitney-Bowes employes have received bonuses so far. The largest was $5,160 for a middle manager; the smallest, $2,715 for a technician. Mr. Sasso says the plan gives employes an extra incentive without burdening the company with a permanently higher salary commitment. "Yesterday's performance shouldn't have to be paid for on a continuing basis," he reasons.

A number of employers are giving their merit pay plans more punch by reviewing salaries more frequently. Sibson Co., a New York City consulting firm, surveyed 250 companies in the fall of 1976 and found 21% considered granting merit raises more often than once a year; a year earlier, only 11% of the companies were reviewing pay that frequently.

Such changes reflect growing management concern that the established "merit pay" allotments in company budgets haven't proved to be the reward systems they imagined. "Top executives have begun to question the whole system of pay for performance," says David A. Weeks of the Conference Board, an economic research organization based in New York. Executives are worried whether they are getting "any increase in productivity for the rapid increase in pay," he says.

Mr. Weeks recently surveyed pay practices of 493 companies; one-third had fewer than 1,000 employes and 51 had 25,-000 or more employes. He found that more than half of the companies have revised their employe evaluation systems in recent years. Many others are setting up new appraisal systems. Some are experimenting with new ways to reward productive workers, and to identify and motivate poor producers.

The task is challenging. Effective merit pay plans are difficult to install for several reasons: Supervisors often are reluctant to issue harsh judgments that bar underlings from getting raises. Job performance can be tricky to measure. Growing use of cost-of-living adjustments in union contracts puts pressure on the managers to give unorganized white-collar workers similar across-the-board raises, and thus funds available for merit increases are reduced.

And there's evidence that typical merit pay plans seldom truly reward superior performance. At many companies "you can explain maybe 95% of the variation in pay by using factors such as the level of the employe in the organization, the number of employes supervised, or the length of service," says Graef Crystal, vice president of Towers, Perrin, Forster & Crosby, a New York management consulting firm. "Not one of the factors is the employe's performance."

Executives have been distressed to discover that employes' immediate supervisors often block efforts to tie pay to performance. "Nobody wants to be the bad guy that sits across the table from an employe and says, based on their level of performance, they aren't entitled to a merit raise," declares Mr. Pilenzo of International Multifoods.

Mr. Weeks of the Conference Board, in his survey, found such reluctance widespread. Pay and performance "will never truly be linked when the consequence of an honest low rating

must be firing or retirement," he says. "Unless a manager per-
ceives himself to be really free to pick and choose among a variety of rewards, punishments and remedies to follow up his performance rating, he will continue to lump everyone under the
protection of an average-to-above-average rating." The result,
he warns, is "declining white-collar productivity and homoge-
neous salary treatment."

In the conventional approach, says Frederick A. Teague,
vice president of the Booz, Allen & Hamilton Inc. consulting
firm, companies have "tried to pay everybody enough to keep
most of them happy," and to lose "only the barest minimum" of
employes through turnover. In the early 1960s, when consumer
prices were rising less than 2% a year, a company could budget
5% or 6% of payroll for salary increases, and "give a few people
8% and they'd be fairly happy," he says.

But when the cost of living began climbing 9% or 10% a
year, those arrangements turned sour. "You sat down and told
somebody they were getting a merit increase, and they sort of
chuckled under their breath," Mr. Teague says. "The difference
between less-than-satisfactory and very good performance was
often a matter of two or three percentage points in pay." If employers succeed in revamping merit pay, that gap will widen, he
predicts.

One reason for possible success, Mr. Teague finds, is that
"companies are trying to make a far more dramatic distinction"
between levels of job performance—"not just between the stars
and the bums but between the good performers and the less-
than-satisfactory performers." He calls it a "much more offensive pay strategy."

However, the old report-card-like annual reviews, ranking
such considerations as absenteeism, personality, judgment and
quantity of work, are out. "We're trying to get away from that
whole concept," says George Sherman, vice president for industrial relations and personnel administration for Midland-Ross
Corp., the Cleveland maker of industrial equipment. "It either
becomes a valentine from the supervisor or widens any breach
that may exist between the supervisor and the employe."

Instead of "putting on the judicial robes," Midland-Ross supervisors are encouraged to sit down each year with employes and "see what we can do to find out what it takes for them to progress," Mr. Sherman says. If an employe isn't performing, he adds, the supervisor tries to determine whether the reason is "something we failed to do, or whether it is the employe's own doing."

How will employes respond to the new merit-pay approaches? Will the dangling of a plumper carrot for top performers really induce better work? At most companies, it's too early to say. But Mr. Pilenzo claims that International Multifoods employes "have responded well" to the company's new system of setting performance goals. He says: "There is a growing feeling that real performance will really be recognized differently from average performance. People confident in their own abilities welcome that kind of situation."

Whatever the benefits to be gained, many employers will face persistent obstacles in trying to install effective merit-pay systems.

For one thing, across-the-board pay increases for white-collar workers are likely to continue, especially at companies with organized blue-collar employes. Negotiated pay raises in union contracts are still putting pressure on companies to grant similar increases to the rest of the work force. In 1976, for example, Firestone Tire & Rubber Co., while negotiating a contract with the United Rubber Workers, announced plans to begin paying cost-of-living adjustments to salaried employes; the adjustments are similar to provisions won by the union.

Moreover, plenty of skeptics still doubt employers will limit merit pay raises to the truly deserving. Mr. Crystal of Towers Perrin believes that companies dislike dealing with disgruntled employes who have been told they won't get a raise—a decision that, in inflationary times, amounts to a pay cut. He says executives in such situations often say, "Let me quit or fire me, but I don't want to work for you at a reduced salary. If I take a cut, you've cut my bargaining potential with another employer."

Women on the Move

Doris Etelson, 48, a vice president of Howard Johnson Co., lives and works in the Boston area. Her husband, Robert, owns an air-freight company in Newark, N.J. He lives in Pomona, N.Y.

Every weekend, Mrs. Etelson drives or hops on a plane to visit Mr. Etelson in Pomona. Twice a week, her husband takes a plane to spend the night in Boston. Two days a week they are apart.

This is the arrangement that the Etelsons have been living with since Mrs. Etelson was named as the big food and motor-lodge company's first woman vice president a year ago. It is also the price that the Etelsons have to pay to maintain two successful careers.

They have been able to keep to this tiring, expensive schedule because their children are in their twenties and are no longer at home, because Mr. Etelson has encouraged his wife's career, and because they are a highly affluent couple. For many other, younger career women with children or with husbands settled in their own careers, a transfer often is impossible. The result, many women fear, is that talented female executives are likely to see their careers stagnate.

Although the transfer as a route to corporate advancement is showing signs of declining, the fact remains that for the highest-flying people in national companies, the transfer is a clear road to the top. But many companies concede they are loath to suggest a transfer to a married woman because of the fear of provoking a domestic crisis.

The problem of the transfer affects relatively few women at

present. But it clearly is a dilemma that more and more women are going to have to face as the women who were hired in the early 1970s to meet affirmative-action goals gain the experience needed for promotion.

Women have a deep apprehension about moving, observes Janet Jones, chairman of Management Woman Inc., a New York firm that places middle and upper-level women executives. Most, she claims, aim for those promotions that don't involve moving, or they choose fields or companies less likely to require mobility. Even when asked, fewer women than men accept a move, she says. (However, there also is a clear trend for men with working wives to turn down transfers.)

Indeed, only 5% to 10% of the 100,000 employes who were transferred by the 600 largest U.S. companies in 1976 were women, estimates Merrill Lynch Relocation Management Inc., a subsidiary of the holding company for the big brokerage concern. Perhaps half of these women had children, many of them probably school-aged, Weston Edwards, chief executive of the relocation-consulting firm, estimates. Many of the women, he says, were divorced.

Mr. Edwards notes that employes most likely to be considered for transfer earn $20,000 a year or more. The Census Bureau says that in 1976, only 328,000 women, or 1.1% of the 29.8 million women working full time, earned $20,000 or over.

But even many of those women, whose earnings and training clearly qualify them for the promotion that involves a transfer, are blocked by their husbands' careers. An obvious reason why many husbands are reluctant to follow their wives to new jobs is the fear that their own careers will suffer or that they simply will be unable to get another job. Long-distance commuting is possible, but even then, if there are children at home, the problems are legion.

Thus, the "critical issue" for working couples is how to make their "shared vision of equality" a reality, says William Chafe, associate professor of history at Duke University and a student of the American family.

Certainly, he says, couples who want to have both dual ca-

reers and children will never make it to the top of their professions. "It's tough enough to do it in the first place, but it can
never be done in this situation," he says. Prof. Chafe says that
childless couples will have an easier time of it, but not without
sacrifices, such as weekend commuting if a transfer is crucial to
a career. "That can't last indefinitely, and it could cause a split
in the marriage," he says.

Prof. Chafe believes that only a "dramatic change" in business policy will ease the transfer dilemma for working couples.
Such a change, he says, would include flexible working hours,
corporate day-care centers, and opportunities for shared positions to accommodate working parents. "We're talking about a
social revolution," he says.

A few couples, however, do combine long-distance commuting and children. An example is Sharon Kirkman Donegan,
36, vice president of Boyle/Kirkman Associates Inc., a New
York management-consulting firm. In 1975 she married L. E.
Donegan Jr., president of Keydata Corp. of Boston and the
father of a 13-year-old son, Matthew. She says that when they
married "there was never a question" about giving up her New
York job.

But, she says, keeping a 10-room Boston town house and a
New York apartment, flying home on weekends and providing
for household help and part-time child care "costs all you make.
The whole arrangement works because of an incredible amount
of organization and planning, energy and stamina."

Some women complain that they never get the chance to
try to work out the intricacies of a transfer because their companies simply refuse to transfer them in the belief it would disrupt
their families. Mrs. Kirkman Donegan believes that corporate
managers subconsciously discriminate against women in choos-
ing which employes to transfer. Managers, she says, "internalize
and personalize" their decisions by relating them to how they
would feel if their own wives were asked to move. "It's a sub-
conscious, paternalistic attitude, a secret mental process," she
says.

But Joan F. Showalter, a personnel vice president of CBS

Inc., New York, disagrees. As women advance they have the same "option for growth" as men, she says. "We're sophisticated here. There's no discrimination relative to personal considerations." And James M. Shipton, senior vice president of First Chicago Corp. and its subsidiary, First National Bank of Chicago, says, "I've never heard a manager say he wouldn't consider a woman because he wouldn't want his own wife to go."

To counter any hint of prejudice, General Motors Corp. in 1973 put promotions in each plant or division in the hands of a committee of line supervisors instead of one manager. "We still have our share of chauvinists," but now they "only have one vote each," says Gerald Kahler, director of human resources planning for GM. As a result, the number of women at GM who are being asked to move "has increased dramatically," and if a husband and wife work for the company, both are considered for transfer together, says Mr. Kahler.

But at some companies, women are considered a "transfer risk." Because of the large investment involved in training and then transferring an employe, these companies want to guard against the possibility of a woman leaving to get married or to have children. "It's not that we mistrust them, it's that we don't know," says Owen Johnson, a personnel vice president at Continental Illinois National Bank & Trust Co. of Chicago. "The commitment she makes at 25 isn't what it might be in her 30s; it's iffy," he says.

Even so, says Mr. Johnson, Continental Illinois is "taking the risk" by training women for overseas jobs. To date, the bank has sent seven of its women employes overseas, six of them single (the husband of the seventh was a student). If a married woman indicates she can take a transfer, she and her husband meet with supervisors to discuss any problems connected with a move.

The bank, like a growing number of other employers, will help in finding a new job for a husband in the case of his wife's transfer. But often a long-distance commute is the only answer. Take, for example, American Airlines employe Adrianna Boylan, 31, who has risen to manager of advertising and program development from a part-time clerk. Since 1971, she has worked in New York and has visited her husband in Ann Arbor, Mich., on weekends. Her husband, Roger, 37, owns a tennis club.

Mrs. Boylan concedes that weekend commuting "is a strain." She said, "There are times during the week when I am lonely, and at times my husband has said, 'I wish you'd come back.' "

But the Boylans' long-distance marriage could change before long. Mrs. Boylan is hoping for a promotion that will involve a transfer. At that time, her husband says he plans to sell his club and to join his wife. They also plan to have children.

But for the Etelsons, the commuting couple who opened this story, living and working in different cities seems to have produced few anxieties. Mr. Etelson says he is enthusiastic about the arrangement. The one-hour plane flight to Boston, he says, is a lot less taxing than the 70-minute drive from his office to his home.

More than that, he says, the arrangement has opened "a whole new vista" for both of them after years of suburban living. He says he enjoys Boston and has fun "doing local restaurants and visiting the shops." Nor, he says, is he troubled by having an executive for a wife. "I'm satisfied with my work," he says. "I built my company and I'm proud of it. Whatever success she gets, she's entitled to."

Ironically, a person who is opposed to the Etelsons living apart is Howard B. Johnson, chairman and president of the company. The commuting arrangement, he says, "is a risk" for Doris Etelson because it might put "stress on her happy home" or disrupt her discipline on the job. "I'm not happy with it, but if she's willing to make the sacrifice, I'm willing to take the chance. I may not like the idea, but I'm crazy about Doris," he says.

The Etelsons were married in 1950, and for the first years of their marriage, Mrs. Etelson operated a cafeteria in an industrial plant. She stopped working between 1958 and 1961 to care for her two young daughters.

In 1961, she joined Howard Johnson as a food supervisor

for seven restaurants. From the beginning, she says, she had the clearcut goal of going "as far as I could in management and to take it step by step." She became head supervisor for 25 restaurants in 1965, then area manager for seven restaurants in 1968, a "significant step" that "didn't come easily," she says.

She was named staff assistant to a divisional manager in 1970 and advanced to director of administration in 1972. At the same time, she was working toward her bachelor's degree in economics at an extension of the State University of New York. (She graduated in 1974 and now is working on her master's degree in business administration.)

Mrs. Etelson says she realized that her next move up would depend on her willingness to go where an executive job opened up. But because her husband had his business in New Jersey, she couldn't go just anywhere. "It was limiting me, and therefore my value to the company," she says.

She confronted the problem by applying for top corporate spots in New York, Wilmington, Del., and Boston. The jobs would have involved running many restaurants, requiring long and erratic hours. But Mr. Johnson refused to hear of Mrs. Etelson taking on such a job if she would have to make a long-distance commute. "It wouldn't have been a happy ending for her or for the company. I wasn't going to contribute to anything that would make her home life unhappy," he says.

But Mrs. Etelson persisted, and in 1977 Mr. Johnson relented and offered her the newly created post of vice president of service standards. The job involves finding ways of upgrading the quality of customer service at Howard Johnson restaurants. It also carries profit-and-loss responsibility for the restaurants.

Mrs. Etelson says that she simply couldn't have considered her arrangement if her children had been below high-school age, nor could she have accepted without her husband's cooperation. But, she says, "he knew I had devoted time and effort to my career. After all, I have supported him in his business."

The Market For
Divorced Executives

The job would be hectic and the company chairman knew exactly whom he wanted to fill it. "Find me someone who is as unhappily married as I am, so he'll really devote himself to the task at hand," he told the executive recruiter.

Sure enough, the man who landed the $100,000-a-year East Coast job had a stable, but hopelessly dreary, marriage. He liked nothing more than to escape from his family by spending Sundays in the office, says Donald T. Johnson, chairman of Johnson-Smith Inc., the New York executive-search concern that handled the assignment.

As this unusual case suggests, the right family status can still be crucial in getting an executive job. But the happily married executive, who traditionally has enjoyed a hefty advantage in the job market, may be in for a surprise; his favored position isn't what is used to be. Board room prejudice against divorce is declining significantly, and for a growing number of jobs, many companies actually insist upon the unattached, executive recruiters say.

The mere growth of divorce has made it more acceptable in the executive suit. "These days, we couldn't be in business if we only dealt with married people," says New York recruiter William Battalia. At the same time, the divorced, the single and even the married but childless all benefit from the growing corporate complaint that families today resist transfers more than ever before. One corporate response is to resist families.

Take the big multinational corporation in a pleasant Midwestern city that couldn't fill a $50,000-a-year job. As soon as five very capable married candidates learned that the job involved a 40% chance of a transfer, possibly overseas, within 18 months, they "all crawled back into the woodwork," says George G. Atkeson, principal of Ward Howell Associates, executive recruiters retained to fill the job. "We then told the company we would like to concentrate on single and divorced people; as a group, they are much more willing to move than married people," Mr. Atkeson adds. A divorced man soon took the job.

Officially, companies tend to insist that marital status counts for nothing in hiring. Indeed, employment discrimination on the grounds of marital status is illegal in several states.

But talks with executive recruiters, who seek managers for companies on a confidential basis, reveal a great array of corporate strategies, policies, prejudices and quirks on the issue. Sometimes companies seek a married person, but shun a family. Sometimes they welcome a divorced executive, but shun a recently divorced executive.

A declining, but still huge, number of companies still seek the married executive whenever possible. Gerard R. Roche, president of recruiters Heidrick & Struggles, recalls the chairman of one of the nation's biggest companies who rejected a divorced candidate for the company presidency, explaining: "The man who has messed up his personal life is the man who will mess up my company."

Even if he is considered, the divorced jobseeker may be checked more carefully than he realizes for signs of "stability." William B. Arnold, a Denver recruiter who isn't unique in his procedures, says: "If a guy is divorced, sometimes I take him for a drink in a cocktail lounge to see if he can keep his hands off the waitresses."

But the broadest change in recent years is the increased willingness, even preference, to hire the unattached, personnel experts say. Roger Kenny, senior vice president of Spencer Stuart & Associates, recruiters, recalls an East Coast consumer-products company that was "so prejudiced against divorce five or six years ago we generally wouldn't even send them candidates who were divorced." Two years ago, in 1976, Spencer Stuart found the company a divorced executive whom it hired as president.

Sometimes companies even are willing to be a factor in the divorce. J. Gerald Simmons, president of Handy Associates, recruiters and consultants, cites a Darien, Conn., executive who received a job offer from a Midwestern company. The executive told the Midwestern company chairman that his wife would file for divorce if he took the job, but that he wanted it anyway. The chairman replied, "Go ahead, I don't care what you do on your own time—just raise our sales 30%." The executive got the divorce and took the job, Mr. Simmons says.

Statistics show the change too. William H. Clark Associates, a New York recruiting company, says 10% of the executives its clients hire now have been divorced, compared with "2% at most" in 1968. Paul R. Ray & Co., a Fort Worth search concern, says the proportion of divorced executives its clients hire has doubled in the last four years alone.

But single as well as divorced people increasingly are welcomed. In some Quaker Oats Co. sales-management jobs involving future transfers, a candidate's unattached status has been "a deciding factor" in his getting the job, says Paul R. Pearce, personnel vice president of the Chicago company's grocery-products group. "On average, single people are easier to move," he explains.

Increasingly, companies seek unattached executives simply to speed the recruiting process. Oliver & Rozner Associates, a New York search company, recalls seeking only single or divorced executives for a $38,000-a-year sales management job. The position could—and did—lead to two promotions and a $75,000 annual salary within three years. But it also involved constant travel and two relocations, and the company wanted the executive fast. Concentrating on unattached executives "enabled us to reach people who could make a professional decision without making a family decision too," says Burton L. Rozner, executive vice president of the recruiting concern.

Such family decisions are getting tougher, recruiters say.

"With at least 30% to 35% of the executives who receive offers and turn them down, family pressure is the reason," says Robert A. Staub, president of Staub, Warmbold & Associates, recruiters. He recalls an executive earning $75,000 a year who rejected a job paying $50,000 a year more because his 16-year-old son didn't want to leave his home and pals.

This family resistance to moves can create opportunities for the unattached executive. One married New Yorker rejected a $70,000-a-year job in the Southwest, partly because his wife resisted sacrificing her cultural activities in New York. Recruiter William H. Willis found a divorced man eager to fill the slot.

Mr. Simmons of Handy Associates says a Connecticut company seeking a woman attorney preferred a divorced or single candidate. It contended that a woman's career usually takes a second priority to her husband's, and that a married woman would be subject to her husband's transfer.

Numerous recruiters find the increasingly common dual-career couple is especially hard to transfer, R. J. Wytmar, a Chicago recruiter, recalls a Midwestern executive who rejected, after long talks, an offer to be president of a retail concern in another city at a 50% boost in pay. The basic problem was that his wife would have to surrender a nursing-management job she liked. "There's no doubt about it, this company would be much more amenable to hiring a divorced or single person in the future," Mr. Wytmar says.

Many companies long have sought unattached executives for overseas or heavy-travel jobs, but the practice is increasing, recruiters say. One reason is the rising cost of moving a family. Worry about disgruntled spouses is another, recruiters say.

The rising number of Middle Eastern assignments poses a special dilemma, companies find. While spouses often can't adjust to the environment, unmarried executives find their romantic life in the area can be as arid as the desert around them. To deal with the problem, some companies specify married people only, others demand singles only, and still others change their minds.

Mr. Roche of Heidrick & Struggles says one client has an

"ironclad" demand for married managers only in the Middle East. It found singles ended up chasing other executives' wives or "commandeering the company jet to go to Barcelona every weekend," Mr. Roche says.

Thomas C. Amory, president of William H. Clark Associates, recalls a company operating in Kuwait that originally figured executives without wives would soon leave and therefore shunned singles. But the wives who supposedly would keep the husbands happy soon started pressuring them to quit their jobs, the recruiting executive says. Now the company recruits only unattached executives for Kuwait, he says.

Simple marital status isn't the only family issue, however. One company filling a heavy-travel job didn't care if the candidate was married or not. But it excluded anybody with young children "because it felt that really does tie down a person," says Arthur Armitage, another Ward Howell principal. Mr. Rozner, the New York recruiter, says a Michigan client suggested saving time by avoiding executives with school-aged children. As soon as such candidates learned how bad the local schools were, they would reject the job, the company figured.

With divorced executives, timing may count more than the separation itself. "Often there are no negatives about divorce— as long as the divorce has been completed," says Carl W. Menk, president of Boyden Associates, recruiters. Such companies figure that a divorce in progress will drain the executive's effectiveness.

Mr. Atkeson of Ward Howell recalls one client, himself divorced, who rejected a job candidate with a divorce in progress. "Frankly, I was so useless to my company during my own divorce I'm sure he would be too," the client told Mr. Atkeson.

Companies that think nothing of one divorce often think long and hard about a record of two or three divorces, recruiters say. Gerald P. Kent, a personnel official at Western Union Corp., says divorce itself doesn't pose a problem, "but if the guy is shedding a wife once a year, you might get a little gun-shy."

There are still other variables. Recruiters say companies disagree on jobs that are traditionally thought to require a spouse. They say a growing number question the need for a mate. At PepsiCo Inc., marital status is never a hiring factor because the company finds it never makes a difference in actual job performance, regardless of the situation, says Edward Walsh, director of personnel. But many companies still insist that big jobs in small cities require a spouse to entertain and to serve as a community leader, recruiters say.

There is also a variable applied to singles. Even companies that actively seek young singles sometimes reject middle-aged "permanent" singles, recruiters say. Companies commonly wonder if they are homosexual. While they are more willing than in the past to hire homosexual professionals, companies generally try to avoid homosexual managers, recruiters add. Companies in glamour industries are sometimes exceptions, they add.

But even the middle-aged heterosexual executive who has never married often is shunned, recruiters say. Companies wonder if he is a "loner," if he is willing to take responsibility beyond himself and if he will fit into a corporate executive culture dominated by married people. "It's the idea that 'he's not like us,'" says Mr. Wytmar, the Chicago recruiter. He says a divorced executive often is far more welcome than a permanent single.

In corporate America, it's still "better to have loved and lost than never to have loved at all," he adds.

The Takeover Trauma

In January 1976, Microdot Inc. of Greenwich, Conn., agreed to be acquired by Northwest Industries Inc. rather than submit to an unwelcome takeover bid by General Cable Co. "If we had to be acquired," says Rudolph Eberstadt Jr., Microdot's president for more than 16 years, the Northwest executives "were the best people to go with."

And in the aftermath of the acquisition, Microdot in fact has been operating relatively smoothly. The company's divisions still continue to churn out fasteners—everything from nuts and bolts to complicated electrical connecting devices—and ingot molds. Nobody has been fired, and Northwest has made concerted efforts to help Microdot personnel adjust to being part of a huge conglomerate.

But despite such efforts, Mr. Eberstadt announced his resignation mid-way through 1977. The 53-year-old executive, who built a lackluster string of industrial businesses into a successful Fortune 500 company, says he "simply couldn't face being a division manager after years of running my own company." After Northwest took over, he adds, "I felt as if the things I did no longer had any impact."

Mr. Eberstadt's departure may be the biggest change at Microdot since its acquisition, but it is by no means the only one. And as the company struggles to adjust to its new status as a subsidiary, its problems are in many ways typical of those encountered by many companies that have suddenly become a subsidiary or division of someone else. However, many recently acquired companies go through much greater traumas than those at Microdot; often operations are drastically redirected, plants are closed down, hundreds or thousands of workers are laid off, and whole echelons of executives are dumped.

Such upheavals may be particularly likely if the acquisition results from a bitterly resisted tender offer for the target company's stock. Because tender offers evolve rapidly, managements usually have little chance of fending them off unless another suitor can be attracted quickly. And the aftermath of an unsuccessful fight to keep a company independent can be traumatic, especially for the chief executive of the besieged concern, says Robert F. Medina, chairman of Medina & Thompson, a firm of consulting psychologists that has worked with executives on both sides of tender-offer battles.

"During the fight, they may feel exhilarated," Mr. Medina says, "but afterward, when reality hits, they usually have a devil of a time adjusting."

Microdot's fight began in December 1975, when General Cable, also of Greenwich and a maker of wire and cable products, launched a surprise takeover bid: $17 a share in cash at a time when Microdot stock was selling for $11.75 a share. Mr. Eberstadt was determined to keep Microdot independent, and besides he was unimpressed with General Cable's operating record. So he replied with a vigorous defense, which included newspaper ads warning chief executives of other middle-tier companies that "they could be next." The public strategy even included an announcement of a shareholders' meeting to vote on a liquidation of the company.

Behind the scenes, Microdot had another strategy. It asked Goldman, Sachs & Co., the investment banking concern, to find a friendly suitor for it in case all else failed. Goldman Sachs came up with Northwest Industries, among others. Fearing that General Cable would succeed, Mr. Eberstadt reluctantly decided in late January 1976 to merge with the Chicago-based conglomerate.

Since Microdot became a Northwest subsidiary, only minor changes have been made in most of the lower-echelon offices. For example, a wall has been torn down in the headquarters building to make room for a few new office employes added because of the extra work involved in reporting to Northwest. And the switchboard operator works an hour longer because of the time difference between Connecticut and Chicago.

But in the executive suite, the changes are subtle but pervasive. "Nothing has changed, and yet everything has changed," says the slim, partially bald Mr. Eberstadt. "After years of dealing with a board of directors who knew and trusted me, I'm suddenly confronted with having to account to Northwest for all kinds of little details." Among them are capital outlays. Microdot's $14.5 million expenditure budget for 1977 had to be approved by Northwest; also, Microdot must get approval for any individual project over $100,000 and must provide its parent with details at the beginning of each year for any project over $10,000. As for acquisitions, which had been Mr. Eberstadt's forte, "I now have to get permission," he says.

Mr. Eberstadt adds that he particularly misses "the ability to pick up the newspaper and see our stock quoted, and the meetings I used to have with securities analysts to discuss Microdot's future."

Microdot's past also makes the changes especially hard for Mr. Eberstadt. In 1960, he became president of what then was called Republic Industrial Corp., a small, unsophisticated concern operating in a six-room suite of offices on Madison Avenue in New York. "We didn't even have rugs on the floor," he recalls.

In the years that followed, Mr. Eberstadt guided Republic Industrial into numerous acquisitions. Among them was the 1968 purchase of Microdot Inc., a successful West Coast maker of fasteners, whose name Republic eventually adopted in place of its own.

But despite the rapid growth, Microdot is dwarfed by Northwest Industries. The subsidiary had 1976 sales of $335 million and 6,200 employes; the parent had sales of $1.6 billion and 37,000 employes. And although Microdot has retained an atmosphere of shirt-sleeve informality in its small, nondescript offices in Greenwich, Mr. Eberstadt remarks that "it's difficult to duplicate within a conglomerate the proprietary feeling I used to have."

Northwest's more formal way of doing business bothers Michael Becker, Microdot's controller and the person who, next to Mr. Eberstadt, has felt the transition most keenly. Mr. Becker used to prepare a three or four page summary of the company's annual budget for management, but now finds "I have to put together 125 pages for Northwest." He notes that Northwest wants to know about every capital project on a month-to-month basis "so that they can feed it into their computer"—something he views as of dubious value.

But what bothers the 39-year-old Mr. Becker most is that "I'm so busy scrambling for Northwest, I don't have time to take care of Rudy Eberstadt's needs." He adds: "It makes me feel inadequate to have to tell the man I've worked for all these years that he has to wait until next week for something."

Another problem that troubles Mr. Becker is that while Northwest focuses on the broad issues, executives at the parent company tend to overlook more specific ones. "They may ask why the fastener group is going better one month than another, but they don't care about any changes at a particular company within that group." In short, says Mr. Becker, "to Northwest we're just a piece of a larger whole."

Other Microdot executives say the company used to be able to move much more quickly on business transactions. Allan Howell, vice president of corporate development, cites an incident that occurred shortly after the merger.

"I had a meeting with some people about doing an acquisition," he recalls. "It seemed like a great deal, and I got all excited and was about to say 'Yes, we'll go ahead,' when I suddenly realized I was no longer free to give them an immediate response." Mr. Howell says the proposal eventually fell through for other reasons, but he notes that "in business you sometimes take risks which are from the gut, not based on numbers," and this, he says, "is difficult to justify to an overseer."

Another disadvantage in working for a subsidiary is a certain lack of ego gratification. Mr. Howell, who was recently promoted to his current position from financial assistant to Mr. Eberstadt, says that although he is pleased by the promotion, "it would have been nicer to be a vice president of an independent Microdot." The executive rues the fact that since Microdot is no longer a public company, "when we achieved record earnings (in 1976), the only place we could go for recognition was Northwest."

That Microdot is no longer public similarly frustrates Samuel Shaw, the company's legal counsel. He says a lot of his most interesting work "concerned problems relating to Microdot's publicly traded securities"—a function currently handled by Northwest's counsel.

Ben Heineman, Northwest's president, isn't insensitive to the impact that Northwest's size and position have on Microdot's executives. "We've tried to make them feel at home," he says. "Believe me, I understand it's difficult, particularly for someone like Rudy Eberstadt, not to be his own boss." To ease the situation, Mr. Heineman says he usually has heads of newly acquired subsidiaries report directly to him "so they won't feel denigrated." He adds: "We know we have to be sensitive to personalities if we want strong independent executives running our divisions instead of mere office boys."

To foster initiative, Mr. Heineman says (and Mr. Eberstadt confirms), Northwest operates in a relatively decentralized fashion and gives its divisions considerable freedom. Yet even Mr. Heineman concedes that "life for Microdot can't ever be the same as it once was."

In some ways, however, Microdot is better off than in the past. For one thing, while Northwest monitors Microdot's expenditures closely, its financial resources provide the subsidiary with substantially more capital to spend and presumably can help cushion it during future economic downturns.

On a far less lofty level, some Microdot employes have discovered personal benefits from the merger. They are exercising their right to order goods at cost from other Northwest subsidiaries, which include Buckingham Corp., which distributes Cutty Sark Scotch, French wines and tequila; Fruit of the Loom Inc., which makes underwear, and Acme Boot Co. "It's just one of the fringe benefits that go along with being a Northwest subsidiary," remarks a Microdot executive while holding up a pair of newly acquired Acme boots.

Employe attitudes have been affected in other ways, too, "When I used to go out of town on business, I'd always order the cheapest thing on the menu because I felt I was saving money for Microdot," one executive says. "Now I just go ahead and order the filet mignon."

Perhaps the person who will benefit the most from the change at Microdot is Larry Blackmon, the company's executive vice president of operations, who will take over as president when Mr. Eberstadt departs. Mr. Blackmon says the transition "was probably easier for me to accept because I started on the bottom of the corporate ladder, while Rudy started on the top."

Whatever the reason, Mr. Eberstadt feels sure he is making the right decision in leaving Microdot, even though he hasn't any definite job plans. "The company is better off without me," he says. "My heart is no longer in the job."

Executive Dropouts

When we last left Tony Rousellot in 1971, he had given up a successful career as a stockbroker in New York to seek happiness on the ski slopes of Taos, N. M.

Well, Tony says he has found what he was after. Now he is "terribly involved" in raising tropical plants, and he and his artist wife have formed a landscape consulting firm. "I couldn't conceive of going back east—even to visit," he says.

Mr. Rousellot, who is now 42 years old, was one of the people The Wall Street Journal mentioned in 1971 in two articles about people who had dropped out of corporate life. At that time, dropping out was a tiny but recognizable trend in the business world. It seemed to be a predictable extension of currents running through society, particularly affecting the country's youth.

There is evidence that in the years since, the dropout trend has quietly continued, and perhaps increased. Some experts say this is because many of the assumptions prodding dropouts, such as the idea that success needn't, or perhaps can't be defined in corporate or institutional terms, have become accepted tenets of American society.

"We have broken down the ethic that a successful life must be spent in one enterprise or corporation," says Eugene E. Jennings, a business consultant and professor of management at Michigan State University's business school. "We don't any longer believe in the gold watch theory." Mr. Jennings says he has counseled 18 executives who have dropped out in the past three years. More than half "have gone 180 degrees," or completely changed their styles of living. "It's no longer a fad," he says. "I know it's increasing, and it's a healthy thing."

A spokesman for Boyden & Associates, an executive search firm, cites a gradual but steady increase in the rate of executive dropout. He links this to "the loosening up of career planning that stems, really, from the youth movements of the 1960s." This can be the best solution for both the executive and the company he leaves. "The executive who is looking over the rainbow is rarely very effective for very long," the spokesman says.

The yearning for a completely different type of life on the other side of the rainbow is common among executives, according to Mr. Jennings. "Between (the ages of) 38 and 50, men are most vulnerable to stopping and asking that tough question, "What am I doing here?' " he says. "It's like you've been slumbering for 20 years, and suddenly you see what you want to do, and see you've been doing everything but what you want."

Although the feeling that something is lacking in their lives is common to most dropouts, John Turner, a San Francisco psychiatrist and business consultant, says he senses a change from the early 1970s. Then, dropping out often was done "in the rebellious sense." He says: "What we are seeing now is people saying, 'I want to be happy—I want my wife and kids to be happy,' It's a conscious, rational decision."

Still, there is much risk in making such decisions, and forsaking the security of corporate life can be chancy. To see what pitfalls there are—and how dropping out looks once the novelty wears off—The Wall Street Journal located many of those named in its original stories and asked them about their lives since 1971.

"I'd recommend it to everyone," says Marshall Whitfield, now 41, who left the presidency of a Los Angeles venture capital firm in 1970 to become a ski bum in Northern California. Mr. Whitfield spends his winters on the slopes. "I finally got as good at deep powder skiing as I'd always wanted to be," he says. During the summer he did construction and carpentry work. When money became scarce, he sold securities from the portfolio he had accumulated during his business career.

In 1973, Mr. Whitfield met a Los Angeles film maker, whom he married. Through his wife he became involved in financing film productions. This has now become a full-time business interest for him, and he has recently moved back to Los Angeles to pursue it.

Mr. Whitfield says his only big mistake after dropping out came when he "tinkered a little bit in real estate—and disastrously, like most dilettantes." That experience taught him that "if you're going to drop out, drop out completely and really enjoy it."

Marshall Whitfield has been able to drop back into a business he enjoys. Others aren't sure they could ever face the business world again.

"It would be hard to get back into the corporate life," says Bill Lawrance, 56, who was a supervisor with Canadian Telephone & Supply Co. in Vancouver until he quit in 1969 to go sailing. He and his wife Barbara bought the Yellowbird, a 44-foot ketch, and sailed it to St. Lucia in the West Indies. They chartered the boat to vacationers, with Mr. Lawrance as captain, Mrs. Lawrance as crew. "We had an excellent six years down there," Bill Lawrance says. "We worked maybe 14 to 15 weeks a year, but when we did, we worked 24 hours a day. You can put up with that."

The Lawrances left the islands for a small farm north of Vancouver in 1975 after Mrs. Lawrance developed health problems. They now plan to spend much of their time traveling. "We're very, very happy we did the whole thing when we did," he says. "If anybody waited until they were 55 or 60, I'd say it's waiting until too late. You have to do it at least before you're 50."

Someone else unlikely to drop back in is John Koehne. Mr. Koehne, his wife Ann, and some of their children now live in the foothills of the Blue Ridge Mountains of Virginia. They are developing a farm and something they call the "Dharma Self Help and Analytic Center." They moved to Virginia in April 1975, the latest step in a far-ranging odyssey that began in 1969 when Mr. Koehne dropped out after 20 years as an analyst with the Central Intelligence Agency.

After selling their McLean, Va., home, the Koehnes wandered the country in a camper truck. They then bought 160 acres of undeveloped land in Northern California where they established a "growth center" based on principles of yoga. They built three geodesic domes for shelter and lived there until the fall of 1975. An adviser, Yogi Bhnjan of Los Angeles, told the Koehnes the time had come for them to visit the city of Amritsar, a Sikh religious center in northwest India, to do 40 days service at the golden temple there.

"It was a very high experience, but it was a very difficult experience at the same time," the 55-year-old Mr. Koehne recalls. An outbreak of malaria hit most of the Koehne family. While in India they decided to sell their California property and look elsewhere for land more suitable for farming. Eventually they found the farm in Virginia.

Not everyone who drops out heads for the wilds, the slopes, or the sea. Herman Rottenberg, age 60, lives in a plush co-op apartment overlooking New York's Central Park. He dresses well and has enough money to fund two foundations. He lives like the head of a knit-goods company, which is what he was before he liquidated the company in the mid-1960s and, in his own fashion, dropped out.

"I didn't enjoy the business world because I didn't like the morals and mores of what was going on there," he says. "The only thing I enjoyed was that I was successful." Mr. Rottenberg founded a small folk-dance group, which has grown into an 18-member dance troupe. It performs in the U.S. and abroad eight months out of the year, and it is taking up a lot of Mr. Rottenberg's time. "I only spend about eight days a week on it," he says.

Herman Rottenberg's dropping out was cushioned by the savings he could fall back on. But even some well-heeled dropouts say that away from the corporation, finances can be a serious problem.

"One thing I didn't figure on is the amount of savings you need," says Alasdair Munro, 49, who chucked a high-powered New York advertising job in 1970 to move to Vermont. "If someone were going to do this and had kids to educate . . . I'd say to be awfully sure you've got that money tucked away in some form where you're not tempted to borrow from it. That's a great temptation." (The Munros have one child in college and another in prep school. They have been able to handle the costs, but that has been "probably the most worrisome" thing about dropping out, Mr. Munro says.)

Mr. Munro dropped out not so much to flee from business pressures as to change fundamentally the way he lived. He was a senior vice president in charge of the Coca-Cola account at McCann-Erickson, the big advertising agency, when he quit for a quieter life. "The main reason I dropped out wasn't dissatisfaction with the corporate life, but with the life style I was forced into. I've certainly seen more of my children over these last years than if I'd still been in the corporate world. And I went home for lunch today. I certainly couldn't do that in New York."

But Mr. Munro has found life on the outside tougher than he expected. He got into real estate in Waitsfield, Vt., but his new business suffered some reversals, and in the recession of 1974 went into "a very, very tough slump." The Munros tightened their belts as "the economic realities of life became somewhat grim."

Things got so bad that the dropout "poked a toe in the water in New York" to inquire if he could drop back in, but the recession-racked agencies weren't doing any hiring. Mr. Munro says the experience taught him that "it takes a lot for a large corporation to get to the point where it's really in tough shape financially, but in your own business it can happen before you realize it."

About 18 months ago, the real estate business started looking up in Vermont, and now things are "going swimmingly" once more. He and his partner are opening a second office in nearby Burlington. Mr. Munro now advises the would-be dropout: "Pick the time in the business cycle when you're coming into an upswing, rather than going into a downswing."

Some dropouts say they've managed to transcend the pitfalls and find real happiness. Such is the case with Tony Rousellot, the stockbroker, who in 1970 quit his job with Neuberger & Berman, sold his upper east side co-op apartment and his Massachusetts country home, and headed west to the ski slopes of New Mexico.

Today, "we're so delighted with where we are and what we've done that I can't think of anything negative to say about it," he says. "I think I'm a totally different person in terms of how I look at life and other people."

Mr. Rousellot became a ski-school supervisor and a director of the ski association in Taos. Last winter, he boasts, he was outdoors "every single day" of the ski season. He and his wife designed their own house and formed the landscape company. But Mr. Rousellot took such a liking to propagating and raising tropical plants called bromeliads that he is planning to go into that "full tilt." The Rousellots will soon move to Santa Fe, in part because there is more cultural life there.

For Tony Rousellot, New York was "the salad days—when you wanted something, you bought it." Now there is less money —but less is needed. "If I had to have eight suits in New York, out here I have to have eight pairs of blue jeans. And blue jeans last longer than suits."

The initial phase of dropping out was a bit difficult, he says. "But after the realization that things are just different out here, that the pace is different, I was perfectly content. You have to work at it . . . to create your own niche."

SOURCES

The following consists of a list of the authors and titles of *The Wall Street Journal* articles on which this book is based.

Jerry E. Bishop, "Inventor's Odyssey: Ovshinsky's Theories Finally Win Approval in the World of Science," July 7, 1977.

Terry P. Brown, "Passed-Over Employes Are Suing Their Firms To Demand Promotion," April 29, 1977.

Terry P. Brown and Liz Roman Gallese, "Quiet Operator: Max M. Fisher Moves in Powerful Circles And at a Hectic Pace," February 8, 1978.

Harlan S. Byrne, "Take-Charge Guy: He Likes Setting Goals, And His Next Big Goal is Two Billion Dollars," May 16, 1978.

James Carberry and Liz Roman Gallese, "Top Banana: Who Is Mr. Milstein? Head of United Brands is Keeping Low Profile," May 13, 1977.

William M. Carley, "Empire Builder: How Harry Gray Chose and Then Pushed Latest Takeover Offer," June 17, 1977.

Lindley H. Clark Jr., "Frank Filling Discovers That Banks are Ready to Aid Small Concerns," November 23, 1977.

Mark N. Dodosh, "Money For Hire: Cleveland Bank Sends Its Branch Managers Hunting for Borrowers," September 2, 1977.

Liz Roman Gallese, "Women Managers Say Job Transfers Present A Growing Dilemma," May 4, 1978.

David Gumpert, "Archie Williams Aims His Black-Run Firm At White Community," December 7, 1977.

Roy J. Harris Jr., "Quiet Growth: A Giant Now, Teledyne Is Still Just Tele-Who To a Lot of Investors," January 16, 1978.

William D. Hartley, "Mr. Hull's Job Search Illustrates the Anguish Of the Fired Executive," May 7, 1977.

Bill Hendrickson, "Master Marketer: Norton Simon's Chief Is Likely to Prod Avis To Try Even Harder," July 20, 1977.

James C. Hyatt, "More Firms Link Pay to Job Performance As Inflation Wanes," March 7, 1977.

Frederick C. Klein, "Doyle Hayt Survives Bankruptcy, Succeeds Second Time Around," November 29, 1977.

June Kronholz, "Mr. Hoffman of Atlas is Big Gun at His Plant But Not In Company," April 21, 1977.

Jonathan R. Laing, "Maverick Banker: Abboud Has Stabilized First Chicago, Making Few Friends In Process," May 19, 1978.

Joann S. Lublin, "Employe Lives Change As More Firms Adopt New Work Schedules," February 16, 1977.

Joann S. Lublin, "Mrs. Lowe Has to Deal With Stress and Sexism As Bank-Branch Head," April 26, 1977.

Joann S. Lublin, "Strong Medicine: Brash Don Rumsfeld Tries His Prescription To Turn Searle Around," January 25, 1978.

John R. MacArthur, "The Early Bird Gets Not Only the Worm But Also a Better Job," September 20, 1977.

Daniel Machalaba, "Bob Dallas Is Fighting Chains and Exhaustion With Small Restaurant," December 2, 1977.

Susan Margolies, "Sleeping Giant: Despite Vast Assets, International Paper Fails to Lead Industry," August 30, 1977.

Susan Margolies, "Microdot Officials Find Jobs Dull After Firm Is Sold to Big Company," February 25, 1977.

Richard Martin, "Mr. Armbruster's Job Is Complex, Mysterious But Positive for Profits," April 18, 1977.

Roger B. May, "Joan Massey Struggles To Keep an Idea Alive on Bare-Bones Capital," November 14, 1977.

Gay Sands Miller, "Displacing Steel: How a Salesman Urges Auto Companies to Use More Aluminum Parts," June 13, 1977.

Eric Morgenthaler, "Men Who Left Work to Seek Happiness Express Few Regrets," December 27, 1976.

Eric Morgenthaler, "Women of the World: More U.S. Firms Put Females in Key Posts in Foreign Countries," March 16, 1978.

Roger Ricklefs, "For a Businessman Headed Abroad, Some Basic Lessons," January 16, 1978.

Roger Ricklefs, "More Managers Are Hiring Executives in Their 40s For Slots in the Middle," May 3, 1977.

Roger Ricklefs, "Single-Mindedness: Firms Become Willing—or Eager—To Hire Divorced Executives," May 18, 1978.

Richard A. Shaffer, "How Fusion Systems Blundered to Success With Exotic Product," November 17, 1977.

Janice C. Simpson, "Turnaround Artist: Wilson of Memorex Revives Its Profits, Cuts Its Debt Load," August 25, 1977.

Jeffrey A. Tannenbaum, "Branching Out: A Zealous Boss Puts Once-Stuffy Colgate On a Bold New Course," July 11, 1977.

Ray Vicker, "Innocent Abroad: How a GM Man In Iran Tackles Costs, Customer He Never Saw In U.S.," July 12, 1977.

The Wall Street Journal, "Time-Zone Trauma: Every Traveler Has A Therapy For Jet Lag, But Malady Lingers," March 7, 1978.

Joseph M. Winski, "Flour Power: Staid Old Pillsbury Is Poppin' Fresh Now Under Aggressive Boss," December 6, 1976.

Bernard Wysocki Jr., "Mr. Newton's Foundry Spends Time, Money Coping With Red Tape," November 21, 1977.

Victor F. Zonana, "Norgren Co. Juggles Its Schedule to Boost Efficiency and Morale," February 17, 1977.